Brea:
Celebrating
75 Years

"Let us gather up our heritage,
and offer it to our children."
—Will Durant

Premiere
Editions

On the Cover:

GETTING INTO THE BIG PICTURE:

 Brightly attired Breans gather at the old city hall to celebrate the city's Diamond Jubilee. Pictured, alphabetically (you find them!)
Edna Pauline Adams, Tina Brianne Adams, Alva Anderson, Gerald Anderson, Alexis Arczynski, Andrea Arczynski, Barbara Arczynski, Milton J. Armstrong, Jim Baker, Elsie Bergman, Walt Bergman, Brittany Bitrich, Adam Boch, Andy Boch, Brian Boch, Elizabeth Boch, Jason Boch, Janae Brolin, Beverly Cary, Ruth Christie, Eunice Conliffe, Evelyn Corollo, Judy Coulson, Marci Coulson, Ruth Hodkins Daugherty, Connie Davies, Christine Davis, Joanne Davis, Frank Day, Virginia Day, Marie Domenico, Denise D. Ehrle, Melissa Ehrle, Aaron Eseltine, Karyn-Leigh Eseltine, Mary Eseltine, Don Fox, Pat Fox, Susan George, Dr. Catherine A. Greene, Amy Hampson, Brandon Hampson, Elizabeth Hampson, Gary Hampson, Teresa Hampson, Hiro Hayashi, Leo Hayashi, Karen Hopkins, Bill Hunter, Wanda Hunter, Harold Ivy, Beth Jones, Leon R. Jones, Adrienne Keller, Andrew Keller, Jill Kimble, Dennis Kimbrough, Joseph Kimbrough, Sarah Kimbrough, Louis Knappenberger, Marjorie F. Lally, Eileen Leyland, Nicole Leyland, David S. Markson, Erin R. Markson, Joshua W. Markson, Nancy C. Markson, Betty Millen, Dean Millen, Kimberly Moeller, Jane O'Brien, Patrick O'Brien, Glenn Parker, Mary Jo Parker, Bev Perry, Garry Phillips, Monica Phillips, Ella Armstrong Post, Kara Ralph, Kathleen Ralph, Gill Realon, Brigid Ricker, Herc Roeser, Reine Roeser, Edward A. Rose, Brian Saul, Miguel Saul, Miiko Saul, Andy Scheffler, Susan Scheffler, Frank Schweitzer, Ruth Schweitzer, Barbara A. Scobie, Terrie Shore, Thomas Shore, Gene Slaughter, Rosie Slaughter, Audrey Smith, Jack Smith, Colleen Snyder, David Snyder, Jeff Snyder, Rick Snyder, Timmy Snyder, Marie Sofi, Brandon Spencer, Justina Spencer, Toni Granes Spencer, Dean Stough, Dorothy Stough, Betty Sutton, John Sutton, Viola Swindle, Al Tremayne, Pat Tremayne, Dora Varner, Karen Vitkus, Lisa Vitkus, Dr. Robert E. Washbon, Carol D. Weddle, Laura Williams, Mark Williams.

Cover photo by Bill Strickland

Special thanks for assistance with Brea's "Big Picture" to:
The Brea Bistro, Brea Nissan, McDonald's, Bill and Wanda Hunter

On the Facing Page:
Country Corner
Looking north from today's Brea Boulevard and Central, circa 1919.
Brea Historical Society

Premiere Editions
Placentia, CA

Produced in cooperation with
the Brea Historical Society

Brea, California

Brea:
Celebrating
75 Years

An Illustrated History by Teresa Hampson

Brea Historical Society
•401 S. Brea Boulevard •P. O. Box 9764 •Brea, CA 92622 •(714) 256-2283

Premiere Editions
909 E. Yorba Linda Boulevard, Suite H2400
Placentia, CA 92670-3623
FAX (714) 572-3868

Staff for *Brea: Celebrating 75 Years*
An Illustrated History by Teresa Hampson

Project Director, Sharon Dean
Pictorial Editor, Brian Saul
Managing Editor, Irene L. Gresick
Designer/Production Artist, exclusive of color, Karen Vitkus
Assistant Designer, Teresa Hampson
Design/Production Art, color pages, Prototype Graphics, Inc.
Cover Photography, Bill Strickland
Color Separations, Colortec
Halftones of Rare Photos, Checkmate Photo/Graphics
Corporate Biographer, Cynthia Simone
"Partners in Progress" Representatives:
　　Irene Gresick, Karen Vitkus, Clair Freeman and Elizabeth Hammond

Printed in the United States of America
First Edition
Library of Congress Catalog Card Number: 92-061361
ISBN: 0-96338180-6

Top of the Town
High on a northwestern hill, the Orange Oil Lease, circa 1919. Later bought by Shell, this rich field continues in production today.

Contents

Acknowledgments

*T*his book has been a community project, produced almost entirely by local labor. My thanks to those whose efforts have helped it happen:

To Sharon Dean, former president of the Brea Historical Society and manager of the society's first publication venture. Her continued support of this project kept it alive through difficult times.

To Jane O'Brien, current Brea Historical Society president, whose energetic efforts helped guide this publication to print.

To Irene Gresick, co-creator of the publishing plan that carried this project to completion.

To Karen Vitkus, co-creator of the plan, sales representative and production designer. Her creative layout helped bring the story to life.

To Brian Saul, pictorial editor and text researcher emeritus: the man with a million files. Through it all, a staunch supporter and a dedicated co-worker.

To Inez and Karl Fanning, lifelong guardians of local lore, for editorial assistance and photo research.

To Leon Jones, for publication plan financial advisement.

*T*o Dean Millen, whose idea inspired Cal State Fullerton's Brea Community History Project. As chairman of the Brea Historical Coordinating Committee, Millen supervised fund-raising and the gathering of local historical materials for this CSUF project, which spanned the years 1980-83 and resulted in the publication of 36 Brea oral biographies, a major source of material for this book.

To Brea Community History Project Director Dr. Leonard DeGraaf;

the coordinating committee: (the late) Dyer Bennett, Karl Fanning, Patricia Fox, Dean Millen, Leo Piantoni, (the late) Lloyd Reese, Frank Schweitzer, Catherine Seiler, Voloney Siebenthal, (the late) Lois Muzzal Smith, Jessie Thompson, Barbara Vasquez, Vivian Weddle, Wayne Wedin, Harry "Frog" Winchel and Priscilla Hutton.

To the CSUF students involved in interviewing, transcribing, editing and indexing the CSUF Brea Community History Project's oral biographies, as well as those who sorted and labeled documents, pictures and other local memorabilia.

To the California Council for the Humanities, Security Pacific Bank Charitable Foundation, Brea Lions Club International, Union Oil (Unocal), Alan and Gary West, the Don McBride Co., Kirkhill Rubber, the Brea Soroptimist Club and others who financed this project, and to Dr. Arthur Hansen, current chairman of the CSUF oral history program.

*T*o Marilyn Morgan, anthropologist with RMW Paleo Associates, Mission Viejo, for editorial assistance with Brea's prehistoric era.

To Paul Apodaca, Curator of Native American Art at the Bowers Museum, and to Richard Buchen, reference librarian at the Southwest Museum, for assistance with the history of Southern California's Native Americans, Spanish exploration and mission era.

To author Virginia Carpenter, for editorial assistance with the rancho era and Juan Pacifico Ontiveros.

To Brea artist Kathi Wahl, for her sketch of the Ontiveros rancho, and to Shirley Christian and Jack Slota of the City of Placentia for its use.

To Carolyn Kozo, reference librarian for the Los Angeles City Library, Elizabeth J. Schultz, Emeritus Member of the Anaheim Library Board, Gloria Scott of the Corona Public Library's Heritage Room, Dace Taube of the University of Southern California Library's Regional History Center, and Jenny Watts of Huntington Library's Rare Book Department, for photo assistance.

*T*o Unocal's Stearns Lease Production Foreman Eldon East, for a visit to this prolific local field and facts on its long history, to Michael T. Hogelund, Unocal Corporate Community Programs Manager, for photo assistance, and to Senior Production Engineer Matt Evans of Unocal's Santa Fe Springs Pipeline Division, for information on the Landa Family homestead.

To Stephanie Harrison, executive secretary to Assemblyman Ross Johnson, for facts on the legislative career of Olinda Assemblyman Joe Burke.

To Archivist Dennis McGuire and Archive Technician Ana Christensen of the Orange County Historical Archives, for assistance with the maps and memorabilia of Randolph/Brea's earliest years.

To Brean Bernie Swart, agricultural photo consultant.

To Research Librarian George May of the Ontario Public Library's Model Colony Room for photos and information on the Chaffey Family, and to Robert Ellingwood for further facts on this topic.

*T*o author William Myers for editorial assistance with regional railways and early electrical service. Additional thanks for railway information to Paul Hammond of the Orange Empire Railway Museum and to Ralph Melching and the Interurban Press for photos and maps.

To the National Archive, Southwestern Region, at Laguna Niguel for official logs of the *S.S. La Brea Hills*.

To my longtime friend, Ray Cole, his friend, Bill Bonzer, and his friend, Tom Lewis, former commander of the Brea Nike Base, who provided leads in the search for Ajax and Hercules missile pictures; and to Terrie Cornell, Registrar of the Air Defense Artillery Museum, Fort Bliss, Texas, for her time and patience in securing a photo.

To the late Ray Wolfert and Daphne Wolfert Miller, for information on the proposed Brea Nike Base Park.

To Thelma Hyder Reahm, for her beautiful Brea stories.

*T*o Susan Gaede, the *Brea Progress'* "Newsy Susie," for some special photos and a fascinating store of Brea facts. Additional thanks to reporter Brian Hall and sports editor Bob Cunningham for editorial assistance.

To the former *Daily Star-Progress* which (during its recent move) offered nearly 50 years of old newspapers to the Brea Historical Society, and to Brian Saul, who weighed down his car to haul them home. Without this timely donation, most of the old advertisements reprinted in these pages would not have appeared.

To BOHS Boys Athletic Director Ron Hampton, Girls Athletic Director Sharen Caperton and to past and current BOHS coaches Dick Tucker, Phyllis Curry and Mark Trakh for the winning facts on Brea's high-school sports.

To Brea Librarian Emily Moore, Reference Librarian Julie Reardon, Children's Librarian Sherry Toth and Library Assistants Letitia Maitlen and Tina Trombetta for their research and assistance.

*T*o the dozens of past and present Brea city employees who patiently answered questions, searched for photos and otherwise assisted with this project: City Manager Frank Benest; former City Managers Wayne Wedin and Terry Belanger; City Attorney James Markman; former and current City Clerks Donna Rhine and Elaine Capps; Financial Services Director Lawrence Hurst; City Planner Conrad Bartlam and Associate Planner Alan Lawson; City Engineer Sam Peterson; Redevelopment Services Director Susan Georgino; Media Specialists Scott Pettinger and Brian Flinn; Photographer Rich Rivera and Communications and Marketing Secretary Cathy Molino; Maintenance Services Director Pat McCarren and Maintenance Administrative Assistant John Oliver; Community Services Director Ret Wixted, Cultural Arts Manager Emily Keller, Public Arts Specialist Christie Wada, Curtis Theatre Manager Scott Riordan, Gallery Director Marie Sofi, Community Services Special Events Coordinator Pat Tremayne; former Brea Mayors Donald Fox, Leonard MacKain, Carol Weddle and Wayne Wedin; former Fire Chief Bud Moody, former Police Chief Don Forkus and Police Lieutenant Bill Lentini; and to the many assistants and secretaries who lent their help in tracking down elusive bits of Brea's history.

*T*o Dr. Edgar Z. Seal, Superintendent of the BOUSD, for information on the local schools and district history; and to Assistant Superintendent of Business Services Gary Goff, Assistant Superintendent for Personnel, Curriculum and Instruction Peter Boothroyd; and BOUSD Board Members Lynn Daucher, Leonard MacKain and Barbara Paxton for additional facts.

To Brea Chamber of Commerce Executive Director Sherry Norman and Brea Mall Manager James Charter for information and insights on Brea's business community.

To Bill Strickland, Brandon Spencer, Brian Saul, Gary Hampson and That Frame Place for additional photo assistance.

To Jack Smith and Gary Hampson for map assistance.

To the Saul Family: Brian, Eva, Meika, Miiko and Miguel, for promotional assistance.

*T*o my family: Robert and Earline Bernhard, two fine writers and their daughter's very first editors; Betty Hampson, a handy "kidsitter" and a surprisingly fine copy editor; Elizabeth, Amy and Brandon Hampson, three kids any mom would treasure; and Gary Hampson, counselor, editor and mapmaker, a husband in a million.

...And to the dozens of unnamed others who so generously shared their stories and photographs so that this book could better celebrate the best of Brea's past.

Teresa Hampson
March 1993

For the people of Brea…
      those who went before, and
      those who still will come;

And for my family…
      whose patience makes
      all things possible

Class Act
Teacher Vera McDonald's fourth grade, Brea
Grammar School, 1917. Blond Evelyn Manson
(Starkey) sits in the third seat, foreground.
Brea Historical Society

Foreword

The Brea Historical Society's motto is "The Past Belongs to the Future, but only the Present can Preserve It." This sentiment has also become our goal. With the loss of so many structures that were historically significant in the downtown area, the need to preserve Brea's past for the future has grown into an urgent mission.

Realizing that documentation is essential in preserving the essence of our local heritage, the Society saw the need to produce an easy-to-read, fully-illustrated book which could be enjoyed by Breans young and old. Once the decision to publish had been reached, the story became complicated and lengthy. I will, therefore, leave it untold and concentrate, instead, on the people who have given so much of their time, energy and love to this project.

This book is the epitome of volunteerism. In the Brea community, where volunteers through the years have generated many great accomplishments, this publication is a crowning glory. Our author, Teresa Hampson, has labored more than a year in her research and writing of this exciting history — starting from the land's beginnings and taking Brea's story to the brink of our city's tomorrows. Pictorial Editor Brian Saul has spent scores of hours in text research and the pursuit of the hundreds of original photographs that make this book so warm and personal.

Our publishers, Irene Gresick and Karen Vitkus, have guided this exciting project from its rocky start to its successful completion, rescuing it when it seemed lost, keeping it afloat by devising a plan and coordinating a professional team, generating new funding patrons and spending long hours in editing, designing and typesetting what we believe is the best Brea history this society could possibly have produced.

The informative and attractive book you are reading has been crafted with pride for the people of Brea, in a format we believe the entire community will enjoy. To those whose loyal dedication has made this book possible, our deepest gratitude and our most sincere thanks.

Sharon Dean
Project Director
and Past President
Brea Historical Society
April, 1993

Plains of the Past
A well-populated local landscape
Courtesy Los Angeles Museum of Natural History

CHAPTER 1

Shadows on the Land

Before subdivisions or shopping malls, oil fields or orange groves...before Basque sheep ranches, Spanish adobes or Indian villages...before all else that would one day come, the place that today is Brea lay for silent centuries beneath an ancient sea. There on the deep ocean bottom, 20 miles out from shore, today's townsite sheltered a collection of sea creatures whose fossilized remains live on in its soil...

Under the Sea
A porpoise and whale of Miocene era Orange County

The presence in prehistoric times of sea cows, giant sharks, exotic shellfish and other undersea dwellers in what is today Orange County has been documented in the work of geologists and paleontologists, as well as occasional discoveries by baffled building crews whose excavators uncover seashells far from the modern-day shore. Reading geologic structures and fossil finds, scientists can sketch a rough record of local life millions of years past.

Rock formations tell of volcanoes spewing lava along the rim of the sea. Bone fragments reveal reptiles inhabiting coastal lagoons and marshes. Fossil records show ancestors of the crocodile flourished in this subtropical climate, though few finds suggest dinosaurs ever strode local swamps. While these huge lizards dominated most of North America during the Age of Reptiles, small evidence of their presence has been found in California, and some scientists speculate their progress west was blocked by an inland sea.

Some 20 million years ago, dramatic changes began in the low-lying Los Angeles basin as its underground lacing of earthquake faults started to shift and slide. The sea repeatedly intruded and receded, finally forming a deep-water channel from what is now Santa Monica Bay as far inland as Brea. In this waterway, microscopic forms of sea life flourished. Diatoms floated in the warm inland waters, leaving behind glassy shells to create the white sediments now seen in cliffs of the Puente Hills.

Such prehistoric plankton played an important role in the development of Brea. For it was the remains of these plants—compressed under centuries of sediment and trapped by movements far below the surface—which produced the pools of oil still being pumped along the city's northern border.

The Secret of the Shells
Common fossil markers of oil

During the course of the next several million years, dozens of creeks and rivers flowed down from the basin's surrounding mountains, gradually filling the floodplain with sediment and raising it safe from the sea. By one million years ago, tectonic upheavals were forming the region's mountains, and the rough topography of the modern landscape was set.

Evolving into a temperate grassland, the area became suited to new life forms. Fossil finds show an exotic array of animals roamed local landscapes, among them mammoths and mastodons, lions and saber-toothed cats, bison, bears, camels, horses, wolves and 13-foot-tall giant ground sloths.

Climatic conditions during these times were vastly less hospitable elsewhere. While the Southland basked in a relative heat wave, most of North America lay buried under huge sheets of ice. Looming as near as the San Gorgonio Mountains of San Bernardino, the glacier's leading edge never crossed the Orange County line.

Sometime around 10,000 years ago, a trend of warming weather stopped the advancing ice, and the towering frozen masses slowly began to subside. So it was that the Southland basin was spared the desolation other regions experienced in these times. Yet it was not unaffected. For, in the end, it was the Ice Age that brought the area its first man.

N o one knows for certain where they came from, and none can say precisely when they first arrived. What is known of the earliest humans to inhabit this region is that they had taken up residence in select areas of the coastal basin sometime between 12,000 and 17,000 years ago.

Most scientists speculate that North America's earliest inhabitants originated in Asia and first began crossing an intermittently exposed land bridge between Siberia and Alaska as early as 50,000 years ago.

Traces they left behind—the combined stone spear tips and bones of bison and other big-game animals—show that these early immigrants were hunters. Hunters follow the game, and many think it was this pattern which drew them east and then south into warmer regions as their prey ranged ever farther from the icy northern landscape. So it was, probably, that the first humans came to Orange County.

Archaeological evidence discovered in the Los Angeles basin indicates its first Native American inhabitants settled along the coast, probably finding food most plentiful there. Even in these early days, the attractions of Orange County real estate were clear. Good weather, a dependable water source, game in the grasslands, and an abundant supply of fish, shellfish, waterfowl and sea mammals on the shore combined to give man a near-perfect environment. Civilization thrived in places like Upper Newport Bay, and segments of the population gradually moved inland.

The presence of American Indians in the Brea area has been suggested through the discovery of artifacts (including arrowheads in Tonner Canyon and the foothills just west of northern Brea Boulevard), and in the diaries of the Spanish explorers, which describe an Indian settlement many believe was located in the Brea Canyon area. Though little local excavation has taken place and experts feel many archaeological sites have been destroyed, proof that prehistoric man inhabited a portion of this valley has come at a Fullerton dig, where evidence shows a highly developed society thrived between 1,000 B.C. and 1,400 A.D.

Anthropologists seem certain the Brea area's natural resources would have attracted early man. Free of the concrete constraints which today make it almost invisible, Brea Canyon's creek in prehistoric times probably flowed nearly year round, providing a small but reliable source of water. Most of the materials commonly used by primitive people for shelter, clothing and food also appeared abundantly in the plant and animal life of this region.

Perhaps most important, the northern hills and canyons yielded one unique resource—asphalt, a tarry petroleum residue that seeped from the ground at several sites. Prized by early man as medicine, caulking and sealant, this substance was both

A Wondrous Array of Land Animals
(From top) Ground Sloth, Saber-Toothed Cat, Ancient American Camel, American Mastodon

unusual in the basin and valuable in trade, two facts which would have made the Brea area especially inviting.

Anthropologists believe at least two groups of people inhabited Southern California during its prehistoric period: the Hokan speakers, who arrived before 6,000 B.C. and of whom little is known, and the Shoshonean speakers, who followed, beginning about 4,000 B.C. The Shoshoneans who made their home in the valley of today's Brea took the name *Tongva*, and evidence gathered by archaeologists reveals much about life in their time.

Southern California's earliest inhabitants lived in small, self-governing groups of generally no more than 150 people—an extended family clan ruled by an elder head man or head woman. These Indians were not nomadic, but became attached to their land, each family building its own wickiup, a dome-shaped stick hut covered with tules or reeds, plastered together with mud or tar. Their settlements were widely scattered, and spaced in near-exact conformity to food resources.

These early inhabitants had no agriculture, probably because they needed none. With throwing sticks or simple bows, seasoned hunters stalked deer and antelope, while those less skilled captured rabbits, squirrels, rodents, birds and small fish. Women added to the food stores by harvesting wild greens, berries, roots, herbs and seeds, and gathering grasshoppers,

Indian Dance by Ruth Underhill
Courtesy Corona Public Library

lizards, slugs and caterpillars for charbroiling over campfires.

Dozens of manos and metates, the tools used by native women in their daily seed grinding, would be discovered in California in later years. Brea has recorded one such find, that of a single metate—unearthed in the early 1900's on the Yriarte Ranch and today displayed at the Brea Historical Society.

Acorns also became a staple food, and plentiful live oak trees in the Puente Hills offered an ample supply. Women gathered these nuts in cone-shaped baskets and ground them with mortars and pestles to make meal, which was dipped in water heated with stones or cooked in soapstone pots to leach out its bitter tannic acid.

In the temperate Southern California climate of prehistoric times, women wore two-piece aprons made of rabbit skin, tree bark or other plant fibers. Men, on the other hand, wore little at all—except sandals. Cooler weather brought out capes of rabbit and squirrel skin for both sexes, and ceremonies saw men dancing to the music of turtle-shell rattles and deer-bone whistles while attired in ornate costumes of fur, feathers and shells.

Anthropologists believe these early inhabitants were

stocky and muscular, and had skin of a medium brown. Young and old, each member of the clan rose before dawn for the daily bathing ritual, and sunrise saw families drying together before the fire. Then, as now, fashion and vanity exacted a price. Women postponed the effects of aging by decorating their bodies with red-ocher paint, and frequently were tattooed from cheek to shoulder by pricking their skin with cactus spines and rubbing the wounds with charcoal.

Flowers often were used for adornment, both as boas and in the hair, and every girl owned at least a few shell beads. Women wore their long, dark hair with bangs and let it hang loose to their shoulders, while men parted their hair in the middle, letting it fall loose or braiding it back, coiling the two plaits upward and securing them with hairpins of bone.

Early valley inhabitants owned little, both by custom and because few items were available. Prized objects such as pottery from Arizona and soapstone bowls from Catalina Island (both found in nearby archaeological digs) were acquired from traders in exchange for tar. For most valley dwellers, days were spent gathering and preparing food or engaging in simple diversions. Basking in the sun was a respected pastime among these primitive people, while bathing in warm

Reconstructed Wickiup
Courtesy American Title Insurance Company

springs (like those at nearby La Vida) was the ultimate luxury. Gambling and telling stories proved popular entertainments for adults, while children played cat's cradle and games with a hoop and pole. Ceremonies and rituals gave form to the flow of days, with entertainments and feasts shared by guests from neighboring clans.

Though their art forms were few, these native people crafted finely coiled baskets of great use and beauty. They brewed no intoxicating drink, but smoked a wild tobacco, ingested grasses to invoke ceremonial visions and purified their bodies in sweathouses. They believed in the kinship of living creatures, celebrated the forces of nature and conducted elaborate and painful rituals at puberty—one involving lying down in a bed of stirred-up red ants. Marriage was by mutual consent, often involving a dowry, and the death ritual dictated the deceased's body be cremated, along with its owner's possessions.

Described in writings as peaceful, the native dwellers seldom warred against one another and rarely practiced slavery. Establishing a stable relationship with the environment, they gradually increased in number. By the late 1700's, as many as 15,000 Native Americans inhabited the waterways, valleys and canyons of Southern California, creating one of the most densely populated Indian regions in the United States.

But one day, few would remain or remember, for history was not kind to these native people. Of the 15,000, nearly all lost their lands and their lives, including the clans that for centuries claimed the place where Brea now lies.

They welcomed them warmly...so the diaries say. Arriving from the south, the light-skinned Spanish travelers were accepted in friendship by the people they called Indians, and invited with excitement into each village they passed. For natives and newcomers alike, a new era was beginning. The year was 1769, but the real roots of the story stretch back several centuries.

The events which led to Spain's first inland exploration of California did not, of course, happen in isolation. New World beginnings inevitably lead back to Columbus, and follow the paths of those who furthered his work: Balboa, discovering the Pacific; Cortes, conquering Mexico; Coronado, searching the Southwest for cities of gold; Cabrillo, sailing the California coast...All these and more opened up the minds—and the pocketbooks—of Spain, and led to ever greater discoveries.

Claiming new lands wherever they went, these explorers were so successful that, during the early 1500's, the size of Spain's empire increased 100 times in a period of only 30 years. In this glut of property, the realm's remotest possession—Upper or *Alta* California— easily was overlooked as a place worthy of attention.

Discovered in 1542, the distant land probably took its name from a popular Spanish novel describing an island paradise inhabited by griffins and gold-laden Amazonian women. Such fanciful stories did little to spur interest in California's settlement, however, and no attempts to explore or colonize it were made for almost two centuries. In the end, only the threat of losing the land to others finally forced Spain to act.

So it was that, amid the ringing of bells, a party of Catalan soldiers, priests and Indian converts set out by land from Baja California in 1769. Led by Don Gaspar de Portolá, captain of dragoons and newly appointed governor of the northern land, the group boasted many who would become famous, among them two future governors and the celebrated "father of missions," Junípero Serra.

Following a trail blazed by an advance party, the group pressed north for 48 days, plagued in the end by dwindling rations and the death of several Indian servants. They arrived in San Diego only to learn a companion sea expedition had fared far worse—with one ship lost and two other crews decimated by scurvy. Of the more than 300 men who began the journey into Alta California, less than half lived to reach their first destination.

Portolá and his forces established a military garrison in San

On the California Coast
Spanish explorer Juan Cabrillo and his men

Diego before continuing the arduous march north in search of mission sites and Indian converts. Suffering from a lingering leg infection, Father Serra remained behind. On a hillside he built a brush chapel—California's first mission, San Diego de Alcalá.

Sixty-three men—some Spanish and some Indian, some mounted on horseback and others driving mules, moved out from the new presidio at San Diego on July 14. As protection from Indian attack, the soldiers dressed in heavy leather armor and carried lances, broadswords and short flintlock muskets.

Led by Portolá, wearing a regulation military uniform and a non-regulation ostrich-plumed hat, the brigade of gray-robed missionaries, bearded soldiers, mule drivers and Indians moved slowly over the unknown terrain, often traveling only five or ten miles a day. Bearing the banner of Spain into the wilderness, they prayed their provision ship would make it safely to Monterey... and that they wouldn't starve or die of thirst before they reached it.

Several members of the expedition kept diaries, among them engineer Miguel Costanso and priests Juan Crespi and Francisco Gomez. Their words describe the scenery and people of the northern trail—telling of encounters with friendly Indians, of gift exchanges and invitations to celebrations, of ailing native children brought for baptism, and of a series of frightening earthquakes experienced along the banks of the Santa Ana River. Nearly everywhere, Crespi wrote, the Indians "greeted us with a friendliness that was unequalled."

Entering what is today Orange County on July 22 in a canyon they called Los Christianitos (today's Camp Pendleton), the party passed through San Juan Canyon, Trabuco Mesa and Aliso Canyon (all now Mission Viejo), Tomato Springs (Irvine Ranch), and today's cities of Orange and Anaheim.

Trudging across plains carpeted with soft native grasses and through thickets of low, red-stemmed manzanita, they sought shade from the shimmering summer sun on hillsides

Gaspar de Portolá, Captain of Dragoons

dotted with groves of live oak and black walnut and in lowlands crowded with sycamores and willows. Crossing the Santa Ana River and angling northwest toward the hills, the travelers approached by midsummer the place where Brea now lies.

It was July 29, and as the explorers looked out over this new setting, only clumps of cactus and a few stream-fed groves of willows relieved the arid landscape. Even so, Crespi described this place as "a beautiful valley of many leagues of good land." The explorers hunted plentiful game here, and in the cool northern canyons discovered tangles of wild grape vines, blackberries and blooming wild roses.

"We climbed a medium-sized hill, quite steep, and descended to a very green little valley which has a small pool of water," Crespi wrote. Costanso called this place *Los Ojitos* or "little eyes," referring to a small spring feeding the pool, while Crespi gave it a second name, *Santa Marta*, to honor the saint's day.

The men had only begun to make camp when a group of local Indians—more than 70 "friendly heathen"—made themselves known.

The natives were planning a religious festival, and welcomed the travelers to attend, but Portolá declined, stressing their need to move on. That night, he and his men no doubt pondered what hardships lay ahead. For at this site only the people, and not the thirsty animals, had been allowed to drink from the small village pool.

Searching the explorers' diaries for clues, many have tried to pinpoint their passage through this region, but much remains unclear. Some say Portolá and his men camped elsewhere that last night in Orange County, while others—including several noted historians—place the group's final campsite near the mouth of Brea Canyon. A lonely marker, erected on North Brea Boulevard in 1932 by the Native Daughters of the Golden West, pays homage to this locale — the campsite Breans like to believe Portolá chose on his march northward into history.

Though none can say precisely just where Portolá passed, what is known for certain is that in the very last days of July, 1769, the valley where Brea would one day be built was first visited by a handful of men from an ocean away. The Indians met them, welcomed them and probably gave the arrival of the Spaniards little thought, never guessing the changes their presence foretold. For though their numbers were small, their impact on the land would be enormous.

Marking Portolá's Passage
The Brea Canyon Monument

*I*t began on a near-parched plain 11 miles to the northwest. The outline of a large cross pierced the late-summer sky as Indian laborers fell to work building brush shelters. It was the feast day of the Nativity of the Blessed Virgin Mary, Sept. 8, 1771, and Mission San Gabriel Arcangel was being born.

Part of Spain's frugal plan for settling California's vast wilderness, San Gabriel was one of two settlements intended to help close the distance gap between established churches at San Diego and Carmel. Originally expected to rise near the banks of the Santa Ana, the mission instead was built on the San Gabriel River in the area of present-day Montebello. Severe flooding later forced a new beginning even farther to the northwest, but by 1776—as American colonists in the east began their fight for independence—the first buildings were rising on the broad plain where Mission San Gabriel still stands today.

Founded as the fourth of California's missions, the settlement was to be a training center where Indians could be taught religion, social behavior and the elements of agriculture in hopes that they would

one day take control and establish it as a pueblo. Pre-dating Los Angeles by a decade, San Gabriel cast the first shadow of European civilization over an enormous part of the inland basin, dominating all people and lands in nearly half of today's Los Angeles and Orange counties.

Travels on *El Camino Real*

Within the scope of San Gabriel's influence lay the site of today's Brea. In this valley, Franciscan fathers rode out to find well-populated Indian settlements, and began the often difficult task of changing the natives' old ways of life. United under mission

authority, the area's once diverse Indians became "Gabrielinos," a term denoting—at least in the minds of the Spanish—the native peoples' ties to the nearby mission.

Yet the padres soon learned that assuming control of the Indians and controlling the Indians often were two different matters. With enticements of colored beads and bright cloth, many natives were persuaded to leave their homes and journey to San Gabriel.

For others, however, civilization's attractions were far less strong. Many became fearful of the padres, and fled to the nearby hills. Gathering together in roving bands, they kept mission guards busy by periodically raiding the San Gabriel settlement to steal horses, cattle and food.

Some of the more manageable native inhabitants were allowed to remain in the valley, living on *rancherias* and herding cattle or small groups of sheep. Hogs were raised in the south near Coyote Creek, and there probably also was agriculture. Other Indians fared less well. Large numbers eventually were forcibly taken to the San Gabriel site to work as laborers in the mission's kitchens, laundries, tanneries, fields and orchards.

Seldom as idyllic as portrayed in stories of this era, California mission life for the Indian was often dangerous, if not altogether deadly. The poor quality of Indian living conditions at San Gabriel was well known in early California, with at least one visiting governor reacting in "amazement and aversion" to the hardships the natives endured. Cramped together in

Mission San Gabriel
H.C. Ford Special Collections, University of Southern California Library
California Historical Society/Ticor Title Insurance

compounds where food was inadequate, sanitation nonexistent and disease rampant, in San Gabriel, as elsewhere, mission Indians died at a rate far exceeding their birth rate.

San Gabriel flourished. Called the "Queen of the Missions," at its peak it listed as assets 17 ranchos, 3,000 Indians, 20,000 horses, 40,000 sheep and 105,000 head of cattle. Well suited to the California climate, lean, black longhorn-cattle were the key to San Gabriel's success. Fattening on the grasslands of hills and valleys as far east as Riverside, cattle provided a ready store of meat for both padres and Indians, as well as tallow for soap and candles, and hides for leather goods.

Eventually part of a 21-mission system stretching nearly 600 miles, San Gabriel was linked to church settlements on the north and south by a network of dusty trails, one which passed through the La Habra Valley a short distance southwest of today's Brea. Called *El Camino Viejo*, or "the old highway," this path was walked by Father Serra and other early Californians during the days of the missions. Today it is marked by bells as part of "The King's Highway," perhaps better known in Spanish as *El Camino Real*.

The California colony prospered, while in Europe, Spain struggled. Once ruler of almost half the world, Spain in the 1790's faded from the global picture as prolonged wars and eventual invasion disrupted its government and destroyed its armies. New World interests were left untended, and in Mexico, unrest led to revolution. Mexico won its independence in 1821, and California came into new hands. A series of unstable Mexican governments created years of political turmoil, and shades of the struggle moved north over the rich mission lands.

With the tempering influence of a strong government absent, soldiers and politicians cast covetous eyes on San Gabriel. The church had never owned the mission properties, but had used them at the Spanish

The Missions of California

EL CAMINO REAL
SAN GABRIEL
FOUNDED SEPT. 8, 1771

government's pleasure, holding all in trust for the Indians.

An end to church dominance came in 1833, when the missions came under civil control. While provisions of the takeover sought to protect the Indians' rights, in the end the native peoples gained little of lasting value. By the time church rule was lifted from their lives, most mission Indians could not survive without it. Their old ways had been lost, and they were ill-prepared to face the future. For most, both freedom and property passed quickly through their hands. Some took poorly paying ranch jobs, and others drifted to Los Angeles. Many fell victim to poverty and disease, and their numbers were rapidly reduced.

A time of tumult and triumph, the mission era brought new ways to the region where Brea would one day rise. Asked to tame a wilderness, padres came to convert its Indians, and forever altered their world. Both sides suffered losses. Uprisings among the

Indians were common, and several priests lost their lives. Disasters struck the missions, and nearly all were at one time destroyed. Fire or flood claimed some, and most—including San Gabriel—were leveled by massive earthquakes. In the civil takeover, San Gabriel fell into decay, its possessions looted, its flocks dispersed and its fields turned back to wilderness.

But though the mission declined, its lessons of success lived on. Built in a land of weeds and little water, San Gabriel was never expected to grow rich. Yet in a span of 50 years, its labors revealed the region's promise. Soil that had never known agriculture yielded plentiful crops and flourishing livestock, and the worth of the once-untamed region was established.

Such success could not long go unnoticed, and such wealth not long lay unclaimed. The padres and the Indians passed out of importance, and a new group of men took the land as their own.

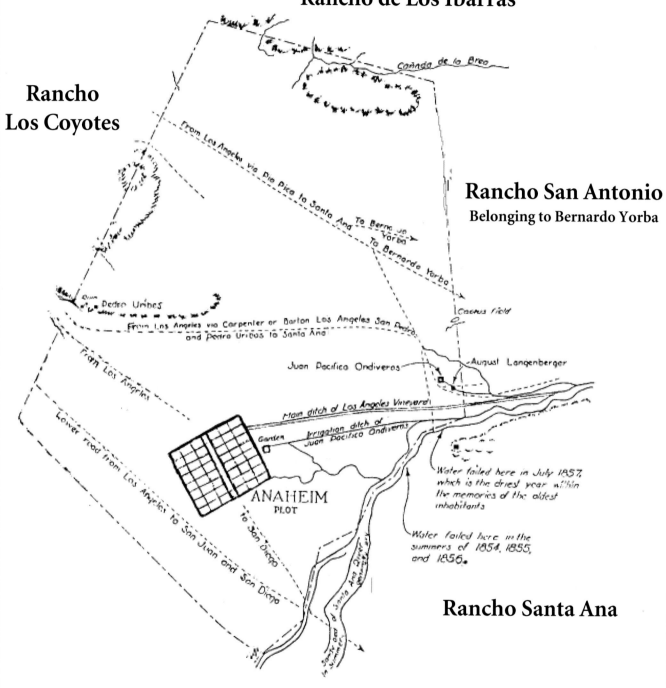

Rancho San Juan Cajón de Santa Ana
Belonging to Juan Pacifico Ontiveros

Rancho de Los Ibarras

Rancho Los Coyotes

Rancho San Antonio
Belonging to Bernardo Yorba

Rancho Santa Ana

ANAHEIM
PLOT

After a map in Los Angeles County Records, Filed 1855.
Note the tar deposits in the north near Brea, and the irrigation channel from the
Santa Ana River to Anaheim—a place Juan Ontiveros indicated wasn't fit to keep a goat.
Courtesy University of California Press

CHAPTER 2

Empires and Owners

*F*or a period of nearly 40 years in the early 1800's almost all of Southern California was owned by only a handful of men, most who gained vast properties from the governments of Spain and Mexico as rewards for military or political service. Sixty-eight years after the first Spaniard rode through the valley of today's Brea, this land came for the first time into private ownership in a grant to Juan Pacifico Ontiveros.

Born in Los Angeles in 1795, Ontiveros counted among his grandparents two members of the small party that had settled the pueblo just 14 years earlier. He served as an artillery soldier, but ended his army career in the 1830's, and followed the popular custom of petitioning for a parcel of land.

Ontiveros paid no ownership fee for the property granted by the lavishly generous Mexican government. Accepting the 35,970-acre estate in 1837, he agreed to meet three requirements: to build a permanent home, occupy it, and pasture several hundred head of cattle nearby.

Taking symbolic possession of the property in an ancient and picturesque ceremony, Ontiveros walked over his new land—pulling up grass, scattering handfuls of earth, breaking off branches of trees and otherwise laying claim to the place he christened, "Rancho San Juan Cajón de Santa Ana."

Near the bank of the Santa Ana River, Ontiveros and his wife, Martina, built their home of adobe, a house long since lost to time. Early maps show the settlement, a few small marks in a vast sea of land indicating a house, an irrigation ditch and "the garden of Juan Pacifico." From here the grass and mustard-laden fields of San Juan Cajón extended 10 miles north to the Puente Hills. Today's cities of Anaheim, Fullerton, Placentia and Brea are built on land that 150 years ago served as pasture for one man's cows.

Land in the rancho era was parceled out in ways almost unimaginable in today's small-space perspective, and Ontiveros' grant was

Juan Pacifico and María Martina Ontiveros
From Disneyland to Diamond Bar, they owned it all in the era of the ranchos.
From the Virginia Carpenter collection

no exception. There were no surveyors in Mexican California, and acreage was measured and recorded according to the accepted yet imprecise practices of the time. A 50-*vara reata* (a braided leather rope of about 135 feet with stakes tied to each end) was used to measure Rancho San Juan Cajón. One side was held

menos (a little more or less) a few hundred acres here or there.

A rancho of moderate size, San Juan Cajón spanned eight square leagues—a fairly level land rising to hills on the north and east. Wild grass, chaparral, mustard and cactus covered the rolling acres, and trees were so scarce that most were noted

close by today's standards, Ontiveros also had neighbors. Rancho San Juan Cajón adjoined the prosperous settlement of Bernardo Yorba, and Yorba's son Prudencio married the girl next door, Ontiveros' daughter Dolores. Considered the finest farmer of the early ranchos, the elder Yorba was greatly admired in his

The Ontiveros Adobe
by Kathy Wahl
One of only a few adobes built in Orange County, the house stood through 130 years of wind and rain, only to be razed for a modern industrial park.
Courtesy City of Placentia

stationary while the other was carried by a galloping horseman till the rope stretched taut, and this process was repeated until the entire rancho was measured.

Such natural features as riverbeds, clumps of cactus and groves of trees commonly served as boundary points between ranchos. In particularly barren sites, borders were indicated with more exotic markers such as stones and knives, or—in the case of one nearby rancho—a single cattle skull.

Not unexpectedly, many markers proved temporary, and rancheros seldom knew exactly where their properties began or ended. Few felt cause for worry. Grants were large and the number of prospective landowners small. There was enough room for everyone, and few cared if their property was *poco mas o*

as landmarks. Gophers, ground squirrels, rabbits, snakes, wildcats and mountain lions vied for space on the plains, while deer and bears kept to the northern canyons. Though 20 miles away, the ocean could usually be seen—and occasionally also heard.

Occupying one of only a few homes situated on the early Los Angeles to San Diego road, Ontiveros and his family frequently were called on to host tired and thirsty travelers, and the arrival of

creaking, supply-laden *carretas* offered a welcome break in the often slow sameness of the days. Though not

time, building a 50-room hacienda that became the social and business center of the Santa Ana Valley.

Ontiveros probably visited at least the closest of several other nearby ranchos, some whose names linger on the land as Los Coyotes, La Puente and La Habra. Perhaps his farthest local travels were to Los Angeles to socialize or buy supplies, riding the old mission trail as it angled northwest through the vast, empty valley of today's Brea.

In this pastoral period of California history, the business of San Juan Cajón and other ranchos was the raising of small but sturdy long-horned black cattle. Ontiveros' semi-wild herds flourished on the rich and unfenced grasslands. By custom, the rancho conducted a round-up each year in late spring or summer, with vaqueros gathering the steadily

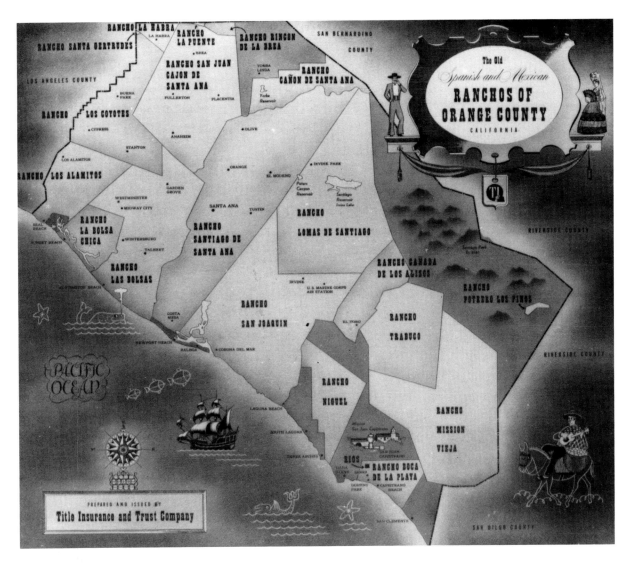

A Handful of Grants
The Ontiveros' property, Rancho San Juan Cajón de Santa Ana, is seen near the north of this map. Tiny Rincón de la Brea (extreme top) was located just over the hills to the northwest, an area still part of Los Angeles County.
Courtesy Title Insurance and Trust Company

growing herds from every part of the remote rangelands. The abilities of both horses and horsemen were tested in the difficult and delicate task of separating cattle for branding. Well-trained horses proved invaluable in this work, and Ontiveros was fortunate to find a ready supply of quality animals in the area's large wild herds. The Californios prized their horses for agility and endurance, and adorned them for special occasions with a small fortune in silver-laden saddles.

The cattle wealth of San Juan Cajón and other ranchos was measured in many ways. Large herds provided a consistent supply of fresh or dried beef, the dietary mainstay. Tallow candles, despite their unpleasant odor, illuminated rancho nights. Hides were used to make saddles and clothing, and became the primary item of exchange in a society lacking currency. Despite laws prohibiting foreign trade, a lucrative hide business sprang up along the coast as ever more *Yanqui* traders

came calling for these "California bank notes."

Situated at the eastern edge of Californio civilization, San Juan Cajón was more vulnerable than most to attack by bands of renegade Indians and Sonoran rustlers who swept down from the Cajón Pass to plague lowland ranchos. The Ontiveros' home, like most outlying ranchos, was designed to resist such raids. Rancho houses boasted adobe walls several bricks deep, with loopholes cut for the firing of rifles. Many rancheros at first used asphalt from the Brea hills to waterproof their roofs, but the tar's tendency to ignite when struck by Indian fire arrows later led to a less explosive architectural style as the now-familiar red-clay roof tiles became more widely available.

Life on the ranchos was predominantly peaceful, however. Days began at dawn with a breakfast of coffee or chocolate and a tortilla, sometimes with a gruel of ground corn. Work was varied, for nearly all the needs of larger ranchos were supplied by resident laborers and craftsmen.

Harness and shoemakers, tanners, carpenters, plasterers, bakers, washerwomen, spinners, seamstresses, dressmakers, gardeners, winemakers, shepherds and more contributed their skills, and wealthy owners employed workers numbering in the hundreds. Many employees were Indians who lived in crude huts outside the main rancho compound, and most fared only slightly better than they had under mission rule.

The land produced plentiful food, and none on the ranchos went hungry. Cooking was done in outdoor ovens, where fresh or dried beef was mixed with tomatoes, onions and chilies in a highly seasoned stew. Soup, beans, tortillas and vegetables accompanied the main course, followed by a dessert of cheese and melon, grapes or berries. Coffee and chocolate were served with meals, and men enjoyed a home-brewed brandy after dinner and at fiestas.

The sheer size of the ranchos made visits between neighbors infrequent. Yet life was seldom lonely. Rancho families commonly numbered a score or more, often including several children and a contingent of live-in relatives.

Both friends and strangers were welcomed with sufficient cordiality to ensure a steady stream of visitors, and fiestas drew a crowd necessitating the barbecue of an entire beef or lamb. Religious festivals featured music, processions, bonfires and fireworks, while secular entertainments included riding and lasso exhibitions, horse races and dancing to the music of Spanish guitars.

Rancho families lived well. Their land and cattle holdings were extravagant, and their tastes not infrequently expensive. Fine furniture and imported fabrics adorned many adobe homes, and earthen floors were masked by costly rugs.

Cattle Brands of the Mission and Rancho Eras

Mission San Gabriel Arcangel

Planned to be built near the banks of the Santa Ana, San Gabriel took a brand commemorating the fearful earthquakes Portolá recorded near this "rio de temblores." The entwined S and T stand for this word.

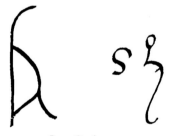

Juan Ontiveros

Two brands are recorded in this name, possibly for Juan Patricio (father) and Juan Pacifico (son).

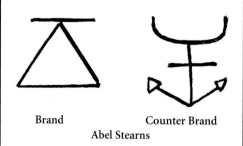

Brand   Counter Brand
Abel Stearns

Stearns bought many of the Southland's largest ranchos, including San Juan Cajón de Santa Ana.

Women dressed in gowns of imported satin and carried shawls of intricate lace, while men wore velvet and silk and bought saddles and spurs of silver. The land was good and the cattle thrived, and the passing sameness of the years seemed proof it would always be so.

By 1840, a number of Americans had settled in and around Los Angeles. Within a decade nearly all were rich, but none nearly so successful as Massachusetts-born Abel Stearns, an energetic and shrewd sailor-turned-merchant who amassed an almost unbelievable fortune in Southland property, eventually counting among his wealth the place that would be Brea.

Stearns' life had all the flamboyance of good fiction. Orphaned at 12, he went to sea on a trading ship and rose in the ranks as a sailor. He reached Los Angeles around 1830 and opened a trading post in San Pedro, gaining control of the lucrative local hide, tallow and fur business. No stranger to trouble, he was stabbed in the face by a sailor in an argument over a barrel of brandy—suffering permanent disfigurement and a lingering impediment of speech. Often accused of smuggling and twice ordered to leave the territory, he escaped sentencing both times when the Mexican government suddenly changed hands.

At the age of 44, Stearns wed the most eligible girl in Los Angeles in the ceremony of the decade. She was Arcadia Bandini: beautiful, rich, and all of 14 years old. Stearns built for her a home so large the locals called it *El Palacio*, and immediately made it the center of Southern California society. Ever an opportunist, Stearns profited by dealing in cash, buying goods, cattle and properties at low prices and offering loans at profitable rates. He made powerful friendships with the Californios, invested widely in land and cattle, financed and encouraged civic improvement, shot his fair share of spurious citizens, and managed not only to survive but to bolster his financial success as California came under American control.

Invaded in 1846, annexed in 1848 and brought into the Union in 1850, California's southern regions were not nearly so quickly or easily Americanized as counties to the north. While gold had been discovered in Newhall even before at Sutter's Mill, no throng of English-speaking prospectors ever overwhelmed the region, and the customs of Spanish society lived on for many years after California came into the Union.

So it was that, in the early years of statehood, rancho life at the Ontiveros and other settlements was little changed by politics, while, at the same time, rancho fortunes were enormously affected by economics. Thousands of Gold Rush miners streaming into the north created an immense new need for food, and the ranchos of the south eagerly met this growing demand.

As beef prices rose to incredible highs, more and more southern herds made their way to northern cities, and the rancheros of Southern California became richer than ever

Abel Stearns
The most spectacularly successful foreigner to settle on Mexican California's south coast.
Courtesy First American Title Insurance Company

before. With excess came excess, however, and many owners outspent their profits. Some had never invested wisely, and most owed money at fantastic interest rates. Few worried. So long as the grass grew and the cattle thrived, the good life lived on in the southern "cow counties."

The first threat to the ranchos came in 1851, when California land

titles came under federal scrutiny. In treaties prior to the region's takeover, the U.S. government had promised to honor grants made during the Spanish and Mexican periods, but the rancheros soon learned keeping their properties would not be so simple. Called before the U.S. Land Commission in San Francisco to defend their claims, owners brought deeds and witnesses in fights for land patents, but many titles proved tangled or flawed, and fully a third were rejected.

Denied his right to San Juan Cajón due to missing papers, Ontiveros appealed to the U.S. Supreme Court, but clear title was not granted for five more years. For Ontiveros and others the battles were time consuming and costly. Bankruptcies grew common, and lists of mortgaged lands filled the papers. And—as the rancheros' debts rose, competition from out-of-state herds caused cattle prices to plummet.

Ontiveros held for 20 years all the land he had been granted, but in 1857 he gave up his Southland home and retired near Santa Maria. He sold a small plot to some Germans, who set to work planting grapes and named their new settlement "Ana-

Roping a Steer
A slice of daily life in Mexican California.
Courtesy Los Angeles Public Library, Security Pacific National Bank Collection

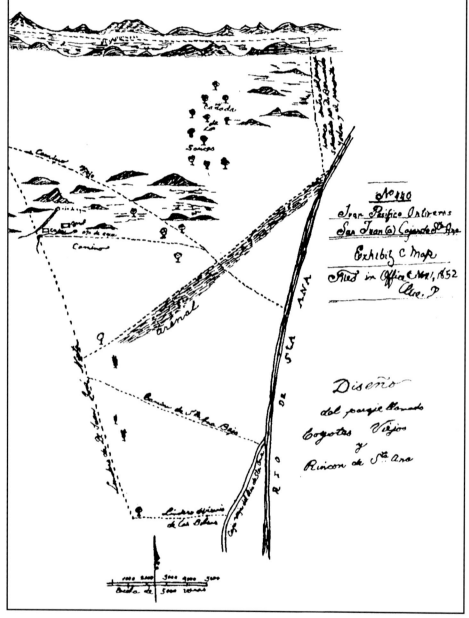

Land Case 440, Rancho San Juan Cajón
Brought as evidence in Ontiveros' 1852 land case, this map and other documents were rejected. Clear title to the land was finally granted by the U.S. Supreme Court, five years after the claim first was heard.
From the Virginia Carpenter collection

statehood. With nearly all the land still held in large ranchos, the countryside held small charm for settlers, and towns were few and poor.

Lacking the amenities of sites to the north, Los Angeles offered little to recommend itself. Treeless, smelly and short of water, the city was unmatched for fleas and seasonally deep either in dust or in mud. Its seedier streets sheltered the dregs of frontier life, a sordid collection of drifters and stragglers, foreigners of questionable character, drunk and degraded Indians and assorted outlaws and badmen. By the 1850's the town numbered 4,000 citizens, less 20 to 30 murdered each month, not counting lynchings.

But by the end of California's first decade of statehood, important changes had reached the Southland. Long cut off from the rest of the country by distance and difficult terrain, the southern regions by 1860 had been connected to the east and north through links of transportation and communication.

Though expensive, uncomfortable and frequently attacked by Indians, the Butterfield Stage became the area's first reliable overland transit system when it opened to passengers in 1858. Nearly nonexistent port facilities received a needed boost that same year when a landing and terminals for stages and freight were built at Wilmington. A sporadically working telegraph was completed between Los Angeles and San Francisco by 1860— and only months later carried the news nearly all had expected.

Word that the Civil War had broken out was greeted with general enthusiasm on the south coast, and more than a few U.S.-born citizens saddled up and headed east to fight. Not many joined the forces of the

heim." Saving for his sons, Juanito and Patricio, only a 3,900-acre plot (today the site of Placentia), he sold the remainder of his rancho to Stearns for the sum of $6,000.

In the Ontiveros-Stearns sale of 1863, the place that would be Brea passed for the first time into the possession of a man born in the United States. Situated near the edge of Stearns' vast holdings, the Brea

site was a tiny northern corner of what would become the largest land empire ever on the south coast. By the early 1860's, Stearns controlled nearly 300 square miles of Southern California real estate from the foothills to the sea.

Only the smallest handful of U.S.-born citizens had come to Southern California before 1850, and few followed in the first years of

Union, however, for most local Americans had emigrated from the seceding states, and sympathies lay almost exclusively with the South. Acting to quell unrest and protect its California investment, the Lincoln administration built two military posts on the Southern California coast during the conflict, installing 3,000 soldiers to control a civilian population of only 15,000.

By 1862, however, few local residents were worrying about a faraway war, for the Southland had troubles of its own.

From the beginning of settlement, water had played a vital role in the region's development. Rainy seasons were short and rainfall scant, and settlements sprang up only in places where rivers ran nearly year round. Since mission times almost 100 years earlier, settlers had depended on the steady pattern of the weather, watching as the hills turned brown and bare in the summers, and trusting the rains to return and the land to grow green again.

On Christmas Eve, 1861, it started to rain, and with only brief interruptions, it continued for almost a month. Sweeping in from the Pacific, one storm followed another, dropping a deluge of water that drained down in floods off the bare mountains and turned lowlands into lakes.

The Santa Ana and San Gabriel rivers overran their banks, altering their courses, destroying irrigation channels and sweeping away cattle and crops. Anaheim's orchards sat four feet deep in water, and Los Angeles shopkeepers scrambled to save their goods. At least 13 people drowned. Everywhere roofs gave way, adobe buildings crumbled, and residents dug themselves out of the mud.

The flood waters drained and the grass returned, but it browned and died early when no further rains came. Rainfall was far less than normal the next season, and the following summer brought swarms of grasshoppers to eat what grass was still left on the plains.

Smallpox struck that fall, terrorizing both ranchos and towns, and killing so many in Los Angeles that the church bell was finally stilled. The skies continued cloudless the next season as well, and smoke from fires in the hills cast an eerie glow on the plains. There was no water and no grass, and starving cattle staggered and died in dusty creekbeds.

For 90 years, growing herds of grazing mission and rancho cattle had been almost the only occupants of the place that would be Brea, but the searing drought of the 1860's brought an end to the cattle era.

Stearns salvaged what he could of his stock, slaughtering thousands for horns and hides and littering the plains with their bodies. Years later, the bleaching bones could still be seen by riders on the Los Angeles to San Diego stage as it rocked its way southward through the valley of today's Brea.

The rains returned in the season of 1864-65, too late for the cattle of the ranchos. Nearly all the herds were gone, but the taxes, the mortgages and the loan payments of the rancheros remained.

The Stearns Ranchos
An empire that drought dried up, nearly 300 square miles of prime Southern California real estate first offered for sale in 1868.
Courtesy First American Title Insurance Company

Basque Shepherd and his Dog
From the Ella Turner collection

trust, and large parts were divided for sale to small settlers.

Promoted in a flamboyant campaign where unseen and empty acres were occasionally advertised as cities, the Stearns Ranchos attracted an assortment of European immigrants and war-weary Southerners, and farming towns rose in places like Santa Ana and Orange. Land to the north was not immediately surveyed or sold, however, and many years passed before large numbers of settlers came to the place that today is Brea.

Assigned a small share in the trust that controlled his ranchos, Stearns provoked his partners by treating the land as his own. A cattleman with an ingrained hatred of sheep, he ironically fought his last major battle over the unauthorized leasing of grazing rights to sheepherders.

In 1870, he entered into a contract with Domingo Bastanchury, a native of France's Basque region who saw in the green hillsides near Brea a place his flocks might flourish. In deep disfavor with his partners and with the sheep issue unresolved, Stearns took a trip to San Francisco, and ended the debate dramatically by dying at the age of 74.

With the cotton industry of the South all but destroyed by the Civil War, the nation's textile mills cried out for wool—and Southland sheep ranchers stepped forward to fill the need. Growing flocks dotted local hills and valleys, and the smoke of herders' campfires rose into starry skies.

A Local Flock, Circa 1925
From the Mildred Dyke collection

Within a short time, most ranchos fell into foreclosure and were sold at sacrifice prices. In the hands of Yankee developers, the immense estates were subdivided, parceled out in small family farms and planted in melons and beans.

Stearns was caught short by debts and came perilously close to bankruptcy, escaping ruin at the final hour by mortgaging his ranchos in exchange for a loan. The Stearns lands passed into the hands of a

Lone shepherds and their dogs kept watch over bleating lambs in isolated grazing areas, their solitude lessened only by weekly visits from the head-quarters' food and mail wagon.

Domingo Bastanchury
The first European to settle his flocks in the east valley's "wild fields and prairies," Bastanchury found success in sheep ranching, and inspired other Basques to follow.
Courtesy Fullerton Library

Shearing time, by contrast, was a community occasion, with everyone on the ranches taking part in the tax-ing work. Large traveling bands of colorfully dressed Mexican and Indian shearers erected pole sheds shaded by palm fronds before tackling the tricky job of clipping, then dipping, the less-than-willing animals.

Once unencumbered, the sheep were allowed to run free, while their heavy fleece was gathered, tied, tightly packed into 300-pound bags and sus-pended from the sheds' ceilings.

Well traveled before their journey's end, these bags were carted to Anaheim Landing (near Seal Beach) and shipped to San Fran-cisco, then loaded into train cars and hauled east on the new transcontinental railroad. Shipping was simplified in later years when train ser-vice reached the Southland.

Bastanchury became the area's most successful sheep rancher, leasing between 10,000 and 20,000 acres and running a flock numbering

nearly 20,000. Other Basque ranchers followed, among them the Toussau Brothers, and the Arroues, Landa, Sarthou and Yriarte families.

Bastanchury's adobe home (located on a knoll near the site of today's Fullerton Municipal Golf Course clubhouse) became a popular meeting place for the closely knit Basque families. Open-pit barbecues found them gathered over well-spiced soups and stews or plates of beef, pork, chicken or the ubiquitous lamb, all served with local wine and loaves of round, crusty sheepherder bread cooked in eucalyptus-fired outdoor ovens.

Holidays brought dances, while Sundays were reserved for Basque "handball" games played on special courts. Spectators cheered on their favorites during these fast-moving competitions, shouting encourage-ment in their native Basque language, French, Spanish, and, in later years, English.

A severe drought in the mid-1870's wiped out many of the Southland's sheep, much as the drought of the 1860's had destroyed its cattle. When the rains failed, sheep

wool prices proved daunting to many sheep ranchers, and the Southland's last pastoral age soon slipped silently into history.

Much of Southern California became settled by small landowners during the decade of the 1880's. While the Southern Pacific Railroad had reached Los Angeles several years before, sky-high ticket prices at first denied train travel to all but the rich. Starting in 1886, competition from the Santa Fe Railroad sparked a period of rock-bottom rail rates, and thousands of immigrants headed West to oranges and opportunity.

Whittier was founded in 1887 and trains reached Fullerton by 1888. The growing south coast won its 20-year war for independence when, in 1889, the County of Orange was carved from Los Angeles.

By the early 1890's, a small tide of farming settlers was moving both north and east toward the place that would be Brea. The Basques who had come as sheepmen now also stayed to grow grain, and families like the Hualdes and Yriartes built the east valley's very first houses.

Operating without irrigation

Rancho Viejo
Domingo Bastanchury's First Local Home

died by the thousands, pulled down by predators and piled up in sandy creekbeds. Some survived, and a few flocks grazed the prairies and hills of Brea far into the 20th century. But natural disasters and plummeting

and keeping an eye on the sky, these and other early area "dry farmers" soon began sowing barley and harvesting hay. And in the northern hills, an old phenomenon sparked new interest.

The Long and Winding Road

Before straightening, Brea Canyon Road followed the meandering canyon creek, and a journey through the hills was a grueling nine miles long. Though evidence is inconclusive, one of the two white buildings in the distance may be the first Randolph School.

From the Alberta Shafer Terrell collection

CHAPTER 3

Decades of Discovery

Nature had never kept secret the oil in Brea's hills. Squeezed to the surface by forces far beneath the earth, it oozed from cracks and pooled in seeps in the canyons of the north, and was claimed by local inhabitants in a changing array of ways.

In the early American years, Basque herders mixed tar in ointments to soothe the skin of sheep, and increasing numbers of residents used the oil-soaked soil as fuel. A rough path was worn into Brea Canyon by the late 1880's, and sounds of picks and shovels echoed through the hills. Chipping away at the tar, settlers carved the oily earth into blocks, hauled it home in horse carts and burned it to heat their homes.

Many people exploited these northern lands during the area's long years of settlement, but few could read the clues to an unseen wealth below. Everyone claimed the tar, a few hoped to find coal, and some even searched for rumored Spanish treasure, while the real riches of the region remained untapped. Not until 1860, as an infant industry rose in the east, did men with an instinct for profit turn their eyes to Brea's hills.

Oil fever first struck the nation in 1859, when the sinking of the country's first successful well in Pennsylvania began a near panic in petroleum prospecting. California's earliest well was drilled far to the north by 1861, but one of the first oil wells in Southern California—now ranked among the most productive of all petroleum regions—was bored only five years later in the hills just north of today's Brea.

Impressed by Eastern oil discoveries, Abel Stearns joined George Hearst and German "Major" Max von Strobel to form Santa Ana Petroleum, and in 1866 leased rights

Max von Strobel
Though not a military man, Strobel called himself "Major"—and everyone else did too. A flamboyant personality, he came to California with John C. Fremont, dabbled in oil at Brea and served Anaheim as its first mayor.
Courtesy Anaheim Public Library

The Treasure of Tonner Canyon

Sunken ships and brazen pirates, midnight raids and gleaming gold—Though Disneyland is still ten miles away, Brea has a few sharp stories all its own.

"Aye, Matey, and if it be treasure ye seek..."

Buried treasure out in Tonner Canyon has long been an interesting legend throughout Southern California. The story is that, back in 1775, a ship laden with Spanish gold was wrecked off the coast now known as Newport Beach. The captain and his crew were saved, and the men managed to salvage their treasure from the sinking ship. Since the crew had suspected for several days that they were being followed by a pirate ship, they were anxious to get away from the open beach as quickly as possible.

After resting a short while, the sailors loaded their treasure on an ox cart and started northward on foot. Darkness came on as they reached Tonner Canyon, and they decided to make camp for the night.

An Indian woman soon arrived to warn the sailors a band of pirates was approaching. Playing it safe, the men hid the treasure at a location not far from camp.

Discovered and attacked later that night, the sailors all were killed, leaving no one alive to tell of the treasure's whereabouts. For unknown reasons, it was later said to be buried near a well or water hole.

This story was told by H.T. Green, an early Walnut settler who owned extensive land in the canyon. Green said he heard the story from his father when he was a boy. Apparently at least the elder Green and his neighbors believed it to be true, for they spent much of their spare time digging for buried treasure in the hills and canyons for many miles around.

—Adapted from the <u>Brea Progress,</u> April 8, 1938

on Rancho San Juan Cajón for the mining of oil and brea. Eastern oil-veteran A.F. Darling chose a site in Brea Canyon and hand drilled a shallow well, while the partners predicted quick profits and planned a railroad southwest to the sea.

But no ties were ever laid. After several hundred feet of laborious drilling, the rope holding the bit gave way, dropping the tool down the shaft and abruptly ending the venture. Against Darling's wishes, the well was abandoned—a failure at 650 feet.

The drilling equipment was removed from the canyon, and its owners went on to new ventures. Hearst became wealthy in mining and served in the U.S. Senate, while Strobel led the south coast's first attempt to separate from Los Angeles, and gained fame as the "Father of Orange County." Brea's oil fields, however, lay forgotten for 20 years. Rights to the land or minerals were sold and divided, and the brea was harvested by new hands. Brought to Los Angeles in the 1870's in an experiment for fueling gaslights, the tar made headlines with its offensive smell, and instead ended up in insecticides.

Economics kept crude underground in the decade of the 1870's. Small profit was possible when uses for oil were few and refining knowledge still poor. Distilling attempts in these early years often ended in disaster. Devastating fires commonly were sparked by the explosive byproduct of crude, an annoying and "useless" substance that would come to be called "gasoline."

Attempts to tap oil returned in the 1880's, as complex machines were invented, refining methods improved and California crude found use in lubricating gears and firing engines. In 1883, the team of Burdette Chandler and J.G. Bower leased a site near the mouth of Tonner Canyon, hired their first "roughneck" drillers and built a small town called Petrolia. Relying on muscle power and primitive machines, the men of Chandler Oil set to work pounding holes in the hardened earth.

Celebrating Puente's Success
The plaque (now missing) that
once marked this pioneering field.
Brea Historical Society

Articles in the *Anaheim Gazette*
gave readers a running account of
efforts to "kick down" Petrolia's
wells, predicting in 1883 that within
months, "a forest of derricks will
stand like sentries on the mountains"
and "rocks will pour out rivers of
oil." Petrolia flourished for a time,
its shallow drilling producing the
area's first gusher, and yielding 5,000
barrels of crude by 1884.

Operations expanded to include
asphalt, which was melted, cleaned
and carted to Los Angeles for use in
paving streets. In 1890, Chandler
Oil's owners pooled their resources
with those of Pennsylvania wildcat-
ter Lyman Stewart, and the Brea
Canyon claim became part of an
infant Union Oil Company. Bigger
fields soon beckoned, and the little
town of Petrolia fell into decay.

To the west, on a hilltop above
today's Site Drive, a new kind of oil
exploration met growing success at
wells drilled by W.E. Youle on the
lease of Puente Oil. Initiating the use
of heavy equipment for deep drilling, Youle made a huge strike in
1884, considered by many to be the

earliest successful well in Southern
California. Once marked by a plaque
presented by the Petroleum Production Pioneers, the Puente site was
credited as "providing the stimulus
for further significant oil development in the Los Angeles basin."

A small settlement called Puente
Wells grew up near the Puente Field.
Oilmen with families moved into
small clapboard cottages, while their
unmarried counterparts boarded in
bunkhouses. The area's first school
was built on the hilltop at this site,
and early religious services were
held here. The oil lease families
became well known for their celebrations, hosting frequent picnics and
welcoming residents of nearby
communities. Setting up long tables
under shade trees high in the hills,
well-dressed neighbors and newcomers crowded together, feasting on
Puente's famous tamales and barbe-
cued beef.

From its wells on this lease,
Puente Oil sold petroleum in bulk to
Los Angeles utilities, built the basin's
first oil pipeline (to a railroad terminal in La Puente), and supplied the
region's first refinery, built in Chino.
Puente and Columbia Oil merged in
1904, and the company was later
bought by Shell. Its rich fields
remain in production today after
more than a century.

One new field followed another
in the remaining years of the 1880's.
Drilling in Brea Canyon, Union
produced a half million barrels on its
Stearns Lease before the turn of the
century. Already on its way to
establishing a statewide empire, Union
was joined in local drilling by a host of
smaller competitors, with Birch, Brea
Cañon, Chanslor, E.L. Doheny,
Columbia, Graham-Loftus and
Wonder all counting claims before
1900 in or near today's Brea.

Title disputes over the valuable
oil lands grew common, and several
boundary lines were drawn in judicial
ink. The work buildings and small
cottages of another oil settlement
sprang up along Brea Canyon Road,
and more and more workers came
west to share in the land's new wealth.

Canyon Chronicles

*Though promise lay in the north-
ern hills, not all who came could find
it. Some had poor tools and some poor
timing, and some just had poor luck.*

*Drilling in Brea Canyon in 1866,
local petroleum pioneers Stearns,
Strobel and Hearst became so disappointed with a series of dry holes that
they gave up forever on such ventures. A few feet and 30 years away,
the same site roared in as a gusher.*

*A twosome of canyon landown-
ers who got together in business had
their share of tough times as well.
Partners in a Los Angeles bank, William Workman and F.P.F Temple
became rich, then lost all they had in
a bad deal. Workman committed sui-
cide after their bankruptcy, and
Temple later died, destitute and alone,
in a lonely sheepherder's hut.*

Portraits of Puente Wells, 1910

Grandpa's Girls
James Kinsler with grandchildren (from left) Arlene, baby
Mildred and Thelma.

"Old Tom"
Charles Kinsler's horse takes a shine to the camera as
Grandpa James Kinsler looks on.

Cousins
Maynard Thayer and Thelma Kinsler pose in the "backyard"
of the Kinsler home.

Best Friends
Cousins Thelma Kinsler (left) and Pauline Thayer, at play
behind the Kinslers' Puente Wells home.

From the Kinsler Family collection

Just over the hills to the east, an untapped field drew growing interest as oil-industry pioneer Edward L. Doheny took up Union drilling in a farming site known as Olinda.

Today's Olinda Village lies nearly two miles east of the original Olinda townsite, which took root as an agricultural community and grew into a thriving oil town. Incorporated since 1960 within the city limits of Brea, Olinda predates its one-time neighbor by more than 20 years.

Two stories explain the origin of Olinda's name: that it comes from a Portuguese word meaning beautiful, or is a mixture of the Spanish word *linda* (meaning pretty), forever expanded by an "O" when an unknown early settler gazed at the valley and exclaimed, "Oh, *linda*!" Following the annexation of California, land courts found this area to be *sobrante*—leftover property not owned by any rancho. Like other nearby sites, Olinda came under the sway of Abel Stearns and later his widow, and was held within

Life in a Canyon Called Brea, 1910

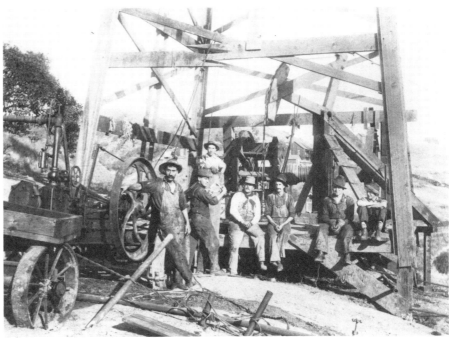

ABOVE: Taking a Break
The shift was 12 hours, the workweek six days long. Lunch was carried in a black metal pail and included hearty sandwiches, homemade pie and lots of strong, hot coffee. G.A. "Bert" Shafer is pictured second from the right in this Brea Canyon drilling crew.
From the Alberta Shafer Terrell collection

BELOW: Canyon Family
Mrs. Fred Gholson and son Billy pose in front of their Brea Canyon tent house.
From the Kinsler Family collection

"It took a special breed of man to build a wooden derrick. He had to be big, he had to be rough, he had to be strong and he had to have experience. Two men would walk up beside that derrick and, in the elbow of one arm, holding on with one hand, they would carry a timber that weighed 300 or 400 pounds up the side of that derrick. The beam just sat in their arms just like that, I'm telling you. Then, when they got it up there, they had to nail it on. Special breed of men, yes."

*—From the memories of
Brea oilman Dyer Bennett*

At the Top of Their Field
The seven-man oil crew at work atop a towering derrick. G.A. "Bert" Shafer stands on the beam, right. "Tower work" was a novelty for most men, but a hazardous one as well. Note the lack of safety precautions on this early rig.
From the Alberta Shafer Terrell collection

The Ghost Rancho of Cañada de la Brea

*Alone among California's vast and valuable Mexican posses-
sions, a small but important stretch of land along Brea's northern
border became the rancho that didn't exist.*

*Originally owned by Juan Pacifico Ontiveros as part of his huge
Rancho San Juan Cajón de Santa Ana, 1,290 acres in the south
Puente Hills were bought, but never sold—all part of a tangled
transaction that erupted in court some 42 distant years later.*

*Popularly known as Rancho Cañada de la Brea (Canyon of the
Tar), the disputed property included all of Tonner Canyon, plus
portions of Brea Canyon and the foothills to its south. Though
evidence shows Ontiveros intended to divide this area from his larger
property and sell it to his friend and in-law Bernardo Yorba, proper
papers for the sale were never filed.*

*Yet for 40 years, no one seemed to notice. Yorba sold the land to
others, and they passed it along as well. Some buyers built homes on
the land and lived there, while others carted away its brea. By 1889,
the property had passed through the hands of 29 such "owners," yet
no protests were ever heard.*

*But in 1891, everything changed. The Stearns Ranchos Co.,
longtime owners of Rancho San Juan Cajón, belatedly realized these
northern lands were oozing great pools of black gold. Seizing the
chance to make it their own, Stearns' management mounted a legal
challenge to the original Ontiveros' sale, and Los Angeles Judge J.W.
Towner ruled in their favor.*

*Though the rancho's name had appeared on maps for 44 years
and its lands had been sold 28 times, the court ruled it had never been
separated from Rancho San Juan Cajón. Wiped from existence by the
very wealth of its land, Cañada de la Brea, Southern California's
ghost rancho, became but a haunting memory.*

the Stearns Ranchos until the land
boom of the 1880's.

Sold in 10-acre plots and soon
turned to agriculture, Olinda Ranch
produced crops and livestock a
decade before nearby areas, attracting
settlers who pastured their cattle,
sheep and burros in the open field
that today is Carbon Canyon Regional Park. Some planted crops in
the canyon's black and red loam,
harvesting lemons, olives, walnuts,
apricots, hay, grain and castor beans
for medicinal oil. But many who
came to farm faced disappointment.
Water supplies from springs and
wells proved brackish and inadequate, and irrigation systems were
contaminated by seeping oil. Nearby
towns promoted at this time, including Carlton (between Olinda and
Yorba Linda) and Richfield
(Placentia's Atwood area) suffered
similar problems, and the fields and
orchards of the 1880's gradually gave
way to the interests of oil.

Established in Olinda by 1897,
Doheny quickly expanded Union
Oil's operation. Forging a partner-

Edward L. Doheny
A true petroleum pioneer, Doheny dug Los An-
geles' earliest oil well with only a pick and shovel.
The first oilman in Olinda, he worked locally
with Union, and later began Brea Cañon Oil.
*Courtesy Los Angeles Public Library,
Security Pacific National Bank Collection*

ship with the Santa Fe Railroad—then pushing for the development of petroleum to power locomotives—he brought a Santa Fe spur line directly into the oil fields. Opened to Richfield on the southeast in 1889, the tracks cut through the present-day dam and park area, ending north of Olinda (now Carbon Canyon) Road.

Before the coming of the railroad, shipping at local oil fields had been done with horse and mule-drawn wagons, loads of building materials and barrels of crude bouncing along over bumpy roads. The coming of the area's first railroad proved a business boon few could resist, and Olinda soon was checkered by new oil claims. Chanslor-Canfield Midway (CCMO), Olinda Crude, Shell, Hall's, West Coast, Columbia, Graham-Loftus, Stearns, Associated and others counted wells in the area, the biggest strike drawing crowds of disbelievers as it gushed 60,000 barrels of crude skyward in the three days before its flow came under control.

AT PRIVATE SALE

The Celebrated

OLINDA RANCH

COMPRISING

5,000 ACRES of choice land in the most productive section of Orange County, about 2 miles East of Fullerton, Orange County, on a well in full bearing.

500 Acres of Alfalfa Land

Under irrigating ditch with perpetual water right, climate unsurpassed. No frost. AND YOU WILL BE SATISFIED THAT THIS **Investigate** is the best opportunity ever offered in the county for a farmer of moderate means to secure a paying ranch on a small cash payment. Our terms are only one-fourth cash, balance on easy payments at low rate of interest. Our prices are within your limit. Write us for maps and full particulars. We will be pleased to show you the property. Apply to...

EASTON, ELDRIDGE & CO.,
MANAGERS.

121 S. Broadway, - Los Angeles, Cal.

Fullerton Tribune, June 24, 1898

Bender Ranch in Carbon Canyon, 1898
Courtesy American Title Insurance Company

ABOVE: Brea Canyon Gusher

The Brea Bonanza

The 2,300 proven petroleum-bearing acres of the Brea-Olinda Field stretch southeast from the Puente Hills through Brea and Tonner canyons to the site of old Olinda.

Formed during the Miocene and Pliocene epochs, this field's vast pools of oil are the remains of countless microscopic marine organisms deposited during Brea's undersea era. Transformed into thick, black crude by time and the forces of heat and pressure, these rich deposits later were sealed deep in the earth beneath layers of folded rock.

Earthquake action on the Whittier Fault gradually twisted and fractured these rock formations, creating channels through which the oil oozed out to the surface. Here it pooled in tar seeps, some as much as a mile in length.

This field's great subsurface deposits of oil vary in depth at differing locations, tapped in early years with wells of a few hundred feet, and pumped today from depths nearly two miles within the earth. Nearly a century of production has marked Brea-Olinda as the Southland's most consistently prolific field.

BELOW: Olinda, circa 1901
Trains approached Olinda from the south through today's dam and park area, crossing north over Olinda (Carbon Canyon) Road.
Brea Historical Society

At Home in Old Olinda
The Kammerer Family poses in front of their board-and-batten house.
(Left to right) Lucy, Archer William, Lollie, baby Phyllis and William.
Brea Historical Society

Where Carbon Canyon Regional Park's green, manicured acres today nestle in the shade of surrounding hills, the community of Olinda rose among towering wooden oil derricks. A boomtown by the turn of the century, Olinda became Orange County's top petroleum producer, and its population swiftly swelled to 3,000. A railroad depot, houses, a school, storage barns, a baseball diamond and tennis court were built on today's park site, and development continued north along Santa Fe Avenue (now a private access road) with a livery stable, Methodist Episcopal Church, barber shop, mercantile store, homes, offices, bunkhouses and boardinghouses.

Pumping plants and pump houses stood near the hilltop, and ranches and farms extended far into the nearby hills.

Seven-hundred board-and-batten houses were built in today's park area, along Santa Fe Avenue, and on slopes to the north and west, all owned by the oil companies and leased to married workers. Rents were low and amenities few. Water was piped to kitchens, but bathrooms were built outdoors. Gas from the fields provided fuel for heating and cooking, as well as lighting in the years

before electricity. Laundry was done by hand with washboards and large tin tubs, the latter used also for bathing. Built as three or four rooms, Olinda's houses slowly grew. Bedrooms or screened porches were added to some, and bathrooms came to all. Yards were fenced in pickets and gardens planted with vegetables and flowers.

Santa Fe Avenue, Looking South
View toward today's park, circa 1920. The company office and social hall appear in the foreground, (left) while the boardinghouse (with tall windows) stands near the center. Baseball great Walter Johnson played catch on this street as a boy.
Courtesy American Title Insurance Company

Santa Fe Avenue, Looking North
Once the bustling center of Olinda's commerce, this street later became a lonely oil field access road north of Carbon Canyon Regional Park. View looks north from Olinda (now Carbon Canyon) Road, circa 1920, and spotlights Stein and Fassel's store, the scene of "a never-ending poker game."
Courtesy American Title Insurance Company

Landmarks of Old Olinda

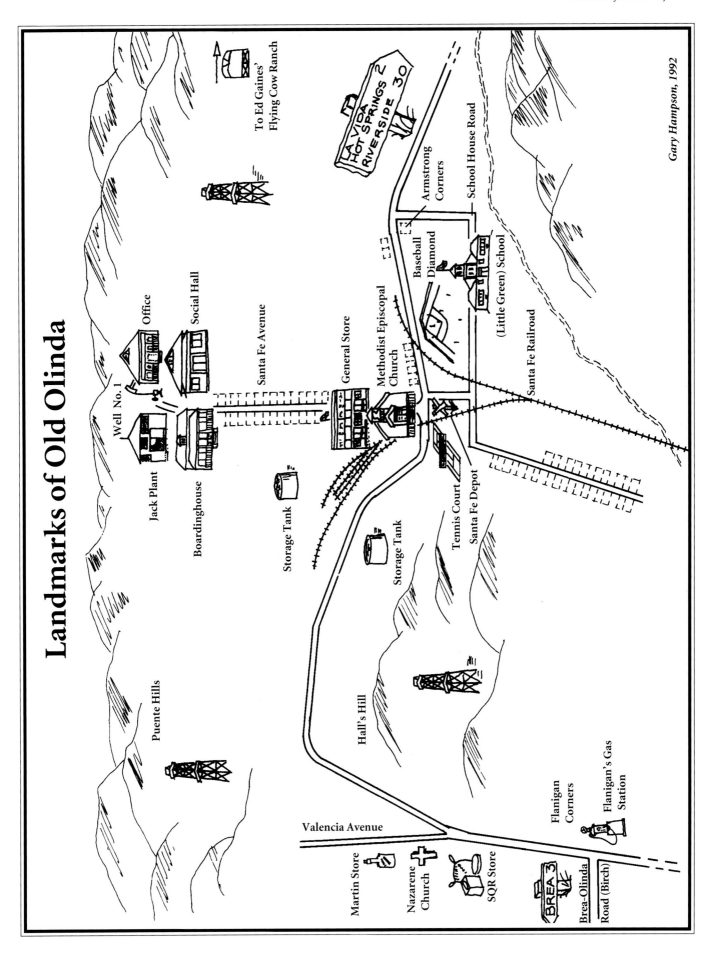

Gary Hampson, 1992

To Ed Gaines'
Flying Cow Ranch

LA VIDA
HOT SPRINGS 2
RIVERSIDE 30

Armstrong
Corners

School House Road

Office

Social Hall

Well No. 1

Santa Fe Avenue

General Store

Methodist Episcopal
Church

Baseball
Diamond

(Little Green) School

Santa Fe Railroad

Jack Plant

Boardinghouse

Storage Tank

Tennis Court

Santa Fe Depot

Storage Tank

Puente Hills

Hall's Hill

Valencia Avenue

Flanigan
Corners

Flanigan's Gas
Station

Martin Store

Nazarene
Church

SQR Store

BREA 3

Brea-Olinda
Road (Birch)

Sunday in the Country
Olindans Julia and Frank Schweitzer (Sr.) in their 1907 Ford.
Ten years later, he would serve as one of Brea's first civic leaders.
Brea Historical Society

The Gathering Place
Olindans assemble in front of the community's social hall, April 30, 1917.
From the Gale Family collection

A Market at the Corners, 1919
The Martin Store, located to the west of Olinda's main townsite at "Flanigan Corners," today's intersection of Valencia and Birch.
From the Robert Bowman collection

Santa Fe Avenue, the site of frequent dances, masquerades, lodge meetings, recitals and graduation ceremonies. Sunday worship services and Wednesday prayer meetings at the Methodist Episcopal Church were well-attended, and, in later years, a Nazarene Church welcomed its own congregation on (today's) Valencia.

Santa Claus came to town in a horse and buggy, driving up Olinda's dirt streets to deliver candy, turkey and toys. Spring and summer brought cookouts, picnics and popular athletic competitions. A sports-minded crowd, Olindans thrived on baseball, with fields built at several sites and each oil lease sponsoring a team. Large crowds of spectators cheered their favorite players, at first from small grandstands near the diamond and later from parked cars ringing the outfield.

Remembered by many who lived there as an idyllic place to grow up, Olinda offered its children a host of simple diversions: hiking in the hills, where slopes were carpeted with wildflowers and breezes were

Some families kept chickens and a cow, and many also had horses.

Olinda's commerce centered on Santa Fe Avenue, with Stern and Goodman Grocery and Dry Goods always a hub of activity. Clerks went door to door each morning, taking orders and delivering them later that day. Goods were charged and accounts settled monthly, and a big bag of candy rewarded those who paid their bills promptly.

Local housewives hurried out to greet the meat man when he pulled into town on his horse-drawn cab. The vegetable man and the ice man also frequented Olinda, and mail arrived Rural Free Delivery (RFD) from Fullerton. The advent of electricity and the arrival of automobiles later changed Olinda's way of doing business. The old store was sold to new owners and a second commercial area sprang up to the west at "Flanigan Corners," today's intersection of Valencia and Birch.

Social life in Olinda revolved around a community hall on upper

The Team to Beat
Always in love with baseball, Olindans fielded some mighty crews, including this 1910 lineup.
Courtesy American Title Insurance Company

**The Little
Red School**
Built near the turn of
the century, Olinda's
first schoolhouse was
too small almost
before its paint had
dried. By 1908, it
served 176 students,
more than the La
Habra and Randolph
(Brea Canyon)
schools combined.
Brea Historical Society

**The Little Green School, Built
1909**
A pot-bellied stove warmed winter
mornings, a creek flowed along out
back and students entered the door
each day to the sound of Sousa
marches. Moved and remodeled,
this building today is part of the
Brea Senior Citizens Center.
Brea Historical Society

Readin' and 'Ritin' and 'Rithmetic: Education in Old Olinda

Kindergarten Capers
The Olinda "class" of 1925-26 strikes a touching pose: (Left to right, front) first three unknown, Violet Nakaya, Earleen Clark, Mildred Phoenix, Edna Schubert, unknown, Catherine Braner, (and back) James Johnson, Eugene Foster, Dick Barman, Curry Charles, Bud McConnell, Elden Smith and Hubert McConnell.
From the Freida Schubert Smith collection

topple, sometimes bursting into flame. Distinctive handbells rang out whenever a lease needed help, and volunteers streamed in from every site to lend their neighbors a hand.

Olinda old-timers remember little rivalry among the disparate oil lease employees. Neighbors in a tightly knit community, Olindans shared bonds of experience and economic equality. The early town had no police force, and few residents locked their doors. Children fell asleep to the steady pulse of oil pumps, counting their rhythm like sheep: "Five dollars, five dollars, five dollars..." the oilman's lullaby. Olinda prospered. While to the west, the town that would one day surpass it slowly stirred to life.

A traveler passing Brea's townsite as late as the turn of this century would have scanned a panorama largely untamed by the efforts of man. Rising gently toward the hills, the valley stood much as it had for centuries, cut by arroyos and a tree-lined creek and dotted with sagebrush and cactus. To the west, a smattering of sheds and a few scattered homes marked the presence of early settlers, and neat patchwork

scented by citrus and sage, wading in cold Olinda Creek and swimming at warm La Vida Hot Springs, or sliding down the steep "gravel-pit" hills after a rain on corrugated metal sheets. Girls took shopping trips with their mothers, while boys hunted jackrabbits, squirrels or snakes, and in later years raced motorcycles over the hills.

Formal education found its first home in Olinda in 1898, when the two-roomed "Little Red Schoolhouse" was built on upper Santa Fe Avenue. The larger "Little Green School" (Olinda grammar, grades 1-8) followed in 1909, built adjacent to Olinda Creek on a site today flanked by the park tennis courts and lake. Olinda's secondary students were transported nine miles to Fullerton's high school, in early times by horse-drawn cab and in later years by bus.

Olinda's oilmen pioneered the practice of drilling with the hole full of water, an innovation widely adopted for shoring up well walls. CCMO crews of "Olinda 96" broke records in 1927, drilling to 8,046 feet—then the world's deepest well. Employed as well pushers (drillers), gang pushers

(foremen) and pumpers (engine mechanics), field men were assigned 12-hour shifts (noon to midnight or midnight to noon), and often worked six days a week. The jobs were hard, dirty, and not infrequently dangerous.

Buffeted by too-harsh winds, the oil-soaked derricks were prone to

Yesterday's Scholars, Olinda circa 1910
While smiles were obligatory, shoes (apparently) were optional.
Brea Historical Society

rows of fields and orchards sprouted green among fallow acres. To the north, the hills spread down in soft folds, dotted by buildings and derricks—the oil fields of the east valley.

Settlement had, by 1890, taken root in both Fullerton and Whittier, and from these sites gradually spread north and east into the La Habra Valley. As elsewhere, access to water and transportation played a pivotal role in development, and the Brea site—short then of both—was slow to draw a crowd. Those who pioneered the land were easterners and immigrants drawn to the valley's mild climate and fertile acres. Clearing away cactus and sagebrush before turning and leveling the soil, these "dry farmers" planted grain crops like barley and oats, and prayed for favorable weather. For the first time in the valley, the clattering of farm machinery split the late-summer silence, and the wind blew sweet from sun-warmed fields.

East valley land was first offered for sale or lease by its longtime owner, the Stearns Ranchos Company, in 1893. Union Oil soon

An Early Farm Family
The Yriartes, circa 1903: (Left to right, seated): Pascuala, baby Ysidoro and Patricio; (standing): Ysabel, Julian, Felix, Agustin and Mary.
From the John Yriarte collection

The Yriarte Ranch, circa 1912
The family's first local home, near today's Elm and State College. The small barn (left) later was moved to Ash and Laurel, where it stood for many years. Pictured (left to right, in car) Patricio and Pascuala Yriarte, Lorenza Lorea Yriarte, Isabel Yriarte Prendiville and Agustin Yriarte.
From the John Yriarte collection

Amber Waves
Cut by clattering mowers and loaded into huge moving
bins, east-valley grain makes its way to the threshing machine.

Machine of Steam
Traveling harvesters gather around a huge
steam traction engine, used to pull both
grain and water wagons. Note the ghostly
worker atop the engine and the "moving"
man on the right.

Photographs from the John Yriarte collection

WHERE IS RANDOLPH

The La Habra Valley Land & Water Co. have just subdivided into 10 and 20 acre lots in the beautiful and fertile La Habra valley 2200 acres of as fine land as ever lay out of doors. It has no superior in South California for oranges or walnuts. An abundance of pure, fresh, soft water is conveyed to the land by 36 inch cement pipe, and distributed on the land by smaller mains.

Your choice of this tract for $150.00 per acre with one inch of water conveyed with every ten acres of land

TERMS: One-third cash, balance on one and two years time at 6 per cent. OFFICE, at RANDOLPH, the new townsite on the tract.

Parties wishing to make inquiries or to purchase lands at RANDOLPH can call on

J. F. ISBELL and CHESTER ROBINSON

Agents for La Habra Valley Land & Water Co., at Randolph, J. C. Hiatt at Whittier, or Townsend & Robinson at Long Beach.

Whittier News, Jan. 31, 1903

The Selling of Randolph…

became the area's largest landowner, with an 1894 purchase of 1,200 acres. While Union retained much of this land (and later greatly added to its holdings), portions of the company's acreage were sold or leased in the early years to several Basque immigrants, among them Francisco Landa, who pastured as many as 3,000 sheep on 600 Union acres in the northern hills; Vittorio (Victor) Hualde, who grew barley and citrus on lands bisected by today's 57 Freeway; and Patricio Yriarte, who raised grain, black-eyed beans and sheep on as many as 1,200 owned and leased acres, including the later site of the city's first high school and the modern-day Brea Mall.

By the mid-1890's, the first vestiges of cityhood had come to La Habra, and—as a new century dawned, the promise of rail and water links to the west sparked growing interest in the place that would be Brea. Prominent among those who saw the potential for

Randolph

2000 Acres

Of choice Orange and Walnut Land, with Water, in this Tract.

Also Lots in Randolph City.

See our Agent on the Grounds, or

…The…

Townsend=Robinson Investment Company

Long Beach, Cal.

Orange County Directory, 1903

developing an east-valley townsite was transplanted Indianian Willets J. Hole, a pioneer La Habra Valley landowner and developer.

Appointed resident agent for the Stearns Ranchos, Hole purchased large tracts of valley land and promoted both these and adjacent properties to investors. Launching La Habra as a "model town" in hopes of drawing newcomers to the valley, Hole built an impressive brick house,

planned innovative irrigation projects, spearheaded construction of the landmark La Habra School and enlisted the cooperation of influential friends like rail magnate Henry Huntington and inventor-engineer George Chaffey to speed up transportation and water ties to the west.

An east-valley agricultural community gained its first measure of reality when Whittier realtors J.F. Isbell and A.H. Gregg signed on as site developers for the Townsend-Robinson Investment Company. By December of 1902, the *Fullerton Tribune* reported surveyors platting 2,200 acres of high ground just south of the entrance to Brea Canyon.

Meanwhile, Chaffey took on the challenge of delivering water to the dusty townsite, striking a deal to purchase the East Whittier Land and Water Company and its assets—a pumping plant, several miles of irrigation ditch and an interest in "water-bearing" land near the banks of the San Gabriel River. Stock was offered to farmers and other investors through the newly incorporated La Habra Valley Water Company, and the vital liquid

Willets J. Hole
An Indiana businessman, Hole brought his ailing wife west for the climate, and stayed to help build Brea.
Brea Historical Society

seemed on its way east at last.

Drilling started almost immediately on new wells, orders for machinery were placed, and surveying began for the laying of cement pipe eastward toward La Habra and the mouth of Brea Canyon, and from there south to Los Coyotes (today's north Fullerton). By early 1903, large teams of men and horses were at work laying pipe, and the gravity-flow line snaked east through the waiting valley.

Work on the water line progressed through the winter, and land advertisements appeared in January newspapers. Promoters selected the name "Randolph" for the new settlement, probably hoping the name would gain favor with Epes Randolph, general manager of the eagerly awaited Pacific Electric Railway.

Billed by promoters as, "as fine land as ever lay outdoors" having "no superior for oranges or walnuts," the Randolph site was touted for its climate, beauty and fertility, and each parcel of land was conveyed with the promise of "an abundance of pure, fresh, soft water." Frequent escorted tours in four-horse tallyho wagons brought prospective buyers from Los Angeles and Long Beach. Randolph's farm property was offered in 10 and 20-acre parcels at $150 per acre and sold briskly, with as many as 50 lots bought in a single day.

Inside the 200-acre Randolph townsite, the smaller "city" lots garnered far less attention, even though Epes Randolph, Pacific Electric Chief Engineer George Pillsbury and Hole purchased choice properties, and newspaper stories celebrated the "fine houses" all three planned to build.

Noting the rapid growth of an eastern neighbor, the *Whittier News* reported, "The new town of Randolph is flourishing: the rain has brightened its fertile acres, and made it look still more inviting to the prospective purchaser," and soon forecast that "schools, houses, churches, stores and homes will dot the (Randolph) landscape, where but

a few months ago barley and mustard held full sway."

By the spring of 1903, new landowners had set out fruit and walnut trees, and newspapers reported lumber from northern forests waiting at building sites. The Pacific Electric completed a scouting survey east through the valley, and Randolph School District was formed—serving a few children from the new farms and larger numbers from the nearby oil settlements, most who previously had commuted to La Habra's school by pony or horse cart.

Epes Randolph
One of the nation's premiere transportation engineers, Pacific Electric's Epes Randolph insisted on a quality line. His Southland rail routes provided the design for a later day's freeway system. *Courtesy Huntington Library*

A grand schoolhouse was proposed for Randolph, but voters found its $8,000 price tag too high, and a one-room building instead was erected in Brea Canyon by Union Oil. Starting in September of 1903, Miss Ellen Dickinson instructed 30 children in this small canyon school. Despite their age differences, all studied together, yet when recess arrived, boys and girls played in separate areas divided by a schoolyard fence.

May saw a large force of men and teams grading an extension of the county road (Central) east from La Habra to the mouth of Brea Canyon, and June brought the grading and oiling of Randolph's first street, Fullerton-Pomona Road (christened for its destinations, later shortened to Pomona Avenue and now known as Brea Boulevard).

Farm news from the community showed Southland "peanut king" C.E. Utt planting the crop his fame was gained for, interspersing peanuts and walnuts on a 50-acre Randolph tract. Land agent John Isbell had planted his acreage in walnuts and popcorn, and a "Mr. Ford" of Fullerton had built a windmill.

Six exhaustive months of work came to an end for pipe layers in June as the first phase of Randolph's irrigation lines reached completion, and materials were readied for a pumping station. No one present was prepared when, in mid-August, the water system's grand debut proved the line to be fatally flawed. Though records of what happened remain sketchy, many believe water never reached Randolph in quantities sufficient to sustain its growth.

The development of Randolph, begun with such success just nine months before, now ended almost as quickly. The failed irrigation project was cancelled, and settlers tried unsuccessfully to build their own new system. More trouble soon followed. Randolph's second great hope—speedy completion of an east valley rail line—was blocked by land disputes and business reverses.

Too many troubles in too short a time dimmed the hopes of all but a few, and delayed for several years further development in the east valley. Land promotions no longer graced the papers, and many who had come to farm sold both their property and its promise. Others stayed—confident water would flow and train whistles blow in the place that would be Brea.

Brea, 1916

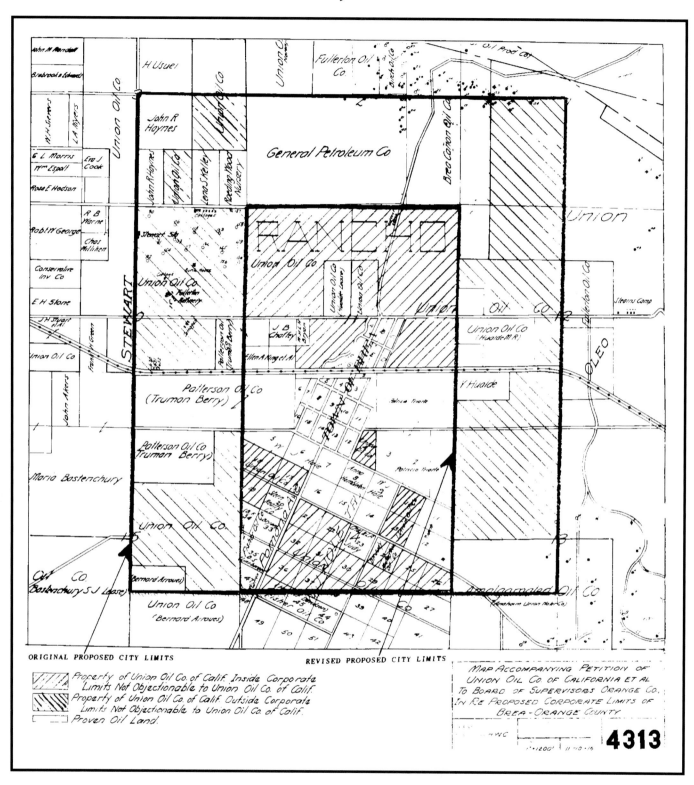

ORIGINAL PROPOSED CITY LIMITS

REVISED PROPOSED CITY LIMITS

Property of Union Oil Co. of Calif. Inside Corporate Limits Not Objectionable to Union Oil Co. of Calif.

Property of Union Oil Co. of Calif. Outside Corporate Limits Not Objectionable to Union Oil Co. of Calif.

Proven Oil Land.

MAP ACCOMPANYING PETITION OF UNION OIL CO OF CALIFORNIA ET AL TO BOARD OF SUPERVISORS ORANGE CO. IN RE PROPOSED CORPORATE LIMITS OF BREA-ORANGE COUNTY

4313

Starting Small

Union Oil's compromise map for Brea's incorporation shows less area (inner line) within the city limits than originally proposed (outer line). Ironically, Union benefited far less than many others in this arrangement, for the company owned two-thirds of all taxable property inside the revised city limits.

Courtesy Orange County Historical Archives

CHAPTER 4

Seeds of Cityhood

In the first years of the 20th century, Southern California enjoyed a system of interurban mass transit second to none in the nation. A consolidation of several smaller railways that together became Pacific Electric, this transportation network played a pivotal role in Southland development—and brought both people and progress to the place that would be Brea.

A few men designed the lines, and many men laid the tracks, but the one man most responsible for bringing train service to the eager east valley was rail-heir Henry Huntington. Robbed of a chance to run his family business—the Southern Pacific—Huntington forged his own empire, purchasing key Southland properties and exploiting them through a network of railways.

Inaugurating service on his Pacific Electric system with a 1902 Long Beach line, Huntington branched out the following year with a second route, to Whittier. Rumors this Whittier "P.E." line soon would stretch eastward into the La Habra Valley sparked land sales in the struggling small town of Randolph, although several frustrating years would pass before rail service became a reality. Caught up in a corporate power struggle, the valley line seemed all but lost when Huntington's partners secretly sold

their stock—effectively handing control of the P.E. to its Southern Pacific competitor.

Daunted but undefeated, the "Trolley Man" rebounded to build again. Retaining a number of prospective rail routes in his own

Henry Huntington
Once a familiar figure in the east valley, Huntington scouted land locations from the seat of a stylish carriage. Resolved and resilient, he united the Southland with his Pacific Electric Railway.
USC Library, Special Collections, California Historical Society/Ticor Title Insurance

The East Valley, 1908, by Charles Lawrence
Union Oil's recently begun Stewart Station rises in the center, the oil camps of Puente Wells
and Brea Canyon hug the hills and a few scattered farms break the valley's otherwise empty acres.
An official Pacific Electric photograph from the William D. Myers collection

name, Huntington formed the new
Los Angeles Inter-Urban Railway.
An ambitious building program
followed, and rails reached out to
sites throughout the Southland.
Among Huntington's holdings was
the route through the La Habra Valley,
where further strides toward cityhood
hinged on improved rail access.

Travel had remained stagger-
ingly slow in the valley's first
century of settlement. Horsemen in
the cattle and early oil eras considered the 25-mile trip to Los Angeles a
good day's ride—though few attempted the return trip before a new
day dawned. Supply expeditions in
the sheep and later oil eras routinely
took twice this long. Westbound
wagoners drove their oxen as far as
the San Gabriel River, camping there
for the night and proceeding to town
the following day. Goods bought,
they turned once more toward the
east, traveling two more days before
reaching home again.

Though the Southern Pacific's
Los Angeles rail route bypassed the
La Habra Valley in favor of the
Pomona, the arrival of Santa Fe
railheads in Anaheim and Fullerton

in the 1880's offered some relief to
local residents. Yet as late as 1908,
the closest train stop for freight and
passengers was still five miles away.

More than ready for rail service
of their own, La Habra Valley
residents anxiously awaited news of
the Pacific Electric's eastbound
"Yorba Linda" line. As early as July
of 1903, local newspapers reported
nearly all right-of-ways were
acquired, yet a series of setbacks

plagued progress. Failure to secure a
few key parcels of land was followed
by widespread financial instability, as
San Francisco's 1906 earthquake
plunged the state into recession.

Finally begun by late 1906, the
plotting of the local line was quickly
followed by the building of culverts
and crossings. A force of 500 men,
most poorly paid Mexican laborers,
graded the roadbed, then laid heavy
wooden cross ties and steel rails.

At Work on the East Valley Line, circa 1910
More than 500 workers and 100 mules labored on the local railway. The wealth of
nearby oil fields provided the major motivation in bringing rail service to Randolph.
Courtesy American Title Insurance Company

Trolleys reached La Habra by late 1908, and tracks soon stretched east as far as Pillsbury, an undeveloped stop near today's Berry Street. Further delays took their toll, but by May of 1910, newspapers reported rails within sight of Randolph, and work began on a depot.

The trolley that rolled into Randolph on a July morning in 1910 arrived late—nearly seven years so, by some accounts, for valley farmers had been watching west for its coming as early as 1903. No grateful crowd of townspeople thronged to greet the train's arrival, for Randolph in 1910 was little more than a sign and some empty fields.

George Chaffey
A brilliant hydraulic engineer, Chaffey succeeded where others had failed in bringing water to the thirsty east valley. His work in the Imperial Valley had already "made the desert bloom."
Courtesy Ontario Public Library

Negligible growth had been seen at the townsite in the years since 1903. With water and train service lacking, backers of the failed first settlement had never recorded the town, and land sales had long since stopped. But as the century's first decade drew to a close, Randolph picked up its pace. In 1908, a townsite plan identical to the original had been filed by Ontario Investment. Now—as Huntington's trains worked their way east, Chaffey's water flowed in from the west. Train whistles sounded and taps were turned on—and town lots came up for sale.

Included in plans for the officially filed first "Map of the Town of Randolph" were 16 blocks and 235 lots bordered on the north by La Habra (now Ash) Street, west by Madrone(a) Avenue, south by Sixth Street (later Cedar and now Imperial) and east by Flower Avenue. Acting to promote local land sales, the Chaffey interests in early 1910 erected the town's first building: a two-story, four-room new Randolph School to replace the overcrowded canyon structure.

While the town of Randolph had languished in the pre-rail period, nearby oil settlements had boomed. Almost 800 people lived in the Puente Wells, Brea Canyon and Stearns Camp settlements, and dozens of new derricks stretched out against the sky.

Rapid change had come to the oil industry in the years since 1900, and that change came home to local fields. Drilling advancements brought production into the modern age as gasoline engines and improved tools pioneered ever deeper drilling, and a new market for crude emerged as the Navy switched its fleet from coal to fuel oil. Huge quantities of crude flowed from nearby wells, some carried in new pipelines to tankers at San Pedro's modernized terminal, and some stored locally in small reservoirs. In 1908, Union began work on its vast Stewart Station—a 100-acre refining, pumping and storage facility a half-mile west of the Randolph townsite.

Agriculture had expanded slowly into the east valley during the pre-rail era. Experimenting with seeds and cuttings, newcomers laid out orchards of fruit and nut trees and fields of grain and vegetables. Citrus, tomatoes, peaches, apricots, apples, cherries, sugar beets, olives, nuts and corn all were tried in these years. Though some settlers continued to dry farm, many tapped underground water with wells, and the whirring blades of windmills spun in the bright summer sky.

Lyman Stewart
Union Oil's founder had a "nose for oil" and a career that spanned 64 years. Stewart's vast property purchases made Union Brea's largest landowner.
Courtesy Unocal

A few harvests were hauled to the Whittier Cannery, but most farmers chose La Habra's new California Vegetable Union, a shipping house built near the rail right-of-way. Prominent agricultural names included the Hualdes and Yriartes, Truman Berry (who bought C.E. Utt's enlarged, 100-acre west-side walnut/peanut farm) and a group of Japanese farmers including Takegawa and Usuei who raised peas, cabbages and tomatoes on the east side of today's North Puente Street.

During these early years a small number of structures took shape in the eastern valley. Dwarfed by imposing barns sheltering important livestock and tools, farm homes started small and sparsely furnished, growing larger later "if and when" farming proved profitable. Able to bring few possessions west, the valley's first settlers made much of little, acquiring items gradually and adding personal touches with curtains and quilts. Exotic flowers bloomed in local gardens, and groves of fast-growing eucalyptus were planted for fuel and shade.

RIGHT: Valley Landmark
Named for Union Oil (now Unocal) founder Lyman Stewart, Stewart Station boasted this crude-oil refinery, built in 1911 southeast of today's Puente and Central. Workers and their families lived in small cottages nearby.
Brea Historical Society

BELOW: Division of Labor
Union Oil's Stearns Camp work force, still heavy on horses in this 1914 photo. This view looks north, near today's Lambert and Wildcat Way. The large building (far right) is a boardinghouse.
From the Jessie Shores Root collection

Holiday at the Hualde House
Famed for their hospitality, the Hualdes host a 1912 Easter gathering. The finest residence in the early east valley, the Hualde home was located just north of today's Lambert near Cliffwood, but was destroyed by fire in the 1960's.
From the Kenny Mon collection

Although Randolph, Pillsbury and Hole had bought large parcels of land in Randolph and talked of building fine homes, no such residences ever rose in the eastern valley. Before the coming of the railroad only one local home boasted a claim to glamor, the $4,500 "Hualde Mansion" built in 1909 on the town's east side.

One of the early Basques who settled the area, Victor Hualde found success growing grain, and later planted citrus. Prosperous among his neighbors, Hualde numbered among his possessions, according to county records, "seven horses, eight mules, two cows, 24 chickens, a combine harvester, mower and rake," though visitors to the Hualde house better remembered its "mighty wine cellar and long table for guests."

Though it was a trolley of Huntington's Los Angeles Inter-Urban that first rocked its way into Randolph, much of this system actually had been built with the help of Pacific Electric. While the

sensational newspapers of the day told tales of heated rail rivalries, the Southland's electric transit systems came together quietly in the end. Not long after the L.A. Inter-Urban reached Randolph, Huntington sold out to Southern Pacific, and the united rail networks formed a vast "new" Pacific Electric network.

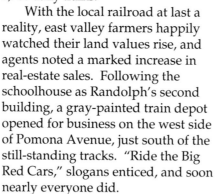

At its peak just 15 years later, this system would boast more than a thousand miles of track carrying 2,700 daily trains.

With the local railroad at last a reality, east valley farmers happily watched their land values rise, and agents noted a marked increase in real-estate sales. Following the schoolhouse as Randolph's second building, a gray-painted train depot opened for business on the west side of Pomona Avenue, just south of the still-standing tracks. "Ride the Big Red Cars," slogans enticed, and soon nearly everyone did.

Passengers relaxed in wood and steel cars furnished with black leather seats, talking together, playing cards and singing songs. Local freight traveled in self-powered "box motor" cars, or was pulled by locomotive engines: outgoing barrels of oil and harvests of citrus meeting incoming lumber, mail, manufactured goods and machinery.

Propelled by hydroelectric power generated in the distant High Sierra, the swiftly moving trolleys whisked their way along the tracks at 50 miles an hour, their overhead lines trailing sparks in the sky.

Once isolated by distance, the valley suddenly was linked to a larger world. No longer a full day away, Los Angeles now was less than an hour's journey, and businessmen, school children and families on shopping sprees ventured west to see the city firsthand. More far-flung excursions followed. Trips to Mount Lowe, San Gabriel Mission, the beaches of Venice and Santa Monica and the citrus groves of Riverside and San Bernardino all tempted local

Alone in a Crowd, 1912
The new town's first building, Randolph School stands surrounded by students, but with no other structures in sight. Knickers and newsboy hats, overalls and big bows—such were the styles when this school was built at the southwest corner of (today's) Brea Boulevard and Lambert. Note Ralph Jepsen (center), the Randolph district's first superintendent, and the school bell, now housed at the Brea Congregational Church.
Brea Historical Society

LEFT: Motorman Nixon
The father of the nation's 37th President, at work in 1908. Many early Breans knew Frank Nixon, a motorman on the Pacific Electric's Whittier line.
Courtesy Yorba Linda Public Library

BELOW: On Track
Long-awaited and eagerly sought, the trolleys became "conjurers of good fortune" for all the striving small cities of the Southland. This rare 1938 photo shows shuttle car 884 in service on the east valley line.
An E.M. Leo photo. From the William D. Myers collection

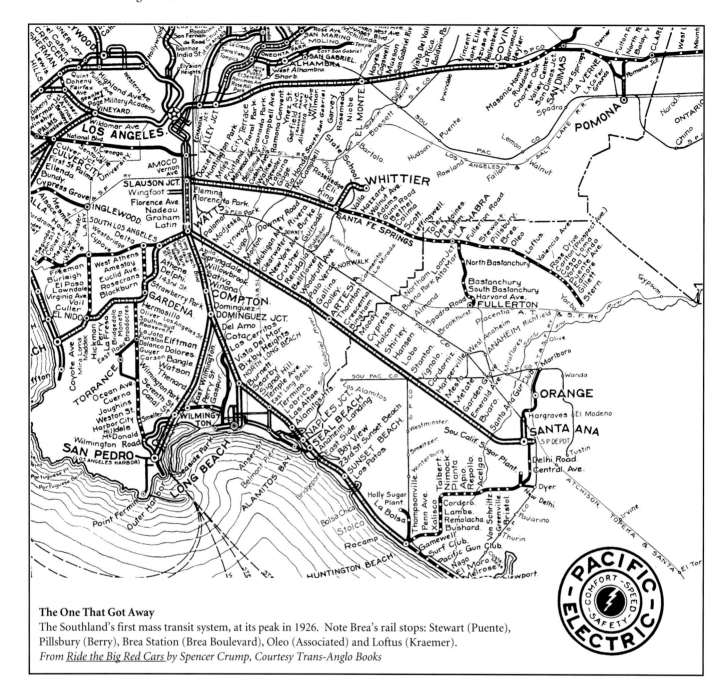

The One That Got Away
The Southland's first mass transit system, at its peak in 1926. Note Brea's rail stops: Stewart (Puente),
Pillsbury (Berry), Brea Station (Brea Boulevard), Oleo (Associated) and Loftus (Kraemer).
From Ride the Big Red Cars by Spencer Crump, Courtesy Trans-Anglo Books

travelers, and, by 1911, the local line had graduated to seven scheduled trolleys a day.

Though initially planned to link Inland Empire trolleys with Los Angeles in a "great circle route" through the Pomona and La Habra valleys, the local rail line never reached its Corona connection. Drama engulfed construction just east of Randolph as the Santa Fe Railroad stepped in to protect its transit monopoly. Seeking to pre-

vent—by armed resistance—the building of a crossing over the Olinda spur (near today's Rose Drive), Santa Fe stationed six boxcars of deputized men to guard the area. A "wild-west" style rail war appeared imminent for several weeks, until the trolley line outwitted its competitor.

Waiting out the Santa Fe by building beyond the trouble spot in Yorba Linda and then backtracking west toward the disputed connec-tion, the P.E. eventually made the

Olinda crossing and linked its tracks together. Yet the struggle proved a turning point for the valley line. Plans for Corona evaporated amid the fighting, and track instead dead-ended at the mouth of Santa Ana Canyon, just 15 miles short of its Inland Empire connection.

Rotary engines installed in electrical substations like Randolph's (built near the tracks on North Orange Avenue) converted incoming alternating current to direct current,

Power to the P.E.
A wooden structure built just south of the train tracks, Pacific Electric Substation 11 was torn down years ago. Not considered an important destination by the railway, Randolph/Brea was the site of modest railway buildings and few official photographs. Note Brea's name on the substation in this rare 1937 photo.
Photo by Ralph Melching

powering the P.E. system. Linked to 600-volt overhead lines, trolleys sped through smogless skies, passing groves of waxy-green orange trees and fields of grain and vegetables. In the first quarter of the 20th century, this rail system transformed Southland development, with every new land venture boasting convenient trolley access. Newcomers rode in on the Red Cars, and small towns swelled into cities.

A mood of celebration marked the trolleys' debut in the eastern valley. With water and rail service, the Randolph townsite at last possessed all the requisites of growth, and development began in earnest in the place that would be Brea.

From the east valley's earliest years of control and ownership under Spain and Mexico, the Spanish word *brea*, meaning asphalt or tar, had been applied to land in the northern hills and canyons. Tonner Canyon was known as Cañada de la Brea (Canyon of the Tar) while land to the west (just over today's Los Angeles County line) was Rancho Rincón de la Brea (Narrow Valley of Tar). With the arrival of the rail line and the departure of city namesake Epes Randolph from its employ,

local citizens sought a new name for their town—but settled instead on an old one.

The townsite of *Brea*, Orange County, California, was officially founded on Jan. 19, 1911, when the 1908 Randolph map was refiled under this new name. Hole continued his stewardship of the infant settlement, arranging the purchase of the 200-acre townsite for $100,000, and raising an additional $100,000 for construction of streets and business buildings, and installation of electric lines and water pipes.

The original 235 homesites were immediately increased to nearly 350 with the recording of a new tract, the "Northern extension of the town of Brea." Owned by Union Oil and subdivided for sale or lease to employees, this expanded acreage spread north from the railroad tracks to Cypress Street between Madrone(a) and Pomona avenues.

Advertisements extolling the new town's virtues quickly appeared in local papers: "The best located townsite in all the country, right in the center of the oil camps, besides being in a fine agricultural and fruit country," proclaimed a *Whittier News* promotion, further

recommending the Brea townsite as "a rare opportunity for businessmen hunting a location."

Priced between $225 and $450, with water piped to lots, Brea property was represented exclusively by the Whittier firm of (C.R.) Thomas and (Fred) Hazzard, assisted by on-site agent J.W. Rouse. Within six months, 25 residential lots and 40 business properties had been sold. A rush of construction found nearly 100 men at work building cottages and business structures, and the sounds of hammers and saws rang out from dawn till dusk. At least one home foundation was laid the same

Boosting Brea
Orange County Tribune. Aug. 2, 1911

Law and Disorder in Brea's "Wild West" Era

"Oh, Brea was a wild country! People carried guns! My father wore a gun in a holster, and the oil workers carried guns too. There wasn't much law, and it was tough country— they used to shoot up the town!

My folks were driving home from La Habra one night when they saw a train get stopped. They watched from the road as that caboose was held up, black handkerchiefs and all.

It got to where there was no police protection, because the only law was out of town. That's one reason Brea was formed. The people wanted to have their own police department and to run the town their own way."

—*Early Brea,*
as remembered by
Thelma Kinsler Henderson

day sale was made. Even so, housing was always inadequate, and many Breans spent their first local months living in a tent.

Almost overnight, a small business district sprang up: several large oil-company machine shops and supply houses on the north, Brown and Dauser Lumber on the east, W.E. Hurst's boiler shop on the northwest, and—at the center of town, (among others) Ed Russell's jewelry store, Ed Peterkin's meat and ice center, Borden and Salveson's grocery, Amos Latch's livery stable, C.P. Griggs' garage, Matt Smith's barber shop and Karl Rudolph's drug store (with soda fountain "to quench the thirst of the dry").

The years 1911-1913 saw major construction in Brea's downtown. The city's earliest large, multi-purpose structures, including the (first) Sewell, Wall, Delaney and McCarty (better known as Brea Hotel) buildings, rose in these years. Taking advantage of street-level commercial space and upstairs accommodations, the latter three

properties offered furnished rooms for rent. Travelers and boarders took meals at Rosalie Rankin's Brea Restaurant or Nellie Alford's Brea Cafe, enjoyed silent movies at Babbit and Tallberg's Brea Picture House or W. E. Richardson's Picture Show, and socialized (if male) at Enoch and Cowden's popular pool room.

Amid the growing trend toward temperance, the city's first properties were restricted against the selling of alcohol, a point celebrated by one newspaper as evidence "there will never be saloons in this townsite." Though oil jobs were commonly considered "hard-drinking, seven-

NEW TOWN OF BREA IS FORGING TO THE FORE

Lots Are Selling Rapidly and Buildings Are Being Rushed

Brea townsite, in the heart of the oil fields in the La Habra valley, is the scene of unusual activity. At the present time about one hundred men are at work, contracts for residences have been let, a bank, lumber yard, hotel and several other business offices are to be put in immediately and the town has an unusually bright future from all appearances.

Beside its favorable location for oil men employ the Olinda, Brea Canyon Hills field, who wish where

Orange County Tribune,
Aug. 2, 1911

days-a-week" work, Brea's practice proved different, due both to the temperament of the times and the religious influence of Union Oil founder Lyman Stewart, a staunch Presbyterian who also started the Union Rescue Mission and the Bible Institute of Los Angeles. In less than a decade, the nation would go dry for 13 years of Prohibition.

The following months saw swift strides, as the tiny town came to life. Brea's business district soon sported new curbs and sidewalks, and improvements were made in the reservoir. On Orange, W.D. Casner's landscaping efforts (the city's first palm trees) offered splashes of green in an otherwise dusty landscape. The aroma of browning bread drifted from Sidney Camm's bakery, and plates of sugared sweets tempted tasters at Ford's Confectionery. The community's first medical man, Dr. V.C. Charleston, hung out his shingle, ladies in plumed hats preened

before mirrors at the new town millinery, Stern and Goodman's store began business with a memorable musical celebration and Brea's earliest financial institution, the "handsome, brick La Habra Valley Bank," began business with assets of $25,000. The town's first post office soon opened in a store adjacent to the bank, with E.S. Glaze as first postmaster.

Residents and visitors alike marvelled at the town's rapid rise. Reporters wrote of Brea's "surprising growth," comparing to "wildfire" the timely transformation of flat, plowed fields into a "thriving new town come to stay." "A city with a substantial present and a most exciting future," wrote the *Orange County Tribune* in 1912, further assessing the budding town as "one of the best of the smaller investment centers in Southern California."

Expansion in the oil industry fostered Brea's growth, as more and more men were hired to staff the region's rich drilling sites. To the northwest, near the mouth of Brea Canyon, Birch Oil hit "the big one" in March of 1911. Gushing $1 million in

BREA THE NEW OIL TOWN
Four miles North of Fullerton, Cal.

ON THE PACIFIC ELECTRIC RAILROAD

GOOD WATER ON EVERY LOT

BEAUTIFUL VIEW
OVERLOOKING THE ENTIRE LA HABRA VALLEY AND IN THE FROSTLESS BELT
You will make money by buying a lot in BREA as
PRICES WILL ADVANCE RAPIDLY
Don't Delay

C. R. THOMAS, Sales Agent

Orange County Tribune, Sept. 13, 1911

Brea Beginnings
Looking north on Pomona Avenue, circa 1912. The buildings are few and the main street still dirt, but the town has begun its rise. Already in business, (west side, from left) the original Sewell Building (featuring the popular Enoch and Cowden Pool Room), the La Habra Valley Bank and (across the street, north) Salveson's store. On the east: Brea Garage and Machine Works, Stern and Goodman store, Rudolph Drug and the Oil Well Supply Company.
Brea Historical Society

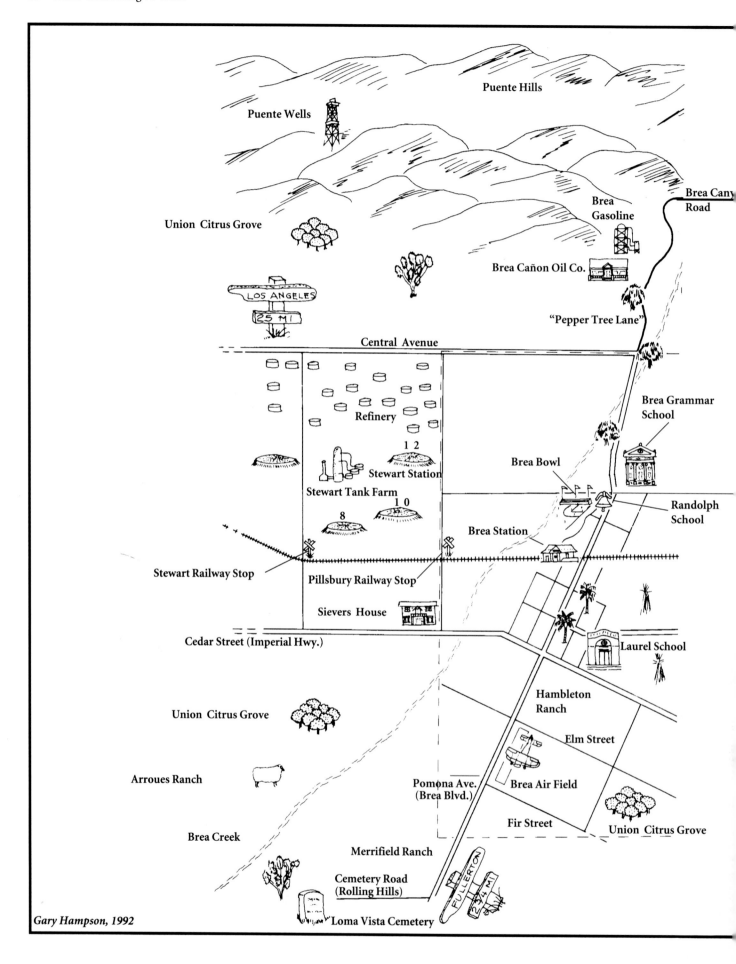

Puente Hills

Puente Wells

Union Citrus Grove

Brea Gasoline

Brea Canyon Road

Brea Cañon Oil Co.

LOS ANGELES 25 MI

"Pepper Tree Lane"

Central Avenue

Refinery

1 2

Stewart Station

Brea Bowl

Brea Grammar School

Stewart Tank Farm

1 0

8

Randolph School

Brea Station

Stewart Railway Stop

Pillsbury Railway Stop

Sievers House

Cedar Street (Imperial Hwy.)

Laurel School

Hambleton Ranch

Elm Street

Union Citrus Grove

Arroues Ranch

Pomona Ave. (Brea Blvd.)

Brea Air Field

Union Citrus Grove

Fir Street

Brea Creek

Merrifield Ranch

Cemetery Road (Rolling Hills)

FULLERTON 2 3/4 MI

Loma Vista Cemetery

Gary Hampson, 1992

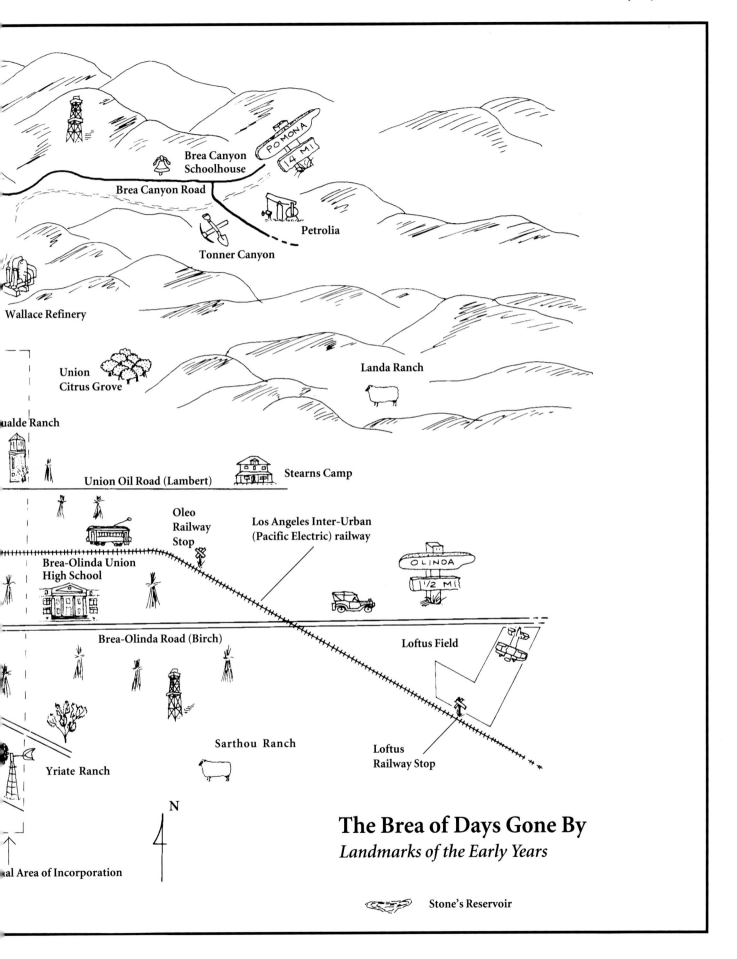

Brea Canyon
Schoolhouse

Brea Canyon Road

POMONA 14 MI

Petrolia

Tonner Canyon

Wallace Refinery

Union
Citrus Grove

Landa Ranch

ualde Ranch

Union Oil Road (Lambert)

Stearns Camp

Oleo
Railway
Stop

Los Angeles Inter-Urban
(Pacific Electric) railway

OLINDA 1/2 MI

Brea-Olinda Union
High School

Loftus Field

Brea-Olinda Road (Birch)

Sarthou Ranch

Loftus
Railway Stop

Yriate Ranch

N

al Area of Incorporation

The Brea of Days Gone By
Landmarks of the Early Years

Stone's Reservoir

Early Architecture
Mr. and Mrs. H.L. Delaney pose in front of their new La Habra (Ash) Street business building, one of the earliest two-stories in town. The Delaney Building's downstairs rentals (circa 1914) include (from left) the first office of the *La Habra Valley Progress* (with editor C.A. Meacham's motorcycle parked out front), Sidney Camm's Bakery and a record shop.
From the Glenn Bender collection

The H.L. Delaneys at Home, 1914
The pioneer couple pictured in front of their house at 119 S. Walnut.
From the Glenn Bender collection

oil during its first year alone, Birch No. 5 would produce a remarkable three million barrels by 1916.

Created by the United States Supreme Court's breakup of the powerful Rockefeller Trust, the new Standard Oil Company of California soon launched local drilling at nearby Coyote Hills, quickly bringing in the Southland's best-producing well. Scrambling to secure more nearby leases, Standard made its entry into Brea on the grain farm of Patricio Yriarte. Encouraged by local prospects, the company expanded its seaside refinery, and soon became not only a producer, but also a large buyer of Brea crude.

The electrification of Orange County's oil fields was pioneered on

Standard's local lease in 1912, when a 10,000-volt distributing system began serving the Yriarte site. Within the next decade, electricity would overtake steam as the favored power source for local wells.

Considered an annoying byproduct in the oil industry's earliest years, gasoline came of age as America embraced the automobile. Olinda had its own small refining plant by 1912, and larger operations followed near the rich Birch field—where one well alone produced more than a million and a half cubic feet of gas daily. Powered by eight eight-horsepower Bessemer gas compressors, The Wallace Refinery (later Pacific Gasoline) was the first plant of its kind in California, extracting gasoline through the compression of natural gas. This refinery's daily production rate of 4,000 gallons soon sparked construction of the smaller nearby Brea Gasoline Company, with a daily capacity of 1,000 gallons.

TOP: The Long Haul
Machinery for The Wallace Refinery's innovative plant plows its way up the "Hog Back" by mule team, courtesy the Yriarte Family.
Brea Historical Society

RIGHT: Canyon Construction
The Wallace Refinery's pioneering plant, circa 1912, on the "Hog Back" slope near today's Brea Boulevard and Canyon Country Road. Brea's William (Bill) Culp managed the plant, which turned Birch Oil's natural gas into gasoline.
Brea Historical Society

BELOW: Lease Life
The ups and downs of oil-lease life were apparent to this Birch crowd. The commute to work was short—but it was tough not to take the job home. Workers' houses line this steep street, northwest of today's Central and Brea Boulevard.
From the Leo Piantoni collection

Canyon Panorama
Brea Cañon Oil's lease near the mouth of Brea Canyon, circa 1915. Local resident Abe Yost served as supervisor during this company's highly productive early years.
Brea Historical Society

Standard Shops, 1914
Fresh from local oil discoveries, Standard built these shops just south of the train station to serve its Brea and Fullerton fields. An old story says company founder John D. Rockefeller once visited Standard's local operation, and shared a picnic with workmen high in the Brea hills.
Brea Historical Society

An incredibly explosive extract, the gasoline produced in these extraction plants was of the highest possible grade. Shipped out in specially prepared tanks, it was blended with lower-grade gases to create a usable fuel. The dry residue of this production process at first was burned off in an open flame, but the gas later was piped into town under the supervision of Brean John Dietzel. Local newsman C.A. Meacham celebrated Brea as "the first town south of the Tehachapis" to be supplied with natural gas, an event

that proved a business boon. The cheap, piped-in fuel soon proved invaluable to local machine and tool shops, and many a Brea backyard was lit by an open torch.

Though local oil production flourished in these early years, Brea gained little recognition for its rich resources. Newspaper writers and oil industry insiders generally referred to both Brea and Olinda drilling sites as the "Fullerton" or "Whittier" fields, and the fame of local production was eclipsed by these larger towns.

Christened in 1901 and 1902 in homage to the fields that fueled them, the *Fullerton*, a 16,000-barrel sail-powered oil carrier, and the *Whittier*, a prototype for 40 years of steel-hulled, steam-powered tankers, more properly should have been called the *"Olinda"* and the *"Brea"*.

Back in the growing town, a local chamber of commerce met for the first time in March of 1913, choosing Stern and Goodman Store Manager Harry Ray as president, adopting the theme "Boost Brea," and doing so by raising funds to build the "Brea Bowl," a baseball field in north town near the

"sand wash" that infrequently flowed as Brea Creek. Fire took its first toll that year, when the original one-story Sewell Building burned to the ground "on a quiet night without a breath of wind."

Up from the first Sewell's ashes rose the two-story new Sewell

Keeping Shop
Business pioneer Ed Peterkin (far right) poses outside his Brea Cash Market in the Sewell Building. Window (left) presumably displayed a collection of ever-popular pigs.
Brea Historical Society

A Wrinkle in Time
Ironing Out the Facts on Brea's Firstborn

Clifford Yates

Every town has a "first" baby story, but only a few—like Brea—have two.

Cute little Clifford Yates arrived earliest among the new town's baby boys, born to Mrs. and Mrs. W.B. Yates on Dec. 2, 1912. The happy news of young Yates' birth was cause for celebration, and newspapers carried the story then, as well as in later years. But in subsequent retellings some facts slipped, and sometimes the story changed.

A 1937 newspaper article spoke of Brea's first son, but gave him his brother's name, while a modern-day history called him Brea's first baby—an honor held by another.

*Though no pinafored-pictures tell the tale, the facts are still quite clear: born on April 20, 1912, **Lois Adams** was Brea's first baby.*

Building, made of brick, with an auditorium and offices upstairs and space for stores below. Dentist C.C. Jarvis (said to pull teeth for $1) set up a second-floor office, while ground-floor space was leased by Sweet's Candy Store (site of the city's second post office, with C.H. Sweet as postmaster), Brea Pharmacy, MacClatchie Hardware and Ed Peterkin's Brea Cash Market, where local youngsters delighted to see live hogs displayed in the window.

The town's earliest electrical connections arrived in 1913, when a 2,200-volt distribution system became operational, and Brea's nights were brightened by the glow of downtown streetlights. Civic leaders acted that year to prevent further fires by building the town's first "fire truck"—an $185 chemical engine mobilized on a chassis offered free from Union Oil. Brea residents passed bonds to promote a regional road west toward Los Angeles, and called on the county sheriff to provide help with a local jail. More than two blocks of businesses and 100 dwellings had been completed, and W.J. Hole's "Brea Annex" offered would-be buyers 24 new homesites between today's Imperial and Date. Town property values had more than doubled in less than two full years.

June 20, 1913 saw the founding of Brea's first newspaper, the *La Habra Valley Progress*. With no rooms to rent for a print shop, publisher C.A. Meacham set the first two months' issues in Ontario, making weekly runs back and forth over dirt roads on his motorcycle. Communication advanced on a second front that year when residents (fed up with Fullerton's phone service and its 10-member party lines) began a 12-year battle for Brea's own local exchange.

Though religion long had been part of local life, it had found few permanent homes. Full-immersion baptisms were recorded in Brea Canyon Creek before the turn of the century, local Methodists conducted Sunday School classes at the Brea Canyon schoolhouse starting in 1910, and several congregations held worship services in sites from banks to pool rooms. Brea's first religious structure opened in 1913 as the Church of the Nazarene (200 S. Walnut), followed by the Christian Church (dedicated in 1915 at 201 W. Ash, now the site of the Brea Missionary Baptist), and the Congregational Church (dedicated in 1915 at the southwest corner of today's Brea Boulevard at Birch).

Both spiritual and social in their offerings, these and other early Brea churches played a significant part in community life, and their influence helped mold local policies. Noted for their activism in the city's first years, Nazarene Pastor J.M. Woodruff and Christian Pastor W.E. Spicer led local battles against prizefighting and in favor of Prohibition.

Sidney Camm, the town baker, soon purchased a lot south of the

Aug. 13, 1915

Sewell Building and began work on the new "Brea Bakery," a narrow, two-story frame structure that would become the latter-day landmark Sam's Place. By 1915, Brea's town center featured several large oil, construction or transfer operations, plus five other two-story structures: the bakery, the rebuilt Sewell Building, and the Wall, McCarty (Brea Hotel) and Delaney buildings. Soon also struck by fire, the Delaney burned as volunteers fought to save it. When pressure proved inadequate, water from hoses failed to reach the second floor, and the blaze at last was extinguished instead by a bucket brigade.

Brea's first all-weather street arrived in 1915, when the county paved Pomona Avenue's thinly oiled dirt surface. The new concrete strip stretched from the mouth of the canyon south through the business district, but was only 16 feet wide, leaving the curbsides bare. Other area roads in this era remained little more than wagon tracks, and wet weather invariably found unwary travelers mired in knee-deep mud. Even so, people were on the move. Hardly a one-horse town, Brea by 1915 boasted several liveries and transfer operations, a bevy of bikes and a few newfangled movers powered by gas or steam.

Though primitive in design and unpredictable in behavior, the automobiles that first sputtered along local streets quickly became status symbols. While 44 cars were registered in 1916, the number leaped to 105 the following year, and every Brean afoot dreamed of owning a Ford or a Chevy. Alarmed over accident rates, city leaders soon acted to make streets safer, passing laws, erecting signs and hiring Brea's first traffic cop. The town treasury took an upturn as daring drivers broke the new local limit—a brisk 15 miles an hour.

Brea's reliance on regional law enforcement ended in March of 1916, when the community won separation from the Fullerton Township. Agitation by chamber of commerce leaders helped Brea gain recognition as an independent township, with the jobs of constable and city judge filled by local residents.

George Bird was selected as Brea Township's first constable, and strolled the city's few streets wearing a star and armed with a nightstick. Isaac Craig was chosen as the town's first justice of the peace, holding court at his family's small white frame house at 338 N. Orange Avenue.

Local improvement took on a leafy look in 1916, as rows of young pepper trees were planted on Pomona Avenue from the mouth of Brea Canyon south to today's Lambert Road. Though greatly

Brea's First Churches

Church of the Nazarene
Services held at Randolph School and revivals conducted in tents led to the completion of this church—the city's first, in 1913.
Brea Historical Society

Congregational Church
Started with a donation from oil company owner A. Otis Birch, Brea's (original) Congregational Church was adorned by a rooftop oil derrick and called "The Oil Man's Church." The derrick later was removed, as pictured.
Brea Historical Society

Christian Church
With help from out-of-towners, Breans erected this "Tabernacle Built in a Day," but the lumber soon found new use in the congregation's nicer "Little Brown Church."
From the Dean Millen collection

reduced in number and now nearing 80 years old, some of these aging sentinels still stand, their massive trunks and graceful green foliage offering a "priceless welcome" to all who enter Brea. Other local tree-planting projects, as well as the city's first official clean-up day, followed later that year.

Local pride led to a change of the school district's name from Randolph to Brea, and voters demonstrated a commitment to education as land was acquired, funds approved and work began on an impressive new school. Built on a knoll at the northern edge of settlement, the imposing Greek Revival structure was christened Brea Grammar School. Unfinished at its dedication in 1916, the $66,000 structure first was displayed for the public at a holiday program featuring a community Christmas tree, children's performances and views of its classrooms, offices and 600-seat auditorium.

Already a respected local educator, teacher-principal William E. Fanning became the school's leader, supervising a staff of 11. Slightly more than 300 students were enrolled in the new school's first year, some walking from nearby homes, and others picked up from the nearby canyons in a converted ice truck, courtesy Peterkin's Brea Cash Market.

Brea residents took pride in their new school, and rallied behind its efforts. Programs were staged,

On the Move
Brea's first ladies gather for the premiere of "jitney" bus service to Los Angeles, 1915. Pictured (left to right, inside bus) Mmes. Mary Dietzel, Eva Jarvis, (unknown) McElhaney and Rosalie Williams; (standing) Mmes. Ted Salveson, Ella Kuenzli, V.C. Charleston, E.H. Peterkin, Sig Salveson, (unknown) Anderson and Art Stickney. Ted Salveson stands at the curbside.
Brea Historical Society

candy sold, and weekly movies screened in the auditorium, all for the funding of enrichment programs. Culture came calling as well. Borrowing copies of 300 famous paintings from a gallery in Los Angeles, the school's art teacher and students

hung them in classrooms and invited public viewing, then staged their own pageant of "living art," portraying the paintings with appropriate costumes, music and lighting.

Money raised in the showing bought more than 20 art prints for

Brea, 1914: A downtown panorama
Presumably shot from the top of the town's first water tower, this photo looks southwest near the intersection of Pomona Avenue and La Habra Street (today's Brea Boulevard and Ash).
Brea Historical Society

Oil Well
Supply Co.   Livery   McCarty Building (Brea Hotel)

Standard Shops   Miller Building

the school's collection, and later classroom competitions allowed additional purchases. One donation, entitled *Springtime*, came from silent-film star Mary Pickford. New projects soon followed. A cabinet-model phonograph and classical record library were purchased at teacher request, a grand piano later was added to the auditorium, and greenery came to the campus with the planting of trees and shrubs outside and the potting of palms and ferns within.

By 1916, Brea boasted nearly all the amenities of an established town. As its population neared the magical mark of 500 required for cityhood, local leaders began a drive for incorporation. A town of some three square miles was proposed in this early effort, an area bounded by (today's) Whittier Boulevard (extension) on the north, the 57 Freeway on the east, Fullerton's city limits on the south and Puente Street on the west. This first incorporation campaign proved abortive, defeated by outlying ranchers and oil company officials who battled to keep their properties outside the city limits to avoid probable tax increases.

Soon countering with a plan of its own, Union Oil submitted a map for a smaller area of incorporation—a move agreeable to nearly all the previously protesting parties. Roughly one and three-quarters square miles in size, this abbreviated

The Butchered Baker

It happened way back when Brea was young and raw, muddy and pretty tough.

The town baker, Sidney Camm, though an expert on the job, was a somewhat excitable type. One morning, covered in a long, freshly washed white apron, he gathered an armload of just-baked bread and set out for the nearby cafe.

For some time before this, Camm and the cafe owner had been tiffing about prices, and an occasional cuss word was heard. This morning, however, a true quarrel ensued, and the cafe man struck out at last. Brandishing a container of ketchup, he swung and the bottle engaged—breaking on top of the baker's head in a flood of tomato-red fluid.

Thinking himself to be killed, Camm fled the cafe forthwith, crossing the street in a panic and barging into the general store. Here a group of shopping ladies took note of the baker's state—and several promptly fainted, falling swiftly to the floor.

Camm, meanwhile, pressed on—dodging out the door and fleeing frantically down the street. Finally overpowered by pursuers and convinced that the "blood" was not real, the baker at long last was calmed.

But—for a time, at least, the cafe served little bread.

— Early Brea, as remembered by Ed Peterkin
Adapted from the <u>Brea Progress</u>, Jan. 13, 1939

Stern and Goodman Store   La Habra Valley Bank   Sewell Building   Delaney Building

Salveson Store   Fire Department   Sullivan Brothers Transfer

Pride of the Town, 1916
An architectural showplace built in a town of modest means, Brea Grammar School later was shorn of both
its ornamentation and its second story. In a much modified form, it serves today as Brea Junior High.
Brea Historical Society

city of Brea would be bounded by
(today's) Central Avenue on the
north, Randolph Avenue on the east,
Fullerton city limits on the south and
Berry Street on the west.

Local chamber of commerce
leaders immediately launched an
"Incorporate Brea" movement.
Attorney Albert Launer prepared the
town's incorporation papers, while
Charles Kinsler spearheaded a
census, tallying an ample 732 residents within the proposed city limits.
An incorporation petition of 55
signatures headed by Kinsler's name
was presented to the county board of
supervisors, who dispatched a
surveyor to confirm and finalize civic

boundaries. Though the county had
reason to oppose incorporation due
to likely tax losses, local Supervisor
William Schumacher lent his support
to the effort, and the board quickly
added its endorsement.

An enthusiastic rally at Sewell
Hall preceded the incorporation
election, with prominent local
speakers promoting the benefits of
Brea cityhood. Launer opened his
office in the La Habra Valley Bank
early on the morning of Feb. 15, 1917,
and local voters came out to cast their
ballots. Anticipating victory, the
Congregational Church's Ladies Aid
Society cooked an Incorporation
Supper. With an overwhelmingly

positive mandate, local voters carried
incorporation 204 to 45, and the board
of supervisors met Feb. 19 to declare
Brea (by population) a sixth-class city,
the eighth incorporated town in
Orange County. Formal notification
of the new city's status arrived from
the Secretary of State's office Feb. 23,
1917—the date since celebrated as
Brea's official birthday.

Held in conjunction with the
incorporation vote, an election of
city leaders saw Isaac Craig, Jay C.
Sexton, P.C. Huddleston, R.N.
Mitchell and M.J. McCarty selected
as trustees, Kinsler as city clerk and
Leon A. Sayles as city treasurer. The
board of trustees convened for the

BELOW: Street Scene, 1916
North Pomona Avenue takes shape as more and more building begins. On the west, Brea Boiler Works, and (on the east, from foreground) the Wall Building (corner, before moving), the Brea Hotel, garages and oil well supply houses, and (top of the hill) the second story of Brea Grammar School. *Brea Historical Society*

first time Feb. 26, electing Sexton as Brea's first mayor, appointing Launer as city attorney and W. J. Renshaw as city engineer.

Rooms 7 and 8 were leased upstairs in the Sewell Building for a city clerk's office and council chambers. Serving just two months, trustee McCarty resigned his office, and Frank Schweitzer (Sr.) stepped in to replace him. Harry Winchel (Sr.) took the oath of office as Brea's first city marshall, swearing not only to keep the peace, but also to collect taxes, impound stray dogs and supervise street repairs.

In early meetings, Brea's board of trustees assessed property taxes, business permits and dog licenses, discussed needs for better street lighting, water service and firefighting equipment, approved renaming streets (alphabetically, after trees), wrangled with the county over promised improvements to Brea-Olinda Road (Birch Street), petitioned the P.E. for a "wig wag" signal at the rail crossing and instructed the marshall to buy a badge and gun.

The next years saw the start of the town's first trash collection and the formal organization of its fire department, with garage owner William (Bill) Culp as first chief. Tax dollars built bridges over Brea Creek at both today's Imperial and Lambert, and funded a modest fire house and an ornamental derrick to house the fire bell.

Local news heated up in 1917 with the entry of a second newspaper, the *Brea Star*, with Archer V. Douglass as publisher. C.A. Meacham's *La Habra Valley Progress* had been bought in 1915 by Tom Baxter, who quickly staked out his circulation area by renaming the paper The *Brea Progress*. Taking a dim view of his new competition, Baxter declared editorial war on the *Star*, lobbing potshots at Douglass and several others before departing with a memorable quote: "The thing I regret most is that having started the job, I am leaving before I had time to show up completely some of the unprin-

cipled crooks of this community." Baxter left, the papers merged, and the much-modified *Brea Progress* continues in operation today.

With the nation's 1917 entry into World War I, the town turned its attention toward Europe, and local citizens responded to the conflict. Many young men volunteered or were drafted into the service, while those at home supported the overseas effort. Women worked at the local Red Cross, rolling bandages, knitting scarves and packing gift boxes for hometown soldiers. Funds for these and other war projects were raised by hosting dances at Sewell Hall, collecting salvage items such as tin, tires, news-

papers and bottles, and staging a concert by the Los Angeles Philharmonic at Brea Grammar School.

Spurred by large contributions from local oil companies, Breans dug deep to finance the war effort through purchase of war stamps and Liberty Bonds. Oversubscribing its quotas in record time for each of five bond drives, Brea set the pace for competition with neighboring towns, stimulating sales and becoming the shining star of all Orange County contributors.

Local patriotic sentiment ran high during the nation's 19 months in battle. Brea's observance of a countrywide "Liberty Day" in April of 1918 began with a spirited game between

The Local Vote: Brea Becomes a City
Courtesy Orange County Historical Archives

local baseball teams, followed by a children's pageant, the playing of "patriotic airs" by the Brea Band and the dedication of a 60-foot flagpole.

Hung high above Pomona Avenue, a home-sewn service banner bore a star for each of Brea's enlisted men. By war's end, at least two were sewn in gold—an honor for Breans Dean Nethaway and Homer Pumphrey, local soldiers lost in battle. Olinda mourned its own fallen soldier, conducting memorial services for lifelong lease resident Joe Reiniche.

Tragedy soon also struck at home, as the worldwide influenza epidemic of 1918-19 reached Brea. With few curative measures available, the disease hit hard, becoming so serious by fall that store hours were limited, social gatherings cancelled, churches and schools closed, and town council meetings called off. Although warnings cautioned the healthy to avoid homes where the illness was present, it spread alarmingly through the winter, frightening local residents and claiming many lives.

Even in the midst of epidemic, news that "the Great War" had

Hometown Help
Taking time out from bandage rolling, letter writing and package mailing, members of Brea's Red Cross for World Service join a 1917 parade in Fullerton.
Brea Historical Society

ended at the "eleventh hour of the eleventh day in the eleventh month" brought Brea's citizens out to celebrate. The town's fire bell and

Government and Finance, Circa 1917
Upstairs rented rooms in the Sewell Building (left) serve as Brea's first city hall, while the La Habra Valley Bank shares its building with a barber shop—also the site of the city's first post office. Downstairs Sewell tenants include (from left) Sweet's Confectionery (the city's second post office), Brea Pharmacy, Ed Peterkin's Brea Cash Market and a general store.
Courtesy American Title Insurance Company

Brea Boosters
The chamber of commerce hosts a regional banquet in 1916 at Sewell Hall. One of the county's largest and most active chambers in these years, the group coined Brea's slogan: "City of Oil, Oranges and Opportunity." Note the stage decoration—appropriately, an oil derrick. *Brea Historical Society*

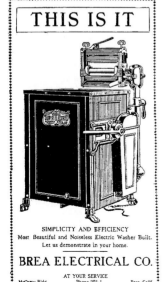

La Habra Star, Feb. 13, 1917

Brea Progress, Sept. 19, 1919

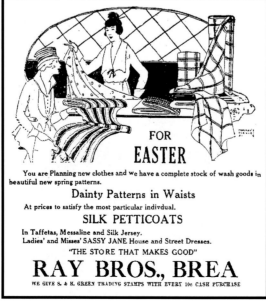

Brea Star, April 10, 1918

curfew whistle were sounded, and a large crowd gathered at the Sewell Building, where Ed Peterkin fashioned a cardboard Kaiser and charged for a chance to knock off his crown.

Far from finished, Peterkin jumped into his delivery van and led an impromptu parade of cars and trucks, all honking their way down Pomona Avenue south through Fullerton and on to Anaheim. Returning at dusk, this group joined others to build a giant bonfire, there singing songs and listening to speeches, and later scattering as far as Los Angeles to continue the night's celebration. By spring, the influenza was dying out and the soldiers were coming home.

Though America's time in the war had been brief, the months had brought great change to Brea's oil fields. Banding together to improve working conditions, local oilmen had affiliated with the American Federation of Labor, forming Gas and Oil Workers Local No. 15731. Rallying for a shortened work day (from 12 hours to eight) and a guaranteed minimum wage, more than 600 local workers enrolled as members in this labor group's first two months. In the patriotic fervor of wartime, rumors flew—some accusing this group of ties to the then-notorious (and often violent) Industrial Workers of the World.

A rival, company-sponsored union soon formed and gained many members, and both groups engaged

LEFT: "Feast and Frolic Friday"
With World War I at an end, Brea returns to more pleasant pursuits. Here, chamber of commerce cooks host a 1919 downtown barbecue.
From the Darwin and Betty Manuel collection

BELOW: Military Markdowns
Brea's own World War I surplus store opens on South Pomona Avenue. Pictured are Mr. and Mrs. Saul Morein, owners.
Brea Historical Society

in spirited finger pointing over loyalties and motives. Though many of these issues remained unresolved, the unions' greater goals met with success. By war's end, better pay and shorter hours had come to the Brea fields.

Enjoying their added leisure hours, Brea's men took part in civic activities, joined the ranks of clubs and volunteered for church and school events. Sporting competitions drew the attention of many, with popular amateur boxing contests at Sewell Hall and lively baseball competitions at the Brea Bowl.

With an end to the war in Europe and renewed focus on efforts at home, the nation entered the 1920's a major world power, far stronger than ever before. Tucked away in its corner of Southern California, the small town of Brea celebrated its second anniversary of incorporation—and, "began to get started."

Growing Along with Brea
Tiny Inez Jones (Fanning) feeds the chickens at her local home in 1919.
From the Inez Fanning collection

Acres and Acres of Oranges
The east valley, as viewed from the Bastanchury
Ranch, circa 1928. Surrounded by citrus groves,
the small town of Brea appears faintly in the
distance.
Courtesy Fullerton Public Library

CHAPTER 5

Seasons of Change

*B*lessed from before its founding by a wealth that flowed from the earth, Brea in the 1920's found new riches in citrus—a treasure that grew from the trees.

In the first decades of the 20th century, vast Southland acres grew into what seemed one single, sprawling orange grove, mile after mile of sweet-scented citrus stretching out to the ends of sight. Sitting on the northern edge of the "world's largest citrus grove," Brea by the mid-1920's branched out into this new industry, its rich acres home to thousands of budding orange, grapefruit and lemon trees.

Long a part of local life, oranges had been planted in the first years of Spanish California, their seeds carried north from Mexico by the mission priests. The introduction of improved varieties in the late 1800's caused a nationwide clamor for citrus, and a boom in orange agriculture transformed the Southland scene. Land promotions lured snow-weary easterners to the promise of frost-free acres and easy profits, and thousands of settlers came west to till new fields.

Though a lack of irrigating water discouraged citrus planting in Brea's first years, the digging of deep wells later solved this problem, and by the end of the 1920's, local orchards were well established. By far the largest of

these groves sprouted from the acres of an unlikely owner—none other than Union Oil.

Starting with major land purchases in the 1890's, and continuing with vast acquisitions through the next quarter-century, Union eventually amassed 15,000 east-valley acres, all probable oil lands. Exploration of these sites often lagged far behind purchase, leaving the property idle—an investment with no return. Taking note of the neighboring Bastanchurys, who had converted huge portions of sheep pasture to citrus, Union in 1925 launched a program to gain from its oil lands likewise—by turning them into orchards.

By arrangement with the Bastanchurys, 2,000 Union Oil east-valley acres were planted in citrus and avocados. More than 800 acres each of lemons and Valencia oranges

The fruit of a local grove, 1992

Serendipity and Citrus
The Olinda Valencia Story

Though the community of Olinda has faded from view, the oil town's name lives on in an important contribution to the citrus industry. In an unusual occurrence, an improved variety of Valencia orange seedling sprouted by chance from a backyard on the Santa Fe lease. Not a cross between old stock, but an entirely new phenomenon called a "nucellar" seedling, the Olinda Valencia proved more vigorous than previous propagations, and many of today's California orange trees originated in bud form from this rare and valuable discovery.

soon took root in the local soil, along with almost 125 acres of grapefruit and nearly 200 acres of avocados. Through a planter's agreement, the Bastanchurys assumed control of Union's new groves, supervising planting, water development and maintenance.

The combined Bastanchury/Union groves covered a vast 5,000 east-valley acres, and set the example for smaller operations to follow. Farmers whose walnut trees had been blighted by recent diseases now turned to citrus as well, and the valley view, in every direction, became one of sprouting greenery.

Thriving on sunny days and frostless nights, citrus could be grown in few places across the nation, and enjoyed great out-of-state popularity—assuming it reached markets safely. Early problems with packing and refrigeration led to diminished profits, but improvements in handling and shipping minimized later losses.

Packing houses in Whittier and Placentia handled most of the local produce, though some lemons were boxed near the train tracks east of town at the old Randolph Marketing building (later operated by Withers Brothers, and then by the Times-

The Sievers House
While other local homes languished in the light of oil or gas lamps, the elegant 1918 J.D. Sievers house became Brea's first residence designed with built-in electrical wiring. Featuring a vast array of appliances, miles of decorative molding and at least one secret passage, the home would serve as the scene of grand parties and political fund-raisers. Later called the Neuls or Durkee house, it was located on a rise northwest of today's Imperial at Berry, but was demolished in the late 1980's.
Photo by Susan Gaede

Mirror Company and Calavo). Union marketed through Fullerton's California Fruit Grower's Exchange, using the famed Sunkist trademark and assigning top-quality fruit the high-octane tag "76".

For Union Oil, the fruits of Brea's groves proved plentiful. A good growing season saw more than 150,000 pounds of avocados harvested from local groves, while the figures for citrus soared far higher. The company's combined annual crop of lemons, oranges and grapefruit filled more than a half-million 50-pound boxes—a total in excess of 25 million pounds.

Though California citrus gained widespread acclaim, its growers faced uncertain futures. Crops were frequently good, yet problems also

Brea Progress, Sept. 24, 1920

plagued the fields. Young trees took several years to bear fruit, provided they survived drought, flood, mold, viruses, a host of insect pests, larger-scale interlopers like gophers and ground squirrels, and that most unstoppable of adversaries, the bitter cold of extreme winter weather. For the decades of the 1920's and 30's, most local growers held their own against these threats—and still managed to show a profit.

As the surrounding groves grew to maturity, the city of Brea took major strides. The town's first decade had seen the provision of basic goods and services. By 1920, Brea took pride in several housing subdivisions, a fine local school, three churches, a variety of shops and oil-related businesses, and a handful of public-works projects. The new decade opened with a spirit of accelerated expansion. There was money to be spent and interest in spending it, and Brea became bigger and better amid a flurry of new construction.

Before building could start, however, the city again grappled with its need for water. Though the successful importation of water had allowed Brea's birth, early municipal systems proved inadequate to serve the needs of a growing town. Over-taxed even in the first years, city pipes often ran dry, and though improvements were made, continued shortages ruled out expansion.

Acting to assure adequate water for the coming decades, Brea voters in 1920 approved $60,000 in bonds for the purchase of the city's water system and 136 shares of water stock. Larger mains were laid, local wells were drilled and success spurred construction of a $40,000 water-storage tank at the reservoir just north of Brea Grammar School. Here a water tower soon stretched skyward, its smooth, metal sides proudly emblazoned "City of Brea" in large letters.

BELOW: Twenties Landmark
A new hall to rival the Sewell, plus space for stores below, the Craig was built by two of Brea's best-known leaders: Isaac Craig, one of the city's first trustees, and his son, Ted, a future Brea mayor and state assemblyman.
Brea Historical Society

TOP: Toast of the Town
George Schuppert, the new town baker,
poses at his Brea Union Bakery.

BOTTOM: Two Generations
The Bakers Schuppert: George and his
nephew Eddie.
From the Sylvia Schuppert collection

Reaction to the city's new water wealth spread swiftly. A building boom was launched, and pipelines rushed out to several subdivisions. Sales were brisk at Brea View, Sunny Crest and Laurel Heights, all to the southeast of the main townsite, as well as at Union Oil's Maxwell Division and the Sievers' Addition, both to the city's west. Barley fields sprouted houses, and a flood of eager oil workers and families vied to buy them as soon as they were offered.

New businesses supported the growing population, and shoppers' choices grew. Four grocery or general stores stood on Pomona Avenue (Brea Boulevard) by the early 1920's, one capturing the spirit of increased competition by calling itself Dailey's "Rock Bottom." The skyline changed as well, with two-story buildings erected by George Schuppert (the new baker), J.L. Fredlihp (the tailor), an out-of-towner named Doolittle and city-pioneer Isaac Craig.

Built in 1921, the Craig Building quickly became a mainstay for local activity, its downstairs housing shops and the twice-relocated post office, and its large upstairs auditorium the site of frequent meetings, parties and banquets. Craig's son, Ted, a recently returned World War I veteran, spearheaded the formation of a local American Legion post (with J. Warren MacClatchie as commander), and both this group and the chamber of commerce soon called the Craig Building home.

The local population took to wheels, and highways were

improved to meet the needs of cars. Brea-Olinda Road (Birch) had been paved to Olinda in 1919, and now was improved farther into Carbon Canyon as La Vida Hot Springs became a popular resort. Whether a cafe at the secluded spot served as a speakeasy during Prohibition remains in question, but Brea's police chief and the county sheriff both told spirited stories of trailing bootleggers "out east toward San Bernardino."

Brea Canyon Road's winding, scenic route was straightened and paved by 1923, better linking the city with Pomona. In town the same year, Pomona Avenue's dirt curbsides disappeared when the full street was covered with a thick layer of asphalt. And by mid-decade, a road destined one day to stretch all the way to the sea was cut as far west as La Habra and given the name "Cedar Street."

By 1920, Brea Grammar ranked as one of the county's best schools, its teachers paid an ample $880 a year—well above the county average. New playground equipment and tennis courts had been added to the site, as well as basement assembly and cooking areas, frequently used for community functions. Hot meals in the new cafeteria sold for a nickel, sandwiches two for five cents.

As the city's population grew, the demand for a second school became urgent, and voters approved its construction. Rushed to completion within six months, the $60,000 campus opened in 1921. A contest to name it drew the attention of many,

and a $5-cash prize was split among several suggesting the same name—Laurel. W.E. Fanning advanced to a new position, taking charge of the district as supervising principal of elementary schools. Local enrollment continued to grow, soon topping the 600 mark, and additions were made at Laurel less than two years later.

Several factors fueled Brea's growth in these years. Early increases in the town's size and amenities attracted many who lived on the nearby oil leases. Schools and shopping were closer in town, streets safer and nights quieter without the constant commotion and clamor of

ABOVE: La Vida
Known and used by the Indians, the Spaniards and the Mexicans, La Vida (life) was only a mud seep until a surprised oil driller first tapped its warm artesian waters. While simple wooden barrels sunk into the ground made up the resort's first spa facilities, later days brought a bathhouse, a hotel, two pools and even a bottling facility.
Courtesy American Title Company

BELOW: Laurel School
Brea became a two-school town with the 1921 addition of Laurel, where Principal Carol Davidson supervised 139 students in the opening term. With the kindergarten rooms still unfinished, Laurel's smallest students attended their first classes in the recently completed Craig Building.
Brea Historical Society

Fast Food, Circa 1920
Brea boys (left) Voloney Siebenthal and Joe Hoskins contemplate lunch, while restauranteer Tom Roche looks on.
Brea Historical Society

Tough Times for Teenagers
A Moving Memory

Today's Brea teenagers, though no doubt burdened by their own share of mortifying moments, can rest assured (at least in one way) things aren't as they once were.

A teenager in the 1920's, Jessie Shores Root remembers her most embarrassing day at Brea Grammar School.

Though she lived in the nearby canyon, Jessie attended the city school, and recently had helped her parents pack for a pending move into town.

Like many who moved to Brea, the Shores family planned to take everything along—clothes, household goods, furniture—and even the walls themselves.

Jessie remembers that one of her schoolmates spied the Shores unwieldy structure as it struggled its way toward town. Possessed of a fact too good to keep secret, he yelled out, "Hey, Jessie—here comes your house!"

—Brea School Days, as remembered by Jessie Shores Root

the oil camps. While a few of the drilling sites were within walking distance of town, some outlying companies offered truck transportation to the wells. Buses were available in other areas, and many workers could afford to buy cars.

Several companies noted the benefits of having fewer families living on their leases and actively encouraged workers to move. Lease houses were offered free of charge or for nominal fees, and dozens of the frame buildings were moved off the hills and out of the canyons, making their way toward town to help ease the housing shortage.

Life in town offered a variety of diversions unavailable on the oil leases. Socials, dinners, dances, concerts, meetings and seasonal celebrations commonly filled the calendars at the Sewell and Craig auditoriums, the grammar schools and the churches. Men joined lodges, becoming Royal Neighbors, Knights of Pythias, Odd Fellows, Masons and Shriners. They played golf at two "grassless" local courses and took aim at the gun club's target range and turkey shoot. Women, meanwhile, joined the ladies-only Maccabees lodge, assisted local men in auxiliaries, displayed their skills in sewing circles or quilting bees and

traded notes on timely issues at the Brea Study Club.

Popular community events included medicine and minstrel shows, parades, traveling chautauquas (musical and lecture shows) and picnics—the largest an annual chamber-sponsored event featuring free drinks and dancing, an

Buy Your
**Family a Ford
For Christmas**

You could not buy a more appreciable gift than an automobile. Wifey has been wishing for it for a long time. Make this Christmas one long to be remembered.

Central Garage
Baldwin, Baldwin & Casner
Ford Dealers
Brea, Calif.

Brea Progress, Dec. 13, 1922

A Feather in Their Caps
Chartered the same year the town was founded, local Lions go native for a 1926 convention. Left to right, (front) Henry Baldwin, Mike House, Forrest Hurst, Hart Chesley, Abe Yost (and back) Bill Craig, Dr. C. C. Jarvis, unidentified, George Henigan, Ed Peterkin, Dan Burney.
From the Darwin and Betty Manuel collection

"east-west" baseball game and lesser events including watermelon eating, races (potato, sack, egg, "dude" and the "fat men's special"), plus a ladies' rolling-pin throw.

Organized in 1920 by a group of World War I veterans, American Legion Post 181 met at several sites before erecting a hall of its own. Active from the start, the group sponsored fund-raising events including picture shows, talent contests and wrestling matches, and held memorable street carnivals featuring fun-zone attractions, games, booths and airplane rides at Brea Aviation Field, a small airstrip just south of town. A women's auxiliary was begun in 1922 to assist local Legionnaires in their work.

Brea became the center of Orange County's growing labor movement in the early 1920's. Membership in Local 27 of the International Union of Oil Field, Gas Well and Refinery Workers swiftly rose to 1,400, more than all other county labor organizations combined. Local women banded together to form the Brea Women's Union Label League in 1918, espousing labor causes, as well as participating in the Federated Women's Club movement. Brea pioneer Charles Kinsler founded and served as president of the Orange County Central Labor Council, and many meetings and social events for this group were held at Sewell Hall.

Local unions joined in 1920 to open a cooperative grocery in a corner of the Stern and Goodman Store, but operating problems and an absence of profit saw it fail within a few months. Improvements in oil-field working conditions in ensuing years gradually robbed Brea of its union clout, and by the mid-1920's, the city had faded as a center for labor activism.

The community showed its support of young people in the early years of the 1920's. Lincoln's birthday, 1921, saw work begin on Brea's log cabin, a youth building erected and today still standing at the rear of 201 W. Ash. Though local boys from the Christian Church's Honor Knights Sunday School class began fund-raising and construction work, community members soon came to their aid—donating sand, gravel and other materials, and moving in massive logs.

More than 100 local leaders were present at the building's dedication four months later, a festive celebration marked by speeches and games. Anticipating the cabin's completion, church pastor W.E. Spicer formed two patrols of Boy Scouts (the city's first) to meet here, but both became inactive. Other youth groups soon found use for the cozy cabin, among them the new Brea YMCA, organized in December with Ben Blanchard as president.

Starting as early as 1918, local music lovers were tapping their toes and tuning up their guitars at performances of the first Brea Band. Though too few musicians and too many saxophones brought something less than success to this early group, an expanded band featuring more members and regular practice sessions was begun by 1921, and soon earned its first applause at an outdoor concert. Performances at major public functions followed in the coming months and years.

Off to an active beginning, Brea's PTA became the county's largest in the early 1920's, well known for sponsoring cultural events and funding school purchases. Expanding its agenda, the group took up a fight for libraries, an effort which led to the establishment of today's Orange County Public Library System.

The persistence of local residents was rewarded in 1921, when the county named Brea the site of its first branch library. With tables donated by the hardware store, chairs contributed

by the oil workers' union and books sent by the county, the community opened its first library in Dexter Martin's Brea Garage on South Pomona Avenue, serving patrons here for seven months before moving to larger quarters at the Delaney Building. Anna McVeigh would be remembered as Brea's first librarian.

The year 1922 proved busy for Breans. The Dramatic Order of Knights of Khorassan (an offshoot of the Knights of Pythias) hosted a huge festival and parade in April, welcoming visitors including future California Governor Frank Merriam. The Lions Club was chartered in August, with banker Jay Sexton as president, and quickly took on the task of building a meeting place for local Boy Scouts, their patrols recently re-formed by W.D. Adkins, and continued by R.H. Lee. Brea Odd Fellows Lodge No. 459 was chartered in April, with 300

A Dream Deferred
With news that Orange County's first branch library soon would open in Brea, newspapers carried sketches of a proposed (but never built) Library, Rest and Recreation Center. Instead, the city's first library opened in a corner of the Brea Garage.
Brea Historical Society

attending initiation ceremonies at Craig Hall, and the chamber of commerce continued its efforts to make Brea's name known, taking top prize at the Anaheim Valencia Orange Show for a display featuring citrus and a miniature working oil well. A silver cup and $250 came home to the chamber for its winning entry.

Brea's prolific oil fields had reached "flush production" by 1923, and not enough men could be found to handle the heavy work load. Dry holes in this era were almost unheard of, and some wells (like Union's 767) refilled a 1,000-gallon tank every 10 hours, "so regular you could use it to set your watch." High wages already had brought hundreds of workers west from places where well-paying jobs were scarce. Even the lowest-level roustabout, relegated to constructing outbuildings and cutting weeds around rigs, brought home a high $5 a day, while those who "pulled" and maintained the wells started out at $5.25.

A Space of Their Own
The Honor Knights Cabin, one of Brea's first community projects—built of local lumber hauled by hometown truckers, its materials and labor donated by dozens of Breans. The cabin served as the scene of many youth activities.
From the Marian Sullivan collection

Physical ability made a driller—the width of a man's back and the size of his shoe, and a certain sense of timing. Derrick work, though less arduous, required agility, and could easily be fatal to a man fearful of heights or bothered by cold, windy weather. Well-maintenance jobs demanded diligence, often invoking around-the-clock duty by workers required to live on the lease.

Improvements in oil tools and production methods transformed Brea's fields in the 1920's. Invented near the turn of the century, the revolutionary rotary drill gained prominence during World War I, and now quickly replaced the less-capable cable tools of earlier times. The decade's next years brought directional and multi-shaft drilling, allowing wells to be sunk cheaply and discretely in areas that before might have been passed by.

Above-ground changes were equally dramatic. Always a worry in high winds, the wobbling wooden derricks of the early years were blown down one by one, and now replaced with safer and sturdier modern rigs built of steel. Field transportation took on its own new look as fleets of draft animals and wagons gave way to an alternate form of horsepower found under the hoods of trucks.

Capitalizing on Brea's proximity to a string of successful wells, manufacturers made the town a mecca of oil-tool innovation in the 1920's. Early local companies like Union Tool and Midway Fishing Tools (builders of equipment to "fish out" tools dropped down a well) were joined by the James E. McGraw & Sons brass foundry, Baash-Ross (which manufactured rotary-drilling equipment at the old Standard Oil

shops just south of the train tracks) and the Brea Tool Works, first founded by a group of local residents and then quickly acquired by town-newcomer William (W.D.) Shaffer.

Soon starting his own shop at Brea Tool Works' former Redwood (at Birch) address, Shaffer launched a company that would become not only Brea's biggest business, but a worldwide leader in the design and manufacture of wellhead production

Auto Center
Whether as a car dealership or a garage, this tile-embellished building at (today's) 146 S. Brea Boulevard specialized in deals on wheels. Opened in 1919 as the Central Garage, it was operated for many years by James and Walter Bergman, and also served as a showroom for an early Ford agency, Barton (and later) Daugherty Chevrolet, and (in recent years) Ed Pawlack Tile.
From the Walter Bergman collection

Inspiration from the East
Named for an Oriental legend, Brea's Red Lantern Theater preceded the Southland's "other" Chinese cinema by a full half-decade. Chinese lanterns greeted guests in the lobby, while inside, two huge cross-legged Buddhas with glowing red lights in their foreheads stared out across the crowd.
Brea Historical Society

and safety equipment. Baash-Ross moved from Brea in 1924, and was replaced by oil-tool manufacturer Duro, which later sold to Enterprise Equipment and eventually became Shaffer Tool Works Plant No. 2.

Construction of an altogether different sort drew attention to the town's center in late 1921, as an ornate and mystical facade took form at 132 S. Pomona. The long-awaited and enthusiastically supported Red Lantern Theater promised Breans an exciting and upscale cinematic experience, its appointments the day's finest, from curly-maple leather-upholstered seats to two of the era's finest projectors and a thundering Robert Morgan Pipe Organ.

Anticipation had been heightened by the city's long wait for a theater. Tired of outside investors who promised and never delivered, a group of Brea businessmen at last took over the project, forming a corporation called Brea Investment and quickly selling its stock, then drawing up plans, hiring a contractor, and pushing construction through to swift completion.

Ground was broken in October for the $50,000 brick structure, which featured an 800-seat auditorium, plus shops on either side. Though construction continued at top speed through the winter, nature intruded

in December, delivering a driving rain that brought collapse to the building's nearly finished front wall.

Taking the disaster in stride, workmen cleared the debris and began again, and the theater threw open its Oriental doors to a grand celebration less than three months later. When the lights dimmed, local film fans were treated to a showing of *A Game Chicken*, featuring popular star Bebe Daniels.

Storefronts on either side of the theater quickly were leased by a confectionery-tobacco shop and a soda fountain, completing downtown's popular entertainment picture. The light of the Red Lantern drew Breans young and old for many years, its combined stage-and-screen facilities the scene not only for movies, but for dramatic and musical programs as well.

Several other local building projects later would be sponsored by the successful Brea Investment Company, for many years guided by president Felix Yriarte, the son of early Basque settler Patricio Yriarte.

Brea Legionnaires honored the fallen of World War I on Memorial Day, 1922, joining other patriotic groups in erecting a polished granite monument at Loma Vista Cemetery. The same year saw the opening of the city's first small emergency hospital, fully equipped with X-ray equipment

frequently used in the diagnosis of oil-field injuries.

The Lions' Boy Scout House was dedicated in January of 1923 on a North Madrona lot secured free of charge from Union Oil. Instrumental in the appropriation was Brea Mayor Harry Becker, who conveniently also served as Union's local superintendent. The city took delivery later that year of its first commercially manufactured fire engine, a $13,000 Seagrave double-combination pumper. Alonzo George Ellis signed on as Brea's first paid fire chief, though the department remained volunteer—its members summoned by the ringing of a bell and picked up at (today's) Birch and Brea Boulevard for a sometimes wild ride through town.

Apart from time spent shadowing traffickers in bootleg liquor, local police professionals in the 1920's devoted their days to patrolling the city's streets, keeping an eye out for errant oilmen known to "overindulge in the grape." A succession of city marshals protected the peace in these years, starting with Harry Winchel—who toured the town in the company of his young son, known by the nickname "Frog." The badge of office passed six times in the years between 1918 and 1923, worn by Marshals I.N. "Pappy" Hurst, D.O Stegman, J.E. Stone, E.P. Rudy and James C. Looney before Charles McClure

took a new oath as Brea's first chief of police.

Law enforcement innovations in this era found officers purchasing a copy of the state penal code, appointing a city night watchman and mobilizing the town's first police vehicle—a cherry-red Indian motorcycle owned by Marshal Looney. Emergency communication experienced its local beginnings when a beacon was mounted on top of the town's water tower. Alerted to trouble by the flashing of a red signal light, lawmen dashed for the closest phone, quickly ringing the station to find out what kind of crime was afoot.

The year 1924 brought Brea its first taste of true fame, as two of baseball's all-time greats faced off on a local diamond. Raised in the oil fields of Olinda, Walter "Big Train" Johnson returned home a legend—a veteran of the Washington Senators regarded by many as the greatest fast-ball pitcher of

Sound the Alarm!

"When the fire whistle went off, everybody dropped everything and got on the main street. The fire truck went by, and you jumped on—that's the way we got together and headed for the fire. I kept a fire suit and a pair of boots. At night, I could jump out of bed, slide into those boots, and pull my pants up. My wife would hand me my coat, and I'd be headed for the door."

—Brea Volunteer Firefighting, as remembered by Walter Bergman

Where There's Smoke
Brea's firefighting volunteers, circa 1925. Left to right (back): Walter Bergman, Bill Atkins, Mac Senn, Louie Crow, Charles Kinsler, A.G. (George) Ellis, Emil Carlson; (front) unknown, Hugh Jones, Fred Boxall, the young Leland "Toad" Kinsler, Gene Crow, Cyrus Young, Carl Passamatek, unknown.
Brea Historical Society

ALL-STAR
Base Ball Game
BREA BOWL
FRIDAY, OCT. 31

WALTER JOHNSON vs BABE RUTH

Bob Meusel and Other
Major League Stars

A CHANCE TO SEE A GROUP OF THE WORLD'S
GREATEST BASEBALL PLAYERS IN ACTION

Brea Progress, Oct. 30, 1924

Something to Smile About
America's favorite batter gives
two youthful fans an afternoon
to remember.
Brea Historical Society

Auspices ANAHEIM ELKS No. 1345
WALTER   BABE
JOHNSON VS. RUTH
BREA - FRI. OCT. 31
2:30 P. M.

Photo by Paul Micco
From a handbill in the Baseball Hall of Fame

LEFT: Friendly Rivals
Baseball greats Walter Johnson (left) and Babe
Ruth warm up the crowd with a bit of pre-game banter.
From the Dean Millen collection

BELOW: Big-League Brea
Johnson, Ruth and their teams slug it out at the Brea Bowl.
Brea Historical Society

all time. Fresh from victory in the 1924 World Series, Johnson was met on the mound by New York Yankee George H. "Babe" Ruth, the famed "Sultan of Swat" who had led his team to three pennant wins and a World Series victory the previous year.

A much-heralded event held on Halloween afternoon, Brea's battle of baseball giants drew combatants from the major, minor and bush leagues wintering in or near Orange County. Staged to benefit the Anaheim Elks' charity fund, the game drew a crowd estimated at between 5,000 and 15,000 to the Brea Bowl, a natural amphitheater near the southwest corner of today's Lambert and Brea Boulevard. Businesses and schools for miles around shut down for the afternoon, and for a few hours "all roads led to Brea."

Flanked by a lesser-known lineup, Johnson and Ruth were cheered heartily by the crowd, though most in the stands stood ready to root for Johnson, a "local boy who made good." Normally an outfielder, Ruth consented to pitch, and the out-of-towner's team stole the show in an upset. The home-run king socked in two crowd-pleasers, one a 550-foot grand slam. Though Johnson's team lost, few local residents seemed to mind. Long after the dust settled and the crowd cleared, memories lingered of Brea's great day in baseball.

Life went on with the celebrities gone, and the town returned to its quiet growth. The American Legion opened a new hall at the corner of Elm and Pomona (Brea Boulevard) that fall, celebrating the event with the community by sponsoring a large street dance. Pomona Avenue was roped off for

THOUSANDS SEE
EXHIBITION
GAME AT
BREA

Enthusiastic Gathering
Greets Noted Ball
Players

RUTH HITS HOMERS

Famous Batsman Knocks
Ball Over Five
Hundred Feet

Witnessed by a crowd estimated at approximately 15,000, Walter Johnson, famous pitcher of the Washington Nationals and a former Fullerton Union High school student, Babe Ruth, world's greatest batsman, and a coterie of big league baseball players, staged their much-heralded exhibition y day

Daily Tribune, Nov. 1, 1924

Back Home Again
Olinda's Walter Johnson, flanked by local friends and former teammates. Among those pictured are Joe Wagner (far left), Fay Lewis (third from left), Bob Isbell (right of Johnson) and Joe Burke (right of Isbell).
Brea Historical Society

the occasion, and the popularly elected "Queen of the Lights" turned on the downtown district's new ornamental streetlamps.

Entering a more elaborate version of an earlier prize-winning display, the chamber of commerce took top honors for exhibits at the 1925 California Valencia Orange Show. The Brea Woman's Club was organized that year with Mrs. A.D. Clayton as president, and quickly turned its attention to expanding library offerings and beautifying the town with trees.

Brea's first funeral parlor opened with a musical program, Charles Haaker's Brea Clay Products (also known as the Brea Brick Company) began casting blocks on East Ash, the Baptist and Assembly of God congregations held their first meetings, and residents won a prolonged battle for improved telephone service when the Brea exchange opened on (today's) East Birch. For the next 23 years, local switchboard operators would assist Brea callers—their familiar reprise, "Number, please?" With the approach of October, all eyes turned toward the sky as the city hosted Orange County's very first air meet.

Airplanes had long been sighted in Brea, for before 1920, the city had not one, but two of the county's earliest airports. Small and primitive, these facilities served the brash biplanes of the time, attracting a fair share of daring young pilots and their flying machines. Located on South Pomona Avenue at the site of today's Brea Heights Shopping Center, a few acres of mowed barley with a windsock was variously called Brea Aviation, Brea Air or Brea Flying Field, while to the east, on Kraemer Avenue at today's Beckman site, lay Loftus Field, later known as Northern Orange County Airport.

As early as 1917, a flight school had opened at Loftus, where an old barn was converted to a hangar. By 1918, World War I pilots training in Riverside frequently were landing at Brea Aviation Field, stirring the minds of Brea boys with thoughts of wings and glory. Opportunities to take flight soon followed, with many residents paying their way skyward

Brea Star, Oct. 31, 1919

for brief, breathtaking trips with barnstorming operations like Bullet, Rex and Mercury Aviation. For $5, local air aficionados could climb into the open passenger compartment and cruise low over Brea's hills and vales. A heftier $10 bought a stomach-churning chase over the same terrain, with a flourish of loops and low passes.

Fame came to Brea aviation in these years, as World War I flying ace Eddie Rickenbacker set down at Brea Aviation Field, drawing a record crowd. Hollywood got into the act when a movie stunt man took flight over a community carnival, performing daredevil tricks and selling rides to thrill seekers. By 1920, flying lessons were available at Brea Aviation Field, and a rush of local residents clambered into the cockpit.

Local garage-owner Dexter Martin helped channel Brea's flying enthusiasm. An accomplished pilot, Martin shared his skills as an instructor, and co-founded the Brea Air Club, the county's first aviation organization. The club quickly

swung into action, sponsoring Orange County's premiere air meet on Oct. 31, 1925. Flight fans streamed in from throughout the Southland, and all were enthralled by daredevil stunts and parachute jumps, high-speed races, the in-flight wedding of a local couple and a breathtaking "dead-stick" crash landing that eerily foreshadowed a later day's disaster.

Sharing credit for the air club and its successful show was Brean Bill Tremaine, former town constable and organization co-founder. It was in Tremaine's Garage at 120 N. Pomona that Brea's great experiment in airplane design took shape, guided by Tremaine and Austrian-born aeronautical engineer Fred Thaheld, and advanced by local money and manufacturing assistance.

In 1925, The team of Thaheld and Tremaine rolled open the garage's double doors and unveiled to the town their creation—the first low-winged, full-cantilevered monoplane ever built in the United States. Christened the *Humming Bird* for its tiny size, the plane performed well in three test

Dexter Martin
One of Brea's aviation greats, Martin later gained national recognition in the OX5 Aviation Pioneers Hall of Fame.
From the Dean Millen collection

Excitement at the Air Show
Trailing yards of billowing silk, parachutist Leo Root lands at a local airfield. Spectators from miles around flocked to the county's first air show—held right in Brea's backyard.
From the Jessie Shores Root collection

circled to the southwest, and had just begun to bank swiftly back toward the field when—without warning—both wings of the lightweight craft suddenly collapsed. Thousands of spectators watched in horror as the plane and its pilot plummeted toward the earth, landing in a twisted mass of wood and metal. Freeman died within minutes, never regaining consciousness.

Distraught by the crash, and fearful of its consequences, designer Thaheld fled from the scene and disappeared, but was later found in New Mexico, and induced to return home by Tremaine. The pair continued to work, taking Pacific Aircraft as the name for their expanded flight-design firm. Building a strong and powerful craft the following year for the $25,000 Dole Hawaiian Air Race, Thaheld and Tremaine sent their plane south to San Diego for required pre-testing by the Navy.

Assigned 13th position in the coming run, the low-winged monoplane met an untimely end in its final test as heavy fog rolled in, obscuring visibility over San Diego Bay. Traveling at high speed, the ill-fated plane emerged from the clouds just short of the Point Loma bluffs,

flights, garnered interest from the military for its speed, and was entered in Brea's second air show, held April 24, 1926 at Brea Aviation Field.

Ray Freeman of Long Beach took the controls that day. Though only 21, Freeman was a five-year flight veteran, respected in his field and well acquainted with its risks. Prior to taking off, he spoke of possible failure, telling bystanders the flight might be his last. Starting his ascent without difficulty a few moments later, Freeman climbed skyward and

RIGHT: The Tragic Crash
Crowds of spectators rush toward the field as the *Humming Bird* falls to the ground.
From the Brian Saul collection

LEFT: Parting Words
Pilot Ray Freeman chats with the crowd just moments before taking flight.
Brea Historical Society

striking the cliffs moments later in a fiery, fatal crash. The plane's pilot and navigator died instantly.

Though unnerved by the two tragedies, Thaheld and Tremaine returned to work, and in the coming years experienced many successes. Together they designed another plane, and then went on separately to new efforts, Tremaine continuing to fly and championing the expansion of Loftus Field, and Thaheld earning nationwide acclaim for later inventions. Local air-enthusiast Dexter Martin left Brea in 1927, taking a job where he could work for speedy passage of federal air-safety regulations, and later serving as president of the National Association of State Aviation Officials. Thaheld accepted a job elsewhere as well, and the pair took with them much of aviation's local glamor.

Like the oil camps before them, Brea's airports were bustling centers of energy and invention, places where impossible notions spun into motion and dreams took flight. Though both saw intense activity in the 1920's and seemed destined for finer futures, both also were abandoned within a few years, surpassed by other airfields. Brea had oil and oranges, and it almost had a major aviation center, but crucial votes in coming years favored other sites, and airfields gradually faded from the local scene.

*B*y the early 1920's, Breans had begun to dream of building their own local high school. Though separate districts in Olinda and Brea offered instruction through the eighth grade, secondary students from both communities still (and always had) attended Fullerton Union High School. Dissatisfied with recent cuts in Fullerton's curriculum—including such locally popular courses as oil production and horticulture—Brea's leaders took a closer look at their growing student population (and the tax dollars following it south to Fullerton), and initiated steps to form a new north-county school district.

Early efforts to elicit help from both the La Habra and Olinda districts went down to defeat. La Habra soon was dropped from the plan, and Olinda lodged protests as well, but Brea's petitions before the county brought the controversial topic to the polling place. Carried by Brea's vote—and over the protests of many Olindans—the Brea-Olinda Union High School District was created on March 21, 1925.

The new district's first board of trustees was elected two months later, with oil-tool manufacturer William (W.D.) Shaffer and citrus rancher John (J.D.) Sievers representing Brea, oilmen George W. Cullen and Milton R. Mears voting for Olinda, and oil and businessman Alonzo H. Brown speaking

ABOVE: Aviation Innovation
Breaking tradition with the standard biplanes of its time, Thaheld and Tremaine's powerful, low-winged monoplane *Spirit of John Rodgers* was to compete in the Dole Hawaiian Air Race.
Brea Historical Society

LEFT: Poised for Flight...
but destined for disaster, the plane later would be lost in a fatal crash.
Brea Historical Society

ABOVE: Set in Stone
Brea's first high school begins its ascent with a ceremonial cornerstone laying. Pictured at this Oct. 20, 1926 event are (left to right) Trustee W.D. Shaffer, Principal I.W. Barnett, and Trustees A.H. Brown, H. Becker, G. Cullen and H.R. Williams. A copper box of mementos was placed behind the cornerstone, its contents sealed away for a future day.
Brea Historical Society

BELOW: Brea-Olinda Union High
Built in the midst of a barley field from block cast in a local brickyard, the new school soon became home to nearly 300 students from Brea and Olinda.
Brea Historical Society

for the other local leases. Mears moved away not long after the election, and his seat was filled by Hugh Williams. While Brea and Olinda high school juniors and seniors continued at Fullerton in September of 1925, 90 freshmen and sophomores attended the new local district's first classes, held on the campus of Brea Grammar School under the direction of Principal I.W. Barnett.

Backed by business leaders, bonds of $320,000 were approved for construction of the new high school, but controversy raged over where it should be built. Three sites were proposed, two inside the city limits on Brea's south side and one just outside town to the east. While most Breans favored one of the "city" sites, Olindans solidly backed the "country" location. District trustees wrangled over the issue, but failed to reach consensus, Board President Sievers resigned amid the arguments, and the decision went to the people. Carried by Olinda's vote, the rural site was chosen, and—by 1926, the community's largest educational institution, Brea-Olinda Union High School, had begun its slow rise from an eastern barley field.

The Practice House
From the 1939 Gusher

A Moving Landmark
The BOHS Practice House

For generations of Brea-Olinda High School girls, it was the gateway to adulthood: a neatly kept cottage near the edge of campus where housekeeping skills were honed.

One-half of a larger facility built at Brea Grammar School (today's junior high) and briefly used to accommodate the Brea-Olinda district's first high-school classes, the Mediterranean-style "Practice House" was moved in 1927 to BOHS's Birch Street campus, where it soon began its long career as a live-in laboratory for future homemakers.

Here Brea coeds came for week-long, intensive training sessions in cooking, cleaning and entertaining. Many approached their scheduled sojourns with trepidation, but the days of sewing and scrubbing, baking and basting gave way to new-found skills and special memories. Years later, graduates would fondly recall the events they hostessed here, from faculty luncheons to senior teas...dinners for doting mothers to parties for nervous boyfriends.

In its day, the Practice House was unique—the only known full-scale, self-contained home economics lab in Orange County. Changing lifestyles and altered expectations led to new uses for the old building by the 1960's, and it served successively as a teachers' lounge, preschool care center, counseling office, classroom and continuation school.

Identified in a 1981 study as "historically significant," the Practice House was spared redevelopment's wrecking ball when the high school fell in 1989. Now temporarily housed on Redwood, it awaits planned relocation on the 200 block of Laurel as part of the downtown redevelopment project.

Pre-election bitterness was forgotten as Breans and Olindans united to make their new school one of Southern California's best. Architect T.C. Kistner's designs, including an ornate portico and columns framing the school's impressive entryway, were adopted with a single change—the elimination of two towers planned to crown the main building. Construction began immediately, and, though problems with the contractor persisted, the primary campus structures (a main building featuring administrative offices, an auditorium, a cafeteria and 17 classrooms; plus a manual arts building and a gymnasium) were completed by June of 1927. A temporary structure built at the grammar school was relocated to the newly opened campus and redesigned as two cottages, one of which soon would be used as the "Practice House" homemaking lab.

The 23-acre, $400,000 campus opened to students on Sept. 14, 1927, offering courses in English, history, science, Spanish, business, art, music, manual training, domestic art, domestic science and physical training, with

ADMIT ONE
FOOT BALL GAME
Brea-Olinda vs. Anaheim
Armistice Day 1930
BREA STUDENT BODY, 25c

Popular Coach
Stewart "Shorty" Smith fielded many a winning team in the high school's early years.
From the 1928 Gusher

additional college-preparatory classes later added following the start of a full four-year academic program. The popular Stewart "Shorty" Smith took up coaching that fall, beginning a trend of sporting success that marked the school's first decade.

Though still under construction in the spring of 1927, the new school nevertheless recorded its first "graduates," when 10 local scholars from Fullerton High were named as the Brea-Olinda "Class of 1927." The officially dedicated school sent forth its own first seniors the following June, graduating 21 students in the Class of 1928.

First published in the spring of that year, the school's annual was christened the *Gusher*, and the area's oil heritage was reflected again in the choice of a campus mascot. Those charged with the task cleverly settled on the twice-right "Wildcat"—the name not only of an animal which once roamed local valleys and hills, but also a term widely applied to independent oil drillers. A stuffed and mounted wildcat (of the former form) took up residence at the school in 1929, along with new Principal Carl Harvey.

An enhanced sense of civic identity settled over Brea with completion of the new high school,

"'Doc' and the 1928 Reo school bus"
From the 1928 Gusher

RIGHT: Brea-Olinda High School
From the 1935 Gusher

its stately columns and stout, stone walls symbolic of faith in the future. The city had come far in few years. Blessed with a wealth in jobs and homes, a vital economy and a spirited citizenry committed to local improvement, Brea by the late 1920's bore small resemblance to the struggling Randolph townsite of a quarter-century before. For a brief while longer, the city would continue this confident growth. But first, it would experience its greatest catastrophe.

BELOW: Sylvan Setting
Youthful Brea-Olinda thespians take to the stage in this 1927 production of *The Gypsy Rover*.
Brea Historical Society

Founders of the Town
Seven Who Led Brea's Way

*I*n Brea's formative years, leaders emerged to guide the growing town's progress. Those who built Brea came from many places and labored at many jobs. Though none claimed expertise in civic planning, all were adept at spotting needs and finding ways to fill them. By the efforts of many, much was accomplished in the early years. Among those most responsible were seven who led Brea's way:

Albert Launer

Born in Illinois, Albert Launer grew up on the site of today's La Habra Civic Center. He came to Brea fresh from law school at the University of Southern California, and opened his first office at the back of the La Habra Valley Bank.

Launer prepared Brea's incorporation papers, and his office was the site of the incorporation vote. He served the community for many years as city attorney, even after he and his wife had moved to Fullerton.

Isaac Craig

A Canadian raised in North Dakota, Isaac Craig came to Los Angeles, and in 1899 took a job building oil derricks in Olinda. He moved with his family to Brea in 1912, and worked as a contractor, erecting such early structures as the McCarty (Brea Hotel) Building and the Congregational Church.

Chosen as justice of the peace in 1916, he worked energetically for Brea's incorporation, and was elected as one of the town's first trustees, a post he held 11 years. In 1921, he built the Craig Building with the help of his son, Edward (Ted), whose formative

years in Brea proved a prelude to later success. The original Craig house, moved to Brea from Olinda, was located on North Orange Avenue. Later homes were built near the intersection of Imperial at Brea Boulevard and in today's Craig Park area. Isaac Craig died in 1955 at the age of 93. His grandson, Tom Craig, today frequents Brea as a landowner-developer.

William (W.E.) Fanning

The group's only native Californian, W.E. Fanning was born in Artesia,

William (W.E.) Fanning

attended Los Angeles Normal School (later UCLA), served in the Spanish-American War and worked as an electrician and a teacher before becoming teacher-principal of Randolph School. "Professor Fanning" acted as Brea's first electrical inspector, served as a director of the Oilfields Bank, helped organize the Lions Club (later serving as its president) and was active in the Brea Chamber of Commerce and Christian Church.

Appointed as superintendent of the Brea (elementary) School District, Fanning established a tradition of community involvement in education. He retired in 1942, and 28 years later attended the dedication of Fanning School, named in his honor. Of this group of seven, Fanning was the eldest (41) at the time of Brea's birth. He died in 1979 at the age of 103, the last survivor of these seven who led Brea's way.

Fanning family members today in Brea include Karl, a retired BOHS teacher, and his wife, Inez (Jones) Fanning, both active members of the Brea Historical Society.

Charles Kinsler

Born in New York and raised in Pennsylvania, Charles Kinsler fought with Teddy Roosevelt at the Battle of San Juan Hill before coming west to Olinda's oil fields in 1899. Briefly relocating to Whittier, he served as major and drillmaster at the State Reform (now Nelles) School, and drove the ceremonial spike when the Pacific Electric rail tracks reached Whittier in 1903.

Charles Kinsler

Kinsler settled on the Puente Lease as an oil worker in 1906, and in 1911 moved with his wife and young daughters to Brea, where they soon began operating the "Kinsler Hotel" upstairs at the McCarty Building (Brea Hotel).

Kinsler took Brea's incorporation census, and was elected as first city clerk. An early member of the local (elementary) school board, he was secretary of Brea's first chamber of commerce, and later became both city judge and volunteer fire chief. Through Kinsler's leadership, Brea's gas and oil workers formed Orange County's first union in 1917. He served both as secretary of this group and president of the Orange County Central Labor Council.

A real-estate agent and insurance salesman, Kinsler was also a joiner— chairman of the local Boy Scouts, and a member of the Imperial Highway Association, a veterans' group and nine fraternal organizations, including the Brea Masonic Lodge.

Kinsler lived with his family at 135 (and later 129) S. Orange until his death in 1934. The Kinslers' adopted son, Leland "Toad" Kinsler, today makes his home in Brea.

Frank J. Schweitzer (Sr.)

An Ohio native, Frank Schweitzer (Sr.) came to California in 1905 and worked in Olinda as a machinist. He and his family moved to Brea in 1912, buying property on Madrona at Imperial and setting out citrus trees. Employed locally as superintendent of Pacific Gasoline Company, Schweitzer helped organize Brea Tool Works, and later served as superintendent of both the Brea Brick Company and Shaffer Tool Works.

Though not a candidate in the city's first election, Schweitzer was soon appointed to replace resigned Trustee M.J. McCarty. He continued his council leadership for the next 21 years. A member of the Lions Club, Schweitzer achieved a lasting place

in Brea fame by developing plans for City Hall Park and designing the "Brea Welcomes You" sign.

Schweitzer and his family lived on Elm Street in a house built by Isaac Craig. His son, Frank Jr., followed his father's lead in local government, serving many years on the Brea City Council, and acting as mayor from 1960-62.

Jay Sexton

A native of Kansas with a law degree from the University of Michigan, Jay Sexton arrived in Brea in 1915. Within months he rose to a position of local power by purchasing extensive property and acquiring a controlling interest in the La Habra Valley Bank.

Elected a trustee, Sexton became the city's first mayor, and served in this post five years. A member of the Knights of Pythias and a charter member (and first president) of the Lions Club, he also helped organize the Hacienda Country Club in La Habra Heights.

Sexton's subdivision of small plots during the local land rush of the early 1920's spurred similar growth efforts, and the town blossomed in ensuing years. Having lived only five years in Brea, Sexton sold the last of his local bank and property interests and moved to Redlands in 1922. He died in 1943.

Jay Sexton

Edward Harland (Ed) Peterkin

An avid entrepreneur, Ed Peterkin got Brea moving—whether by horsecabs, cars, buses or trucks.

Ed Peterkin

A Canadian who became a Fullerton butcher, Peterkin saw opportunity in the new town to the north, and in 1911 bought a lot in Brea for $150 "and a mule team." At (today's) Birch and Brea he built one of the city's first businesses, a meat and ice distribution center. Opening Brea Cash Market in 1915, he soon expanded to transportation, using a converted ice truck to carry canyon children to school, and later replacing this truck with a bus for school and charter use. Peterkin's growing fleet became the Orange County Transfer Company, movers of household goods, oil-field equipment and agricultural products.

An organizer and longtime president of the local chamber of commerce, Peterkin led efforts to improve roads, start a volunteer fire department and a telephone exchange. He was a charter member (and first tail twister) of the Lions Club, helped to organize the Masons, and was first president of the Imperial Highway Association.

The youngest of Brea's "founding fathers," Peterkin was 31 at the time of Brea's incorporation. He and his wife lived on South Pomona Avenue, and later on Walnut at Elm, but moved away after retirement. He died in 1977 at the age of 91.

Brea Ablaze
The Spectacular Stewart Fire
Brea Historical Society

CHAPTER 6

Dedication Amid Difficulty

*P*etroleum invokes power. Harnessed with care, oil fuels much of the modern world. Unleashed—it can set that world ablaze. Brea's first residents knew well the hazards of petroleum production, for many had worked the drilling fields. Safety measures were few on the early oil leases. Workers wore no hard hats or safety shoes, and moved atop towering derricks without benefit of rope anchors.

Danger threatened at every turn. Snapping cables, toppling derricks, steaming pipes, thundering gushers and exploding gases injured many, stealing the lives of a luckless few. In 1918 the whole community came out to mourn popular young Brean H.L. Delaney, struck and killed by a falling plank while working at his own drilling site.

As local oil production rose, new refining and holding facilities further increased early hazards. High-grade gasoline in huge quantities was processed in plants near the mouth of Brea Canyon, while to the west, Union Oil's Stewart Tank Farm stored more than three million barrels of crude in a cluster of earthen reservoirs—four easy targets for disaster.

Near dawn on the morning of April 8, 1926 an electrical storm swept in from the Pacific. Southwesterly winds blew heavy with rain, and the foreman at Stewart Station eyed the sky warily. Fires were burning out of control, he knew, at Union's storage site in San Luis Obispo, struck by lightning the day before. Now, as the leading edge of this same storm brooded over Brea, he told himself nothing of the kind could happen here.

But at a little after 9 o'clock, it did. A single bolt of lightning struck two separate 750,000-barrel tanks of crude, and both exploded in giant fireballs of flame. Jolting the town with the force of major earthquakes, the blasts broke plate-glass windows a half-mile east in Brea's business

An Erupting Inferno
Towering clouds of smoke and flame blacken Brea's skies. Torrential rain and intermittent hail fell during the disaster's first hours, but failed to extinguish the fires.
Brea Historical Society

LEFT: Vain Efforts at Containment
Early hopes hinged on hastily erected barriers of corrugated iron, but the walls were blasted flat as the thunderous boilovers began.
Courtesy Unocal, Pipeline Division

BELOW: Toil and Trouble
750,000 barrels of bubbling crude spew out an ominous smoke signal. Tanks 10 and 12 originally were fired, and later engulfed nearby Tank 8.
Brea Historical Society

district, and sent terrified residents streaming from their homes to stare, disbelieving, as thousand-foot flames shot into the western sky.

Racing to the Stewart site, local firemen were able only to watch as the blazes consumed what they would. Intense heat from the crude-fueled flames made battling the fires impossible, and volunteers instead set about creating roadblocks and otherwise protecting the safety of nearby citizens.

Those who understood oil fires knew that trouble had just begun. While the explosions had been caused by volatile gas vapors collected at the top of the tanks, a far more devastating danger lurked below the flaming crude's surface. The 750,000 barrels of burning oil in each tank floated on a layer of water, and as the fire's heat steadily increased, this water came closer to its boiling point. If either boiled over, other nearby tanks would also ignite.

Field workers arrived swiftly to do what they could. Anticipating an overflow, crews dug trenches to channel burning oil, lining them with galvanized sheeting and packing them with dirt. By 2 o'clock, the dreaded boilovers began. Tremendous flames leaped hundreds of feet

high, creating currents of intensely hot air that hurled the metal barriers skyward "like chips of potato." Further attempts to contain the fires were equally useless. Foam was rushed in by rail, but proved too weak to extinguish the blazes. A huge wind machine was trucked in from a Hollywood film set, but spun unheeded in the field, melting in the fiery heat.

The flames flared and the boilovers followed, catching a third tank later that night. Bubbling over the tops of the three seething caldrons, streams of blazing oil raced down the

land's southerly slope, flowing across the Pacific Electric tracks and through the green rows of J.D. Sievers' walnut and citrus orchards, scorching and blackening all in their path. Nearly everything at Stewart was destroyed—three tanks, a refinery, dozens of lease houses and work buildings. Tongues of flaming oil continued across Cedar (Imperial), consuming more houses and orchards. Bred by the super-heated air, cyclones formed high in the sky and swirled down over neighborhoods to the east, damaging and destroying homes and garages inside Brea's city limits.

In Harm's Way
The Path of Destruction

BELOW: Twisted Tracks
The Pacific Electric rails just south of Stewart Station, melted into flowing curves by the heat of the crude-fired flames.
Brea Historical Society

BELOW: Haunting Homesite
Away on their honeymoon, J.D. Sievers' son and daughter-in-law returned to find their new home burned to the ground. Their unopened wedding gifts lay amid the rubble.
Courtesy Unocal, Pipeline Division

Raining pieces of two-by-four—the earthen tanks' shattered wood roofs—fell as far east as Carbon Canyon and Chino long after the initial blast. The sky glowed like daylight in the dead of night, and even the most exhausted of firefighters found it impossible to sleep.

Enormous clouds of black smoke billowed into the air, alerting residents miles away to the disaster. A steady stream of the curious gathered at prime viewing sites in Fullerton and the Puente Hills, and traffic reached gridlock proportions as an estimated 40,000 spectators came to witness the inferno first-hand. A Hollywood film crew used the spectacular

ABOVE: Raised Roof
The Sutphen home at southeast Cedar (Imperial) at Madrona, heavily damaged by a fire-spawned cyclone.
Brea Historical Society

The Altered Oath
A Story of the Stewart Fire

When the urgency of the fire prevented planning, improvisation sometimes prevailed.

In the first, frantic minutes of the disaster, volunteers were sent to man roadblocks for keeping the curious out. The county sheriff called several hours later to ask if these men had been deputized, but the answer, of course, came back, "no."

Certain this should be done quickly, he explained how to give an oath, and those in charge took careful notes, and set out to get the job done. Yet a snag soon appeared in the plan. A Bible was needed to make the oath legal, and no such book could be found.

The sun was setting and time was short; the group pondered what could be done. Then someone spotted a hefty volume, and everything fell into place.

In the fading light, the guards raised their hands and repeated the needed oath. None ever questioned or ever knew that things hadn't been done "by the Book."

Though the volume they used held the proper words, their arrangement wasn't quite right. For the well-worn tome they had sworn on...was the office dictionary.

—Adapted from a story told by Stewart Station employee Warren E. Griffith

scene to advantage, shooting ground and aerial footage of the towering flames for use in newsreels and movies.

Days later, when the last fire had burned itself out, Stewart Station lay a blackened wasteland. The refinery was reduced to rubble, along with numerous work buildings and cottages. Running straight through the fire area, a hundred feet of train track lay melted and twisted to impossible angles, and farmland bordering the property was burned almost beyond recognition.

Some things were spared. East of the fire scene, the pumping plant and several smaller storage tanks remained safe from the raging blazes. The Sievers house still stood, though nearly all its green groves were gone, and Union bought the entire property in the coming settlement. But while damages were tallied in the millions, losses might have been far higher.

Though three of Stewart's tanks had gone up in furious flame, a nearby fourth still stood intact. Three 10,000-barrel gasoline tanks sitting just south of the train tracks also survived, even though one had sprung a leak while the rivers of fire passed by. Wild rumors of deaths and injuries had flown in the disaster's first days, but all later were branded untrue.

Though between 300 and 400 men had battled the blaze for 48 exhausting hours, not one had been killed. A few narrow escapes were reported and a handful of minor injuries logged, but in the end most volunteers lost only their work boots, mired forever in a sea of soupy mud.

The people of Brea and the oil community of the Southland had banded together in the crisis. Field workers from every oil company in Southern California came to fight the fires, led by many Breans. Even the Boy Scouts turned out, relieving spent traffic officers as the days of the blaze wore on.

Insurance covered Union's losses, and underwriters wrote new rules requiring lightning arresters on oil tanks. Most oil companies soon switched to underground holding sites, protecting the public safety and avoiding new taxes on topside storage.

In the late 1920's, Union's Stearns Lease became the first site in California used as a reservoir for gas and oil produced in other fields. As overpro-

Honors Afloat
Not long after the Stewart fire, Union launched a ship that publicly acclaimed Brea's prolific oil fields for the very first time. For aesthetic reasons, officials dubbed the tanker *La Brea*. *Courtesy Unocal*

duction hit the industry, nearly 600 million cubic feet of gas and 600,000 barrels of oil were pumped back into local wells for long-term storage—much of it remaining untouched until World War II.

With the disaster at Stewart over, Brea breathed a sigh of relief...and went on with its work. A housing crunch continued as more and more lease workers followed the trend into town. To help meet rising demand, a new type of local residence—the town's first apartment building— rose in 1926 on the southeast side of today's Birch at Orange. "Honeymoon Court" soon was followed by a second multi-unit structure on East Ash, an 18-room combination apartment-hotel called the Casa Brea Inn.

The year 1926 found the Masons forming F&AM Citrol Lodge No. 656, choosing the Sewell Building as headquarters and Lester Lee Lemon as first worshipful master. Wayne and Marian Hart teamed with James Hanson the following year to open El Rodeo Riding Club on Valencia at Birch. Later moved to new quarters north of Carbon Canyon Road following the completion of Carbon Canyon Dam, El Rodeo remains in operation today as Southern California's oldest riding club.

Brea's Baptist congregation purchased land on Birch and Flower for its first church in 1927, the same year the city brought a new solution to an old problem by building a $60,000 system of sewage lines and a treatment plant in a southwest wash (today's Arovista Park). The following year saw the Chiksan Company open a small local manufacturing facility, an early step in what would become one of Brea's biggest businesses.

Local finance was enhanced in 1928, when the Oilfields Bank erected a stately stone building at the southwest corner of today's Brea at Birch. A popular location, this site already had known two occupants in its 17 years of use, home first to Ed Peterkin's meat and ice center, and later to the Brea Congregational Church. As the property increased in value, a growing church membership outgrew the site, and the congregation chose a larger location across from Laurel School on Cedar (now Imperial). The old church was moved here and remodeled, and its sanctuary soon was graced by a custom-designed 1,000-pipe organ, a gift of the Shaffer Family.

Brea's financial picture had changed greatly in a decade. Joining the Federal Reserve System in 1921, the La Habra Valley Bank took a new name, becoming the First National Bank of Brea. Always large, deposits at First National dramatically increased with the growth of industry and population, at the same time local banking control was lost through stock sales to out-of-town interests.

Country Cousins
A Tale in Two Parts

My family moved to Madrona Street not long after it was first subdivided. It had all been barley fields before, and there were lots of leggy creatures crawling around. In particular, we were plagued by centipedes.

One time when I was a girl, I remember we were sitting by the fireplace, when—all of a sudden—here came a centipede crawling out through the bricks. My mother was sitting there sewing, and she whipped out her scissors right away. She cut it in two...and do you know—that centipede ran both ways!

*—Brea in the late 1920's,
as remembered by
Catherine Seiler*

Town Newcomers
School District Superintendent Vincent Jaster and his wife, Louise, find their first local home at the Casa Brea Inn.

LEFT: Inner Sanctum
Attention to detail made the Oilfields Bank a showplace of local design. Carved moldings, stamped ceilings and an abundant use of wood created a quietly posh interior where everyone's money somehow always seemed safe.
Brea Historical Society

BELOW: The Oldfields Bank
For 65 years, a landmark on southwest Brea Boulevard and Birch.
Photo Courtesy Dean Millen

In the Common Interest

"The oil people were so honest and big hearted you could almost give them a loan without taking a note. They were dependable with very few exceptions. If you were in trouble, they were right at your side ready to help. When a fellow got in a jam, instead of everybody pushing him down in the mud, they went to him with a helping hand."

—**Business in Brea, circa 1930, as remembered by banker Ralph "Barney" Barnes**

Continued financial growth, coupled with resentment over loss of local influence, led to the 1926 opening of a second Brea bank in a main-street storefront. Organized and owned by Brea residents, the new Oilfields Bank gained wide support, and quickly outgrew its small site. Relocating two years later to an elegant, two-story structure at 201 S. Pomona, the bank drew crowds of opening day well-wishers, and deposits at Oilfields soon

far exceeded those at the older First National.

Though the excitement of local airports had taken wing with their early supporters, hope for a new kind of Brea flying field rose in the final years of the 1920's. Navy engineers scouting sites on the Pacific coast for a dirigible landing base gave Loftus Field close consideration. The city lost out in the first round to a Northern California locale, but Brea boosters banded together to hold the government's interest as the search for a southern site intensified.

The on-again, off-again study dragged on for years, absorbing much local effort. In the end, Navy officials praised Brea for the "best presentation," but chose another location. Labeling

the Loftus land's rolling nature and proximity to oil derricks potential hazards, officials instead selected a site near Santa Ana—today's Marine Corps Air Station at Tustin.

Ground transport came to the fore in these years with the organization of the Imperial Highway Association.

Meeting for the first time at Brea's Olsen and Dyers Cafe and electing Ed Peterkin president, this regional group became a powerful force in the 1930's, influencing construction of the important byway they nicknamed "The Cannon Ball Road." Association members advocated the construction of a major thoroughfare, built "wide for safety, straight for speed and second to none in Southern California," stretching from the ocean at El Segundo east to Corona, and then turning south toward Temecula and El Centro.

Meeting monthly, the highway association lobbied legislators and local cities for support, and quickly obtained major right-of-ways. Construction was slow, but steady. The five-mile link between Brea and Yorba Linda opened in 1938, but not until 1961 were opening cer-

emonies held at the San Diego-Imperial county line for the final portion of the completed highway—at last stretching 225 miles from the desert to the sea.

A new kind of excitement packed punch for Breans in the years of the late 1920's, as heavyweight prizefighter Paulino Uzcundun took up residence at the old Sievers House. Bought by Union Oil after the disastrous Stewart fire, the home had passed to the Bastanchurys, who managed its surrounding citrus groves—as well as the "Bouncing Basque." Though many locals followed Uzcundun's career and considered him a contender, the boxer's tenure in the ring proved brief, and he brought home no titles to Brea.

Twelve years a town by 1929, Brea still lacked a city hall. As early as 1918, trustees had talked of building a

Proudly Posing

Brea's firefighters stand up with their prized 1923 Seagrave pumper in one of old city hall's premiere photos. Details of this building's architecture were obscured in later years by modernization efforts, but it remains in use today as home to the Brea Historical Society. *"Old Susie,"* the Seagrave engine, also continues in Brea, now being restored to her former glory by a team of local firefighters.
From the Kinsler Family collection

Fun in the Sun
Residents flocked to the Brea Plunge in the pre-air-conditioning era. Named to the National Register of Historic Places in 1984, the structure has undergone extensive renovation and remains in use today as the oldest continuously operating civic-owned freshwater pool in Orange County. *Brea Historical Society*

home for city business, but money was hard to come by, and other projects took precedence. In 1922, a site on South Pomona Avenue was selected and designs were drawn for a small civic structure. Yet plans proceeded no farther. Though rumors of parks and pools and city halls circulated

widely in the coming years, not until 1927 did Brea take major steps toward creating a space for recreation and a place for city government.

Voters that year endorsed a bond issue for $60,000 in land-acquisition and building costs for a park, pool and civic center, and these funds were combined with a $15,000 city surplus to begin the long-awaited project. A choice block between Date and Elm was bought below market value from Union Oil, and work began on a Mediterranean-style city hall designed by architect Allen Ruoff.

Opened for business by 1929, Brea's proud new addition became the first true "civic center" in Orange County, combining municipal offices, council chambers, court

facilities, fire station, jail, county library, chamber of commerce and banquet rooms under one roof. Construction of a pool and bathhouse followed, and a smaller bond election provided funds for park landscaping and playground equipment.

The latest in high-tech communication soon found a home at the new city hall as Fire Chief A.G. Ellis assembled Southern California's earliest emergency radio network. An amateur radio enthusiast, Ellis started by building a Brea base station for communication with Los Angeles. A series of enhancements expanded this first system, and, in 1936, Brea pioneered again, this time in two-way mobile transmission between an emergency operator and police and fire personnel in the field. Call letters for this early Brea transmission station were MDAQ.

Brea completed its last civic building project, the popular "plunge," the following summer—an event which proved well timed. By fall, a series of stock market crashes had stopped the boom of the 1920's and started the Great Depression.

The brisk pace of local growth skidded to a halt as the country's financial base crumbled. Across the nation, confidence in government evaporated as factories closed, banks failed and a mood of grim hopelessness took hold. Brea braced for tough times, and they followed not far behind.

Always primarily an oil town, Brea had benefitted economically in eras of both war and domestic expansion. Crude could be refined into fuel oil for Navy ships, or turned into gasoline for Chevys and Fords. But when the government became too destitute to fuel its fleet and drivers became too down-and-out to fill their tanks, the oil industry suffered, and so did Brea.

While some residents lost their jobs during the Depression, few massive local layoffs occurred. When possible, companies split the available work among many employees, hoping all could "squeak by" on less. Everyone was poor, but residents found ways to help themselves—and often helped others as well.

Men from locales hit harder by unemployment frequently passed through town seeking work, and a small hobo camp sprang up near the train tracks on the town's northwest side. On Christmas Day, 1931, a soup kitchen for feeding the hungry and homeless was organized by the Assembly of God Church. In one month alone, 1,300 people, both local and transient, were provided with food and shelter.

With banks across the nation shut down during the state and national bank "holidays" of 1933, both Brea First National and Oilfields banks closed to customers while awaiting visits from government auditors. Deposits were frozen for several months, causing general anxiety in the community.

Though thousands of banks failed and many were closed as potentially insolvent, each of Brea's

Field of Steam
Birch Oil in the 1930's

The Birch Oil lease, like others of its time, held both hazards and charms for the families who clung to its slopes. Homes were built among the derricks, and children of all ages ran barefoot over rugged canyons and hills.

Boiler-powered engines pumped the wells, linked together through lines of tangled steel. One of the first lessons mothers taught their children was to spit on the pipes to see if they were hot, hopefully avoiding scalding burns.

Young boys tagged along with the field workers, "going the rounds" as they checked the pumps. A favorite activity was crossing the swinging bridges that spanned the smaller canyons—stamping on them to cause vibrations, and feeling them sway back and forth. This was a sport guaranteed to impress even the bravest of visiting boys.

—Adapted From the memories of lease resident Leo Piantoni

Roll Call at Birch Oil, Mid-1930's
Hard-pressed by the flagging economy, some local companies resorted to mass layoffs during the Depression, but A. Otis Birch was admired by the town for keeping all his workers employed. Shortened hours allowed everyone at Birch to share in the lessened workload.
Brea Historical Society

Joining Forces to Feed the Hungry

The Brea soup kitchen has served over 3,500 meals since Christmas, it was learned from W.H. Brown this week. Seven local families in two days appealed for help and were aided as far as it was possible to help them. Six local young men, without work or funds, are eating all their meals there, and anyone: man, woman or child, who comes for a meal can get it, whether transient or permanent residents.

A meat market in a neighboring town sends over all the hamburger left on hand Saturday night, and John Gnagy is furnishing practically all the remainder of the meat being served. The Blue and White Stores are regular contributors, and the Safeway supplies most of the vegetables.

Rich's bakery in Long Beach leaves from six to 10 loaves of bread a day, and a mystery contributor from up the canyon comes in every Saturday and leaves a large order of staple foods, but slips away before his name can be learned.

La Habra Star, March 25, 1932

Golden Harvest
Despite the Depression, citrus continued to boom and bloom in Brea, as seen in this grove near the southeast side of today's State College and Brea Boulevard. Romaldo Ruiz drives a D4-Caterpillar tractor through one of Union Oil's extensive orchards.
From the Dean Millen collection

banks had invested conservatively, and both survived the Depression. The stronger of the two, the locally controlled Oilfields, emerged as the city's banking choice by 1934, absorbing the earlier First National and reorganizing as the Oilfields National Bank.

As the nation struggled with disruption and despair, recovery efforts reached out to Brea. Though some of the community's unemployed were able to find temporary jobs with the federal Works Progress Administration, no large-scale WPA projects came to Brea, and many of the city's jobless stayed so. To help the unemployed and their families, a "cooperative" store was set up in 1933 in a large, empty warehouse on the southeast side of today's Brea Boulevard at Lambert.

Participants in the work-share system earned food and clothing credits. Women ironed, or brought in sewing machines and mended or "made over" old clothes. Men were trucked off to distant sites to catch fish or pick fruits and vegetables. Potatoes, carrots, corn, lettuce and citrus—whatever was harvested was brought back, washed and cooked or canned by the women workers. Scoutmaster Les Slauter arranged to have a tractor "demonstrated" in a field on the town's east side, and a huge community garden was seeded in the newly turned soil.

Such efforts were supplemented by government subsidies and local donations. Those owning large stands of trees offered firewood free for the cutting. Barbers contributed haircuts, grocers and growers gave what they could, and those who worked earned points which were cashed in for clothing or food. Records show as many as 200 local families took part in this program during the Depression years.

Larger operations suffered during these difficult days as well. Long pressed by rising debts and falling profits, the Bastanchurys' Sunny Hills Ranch fell into receivership in 1933 and was taken over by the Times-Mirror Company, a major creditor. Times-Mirror assumed control of the land and its citrus, and also took over management of Brea's Union Citrus Orchards, previously overseen by the Bastanchurys. Union Oil's vast orchards were directed successfully into the next decade, first by Herbert M. Bergen, and later by Joe Neuls and Dean Millen.

Bad economic times were compounded by worse weather in the years of the early 1930's. In the first days of January, 1932, storms spread a crust of ice over the hills to the city's northeast, and four inches of snow fell in Carbon Canyon. Record winds that same year blew down a huge vine-covered arbor at Laurel School, while conditions the following winter caused far greater damage. On Jan. 11, 1933, a severe storm with wind velocities up to 80 miles an hour swept through the area, leaving a trail of uprooted citrus, unroofed homes and unseated oil rigs. Fifteen derricks were toppled in the Brea-Olinda district, contributing to more than $1 million in county damages.

Less than two months later, the Southland reeled from a far greater disaster, as Long Beach was hit by a major earthquake. Though many fatalities were recorded near the temblor's epicenter, no deaths

occurred in Brea, and local property damage was limited to a few fallen bricks and broken windows.

The quake struck late on a Friday afternoon, as men were returning from work and women preparing dinner. Many in Brea were looking forward to a mother-daughter banquet scheduled that night at the high school cafeteria. All were shaken as long, rolling waves rocked the area in the first major earthquake since the city's founding. Though planners of the long-awaited banquet bravely attempted to carry on with the event, continued aftershocks frayed everyone's nerves, and the festivities were finally called off.

Many Brea volunteers had reported early to scenes of the earthquake's worst damage. Doctors W.E. Jackson and Charles Westerhout drove to Long Beach to assist the Red Cross, while Dr. C. Glenn Curtis remained behind to man Brea's own emergency hospital. Offers of assistance went out by radio, and a stream of earthquake

refugees quickly poured into the city. In the early hours after the quake, nearly 100 people were fed and given clothing, medical attention and beds at local churches and the American Legion Hall. Through that night and the following day more shaken and homeless victims arrived, all taking shelter and comfort in Brea.

Though few Brea buildings suffered obvious damage in the Long Beach Earthquake, its reverberations soon brought massive change to local schools. Acting to protect students from possible harm in future disasters, legislators rushed through the Field Act, providing stringent guidelines for academic structures. The beauty of all Brea's schools paid a high price for such safety, as their ornate facades were stripped off and their stately columns toppled and carted away.

Inside, more serious repairs were required. At Brea Grammar, the beautiful, two-story combined administration building/auditorium was declared unsafe and destined for

A Downed Derrick
One of several such casualties recorded locally in the record wind storm of 1933.
Brea Historical Society

Behind Bars
Stripped of its ornamentation and subjected to a thorough reinforcement, Brea-Olinda
Union High School would emerge "quake proof" from its bonds nearly two years later.
Brea Historical Society

destruction. Some students from the grammar school were transferred to Laurel during the coming months of construction, but most remained in their classrooms as work proceeded around them.

Built just seven years before, Brea-Olinda High was routed for redesign as well. Extensive repair work at this school forced classes to be held outside, and youthful scholars studied in two huge tents during 20 noisy months of renovation.

The price of repairs at Brea-Olinda High alone tallied $263,000—more than three-quarters of this nearly-new school's original construction cost. Funds fell short for rebuilding at Brea Grammar. Though the modified administration building soon opened as a far plainer one-story structure, nearly two

decades passed before an auditorium again took shape here. All three schools remained in use for many years, but much of the early beauty of their buildings was gone, and newcomers often wondered why they appeared so oddly unfinished.

While the years of the early 1930's were hard, local life enjoyed its lighter moments. Those out for a stroll on Pomona Avenue (Brea Boulevard) smiled at the antics of baby chicks roosting in the window of Gnagy's Market, or swayed to the sounds of big-band music drifting from the collegiate-style Wildcat Cafe. Some chatted with Jack the Hatter, whose traveling outdoor store perked up an empty lot by the theater.

Since few residents had money to travel, camp-type facilities were added to the park, where city-funded sinks and gas plates were arranged in a lighted terrace behind the new American Legion Hall. Brea's PTA contributed picnic tables and the Woman's Club added a drinking fountain, and in summer, both the park and its plunge were almost always full.

A memorable evening in June of 1932 celebrated the opening of Carbon Canyon Road—welcomed as the new gateway between San Bernardino, Riverside, Orange and Los Angeles counties. A crowd of 175 including Lieutenant Governor Frank Merriam, Assemblyman Ted Craig (of Brea), former Assemblyman Joe Burke (of Olinda) and supervisors from all four counties enjoyed festivities at the La Vida Hot Springs cafe of Archie Rosenbaum, former big-name boxer and popular canyon host. Though the hoped-for movie stars never materialized, an evening of enjoyable music was provided by Shorty Smith's "Bear Cat Gang of Musical Hounds."

Long known for its warm springs, La Vida had been a favorite spot for Olinda oilmen, the perfect place for scrubbing off a hard day's grease and grime. The original small shack built on the property had been replaced by a sanitarium in the 1920's, but it had failed financially, and new owners made further changes.

The addition of improved structures and pumps for raising mineral water to the surface brought success, and the secluded site soon was well patronized. In the 1930's it became a popular spot for the Los Angeles Jewish community, with upwards of 1,000 visitors enjoying the waters on weekends. A summer playground for children was established on a high hill west of the highway, its entrance sign (in Yiddish, "The Workman's Circle") often a puzzle to passing drivers.

News from Brea's "other" canyon showed the old Rancho Nogales property just north of the hills had been sold to oilman W.A. Bartholomae, who soon began raising horses and cattle on his 8,000-acre Diamond Bar Ranch. On a sad note, Brea Canyon found its name in headlines when Anaheim Mayor Fred Koesel was stopped and shot by masked bandits while driving from Pomona on the winding canyon road. He later died of his injuries.

Brea tipplers toasted the end to 13 years of Prohibition in 1933, raising tankards of "133" beer, legalized locally by a three-to-one vote. In the first 12 days after passage of the new law, six liquor licenses were issued, one to the B and B Cafe, now better known as Sam's Place.

The year 1934 saw local morale improved with a project sponsored by the Lions. A crowd gathered at 6 p.m. April 5 on Pomona Avenue north of Imperial, and both streets were closed to through traffic. Opening with music by the grammar school orchestra, ceremonies

Camp BOHS
Extensive reconstruction of the school's main building brought open-air classrooms (tents, left and right) to the BOHS campus, where four such wooden-floored structures were erected on the main building's east side. Lacking finished quarters indoors, the class of 1936 held its commencement exercises on the front lawn.
Brea Historical Society

A Gathering of Spirits

The B and B Cafe (sometimes called the Bucket of Blood) was the first place in town to get beer. I had about 12 people lined up on the morning it became legal, and, as soon as it was daylight, I drew all of them a brew. Whether it's good or bad or indifferent, I pulled the first beer in Brea.

In those days the law wouldn't let you order a glass of beer without buying a sandwich too, so the B and B kept a spare on the counter, sealed up in a paper sack. The same sandwich sat on the bar for months at a stretch. Nobody ever ate it—but if anyone were to ask, it was there just in case all the time.

—From the memories of short-term B and B bartender Dyer Bennett

A Home of Their Own
Local Legionnaires and friends happily gather at the groundbreaking of Brea's American Legion Hall. The legion's first building, erected in the 1920's on the northwest corner of Brea and Elm, was replaced in the early 30's by a finer structure, still standing today.
Brea Historical Society

continued with speeches by Mayor Mike Hogue and Assemblyman Edward (Ted) Craig.

In the darkened street, all turned their eyes skyward as Councilman W.D. Shaffer flicked the switch, and the "Brea Welcomes You" sign flashed on for the very first time. Ample congratulations followed for the Lions' architectural committee, headed by Councilman Frank Schweitzer (Sr.), designer of the cantilevered structure.

Brea Welcomes You, 1934
Councilman Frank Schweitzer (Sr.), designed the cantilevered structure, long a landmark on Brea Boulevard.

An immediate success, the two-color neon sign soon became a local landmark, its Depression-era message a comforting symbol of civic pride.

Though funds remained tight through the mid-1930's, the town saw minor construction. Still encased in its iron grid work of post-earthquake repair, the high school found help from the Lions in bringing lights to its (George) Cullen Field. An old structure found new use in 1935 when the Boy Scout House was moved to South Pomona Avenue and remodeled for the Lions and Woman's clubs, and a new sanctuary was dedicated in 1936 at the Christian Church on West Ash.

Civic pride reached new heights in 1935 as Assemblyman Edward (Ted) Craig was elected Speaker of the California State Assembly. The

Little Miss Brea of 1931
Peggy Ann Peterkin (center) is framed by Eleanor Neuls (left) and Helen Hay in this contest of local good looks.
From the Darwin and Betty Manuel collection

youngest speaker in state history at the time of his selection, Olinda's first son of politics had been sent to Sacramento in 1929 at the age of 33, and (in an unusual situation) acted as both Brea's mayor and its district assemblyman between 1930 and 1932.

By the second half of the decade, slight improvement in the local economy was felt, and business rallied on a few fronts. On Pomona Avenue, the old Brea (then Kinsler and later Ozark) Hotel got a new name (the Sherman), a coat of stucco, some awnings, and two downstairs tenants: an Italian restaurant and the Brea Dairy Store. Even bigger news was the move to town of La Vida Bottling Company, which started on a small scale in the canyon and expanded to town in a $100,000 plant adjacent to the Oilfields National Bank.

Already well known for its Lime'N Lemon, La Vida began with a big investment and an even bigger dream. Expecting to soon rival Coca-Cola with its new carbonated creation (a flavored natural water), La Vida launched its Brea venture with a massive publicity campaign.

TOP: On the Line
Workers at La Vida enjoyed its state-of-the-art facilities, and the company thrived for a time under the leadership of Brea's W.D. Shaffer. Though the drink "flowed as freely as water" during at least one city birthday celebration, the company later left town to merge with a Los Angeles bottler.

BOTTOM: Watershed
The tight times of the Depression had begun to loosen not long before La Vida reached town. Announcing itself with a boulevard banner, the company opened a bottling factory at the rear of the Oilfields National Bank building.
Brea Historical Society

Extolling the product's liquid base as one of the world's "few pure waters," company president D.A. LaMar spoke freely of Lime'N Lemon's attributes, claiming it could cure a multitude of ills from colds to indigestion and hangovers.

Billed as both fly-proof and dustproof, La Vida's Brea bottling plant featured a glass front to allow onlookers a view of inside operations. Between 30 to 50 employees worked at this site, and a second facility followed in San Francisco. The drink enjoyed a limited popularity, but the success LaMar forecast proved elusive. La Vida Bottling closed its local doors only three years after its opening—four decades before flavored natural waters became a beverage-industry bestseller.

Better times saw the city's youth involved in a host of activities. Local Boy Scouts marched in parades, hung flags in Brea's business district for patriotic holidays and packed 12 into a pick-up truck for trips to Yosemite and the San Diego World's Fair. The Christian Church's Honor Knights grabbed their gear and

Here Wednesday, November 27
ALANO
DASS
Mystery Man
of India

Special Matinee
for
LADIES ONLY
Friday 2:00 P. M.
November 29

CALLS YOU BY NAME — ANSWERS YOUR QUESTIONS
ASK HIM
ABOUT YOUR AFFAIRS.
Wednesday night in addition to Regular
Picture Program!

Brea Theatre
NO ADVANCE IN PRICES.

LEFT: The Great Escape
When the rigors of the Depression made life seem just too grim, a respite from the world's worries waited at the Brea Theater. No longer known as the Red Lantern, the town's only movie house promoted itself with special attractions and prizes during the lean years of the 1930's. *Brea Progress*, Nov. 21, 1935.

BELOW: Dressed for Success
Always in the forefront of fashion, local Lions boost community spirits during the tough times of the 1930's. Striking chic poses at a 1935 performance of the *Nifty Shop* are Brea's business and professional leaders: left to right (standing) Dr. Glenn Curtis (physician); Arthur Reidenbach (druggist); J.D. Neuls (Union Citrus manager); A.W. Larson (occupation unknown); J.W. Burch (car-dealership owner); Howard Robinson (Union Oil executive); John Daugherty (car-dealership owner); Elmer Guy (attorney); Dr. C.C. Jarvis (dentist); W.A. Hinnen (Union Oil executive); Glenn Gheen (market owner); W.D. Shaffer (tool-works owner); and E.A. Braner (occupation unknown). Seated: E.W. Curtis (Associated Oil executive); Dr. John Holland (dentist); W.W. Hay (Union Oil executive); C.O. Harvey (high-school principal); Mrs. Bernice Curtis (pianist); Mark McMahon (banker); R.E. Barnes (banker); and E.H. Peterkin (market and transfer company owner). *Brea Historical Society*

headed out to Big Bear, and the 100-member combined grammar school/high school marching band donned white pants and white shirts, gold sashes and sombreros, and set off to play at Los Angeles' new Coliseum.

The final years of the decade saw several Brea firsts. Local Girl Scouts got their start under the leadership of Florabell Sage in 1937, the same year Ralph "Barney" Barnes formed a Junior Chamber of Commerce to replace the temporarily inactive general chamber. In 1938, The Brea Rifle Club first set its sights on a target range in the northern hills, and a men's morning social group called the International Coffee Club stirred to life through the efforts of popular physician C. Glenn "Doc" Curtis.

Ralph "Barney" Barnes brought local renown to the big-band sound starting in 1938, launching an orchestra that started out playing for community functions and later expanded to professional engagements. Attuned to local tastes, the band struck up waltzes and fox-trots, and featured a changing cast of Brea businessmen including Barnes (said to play "a mean piano"), BOHS band-leader Lee Auer (on trumpet), Shaffer Tool Works' Don Shaffer (on saxophone), Chiksan's Raymond "Tiny" Thompson (on trombone) and Brea Electric's Frank Holly (on violin and bass fiddle).

Taking matters into his own hands, Dr. W.E. Jackson began construction of the community's first new hospital in more than two decades, fashioning bricks from adobe for a facility built on (today's) North Brea Boulevard. Experimenting several years to discover an appropriate blend of binder and loose material, the physician finally hit on a non-cracking formula for his "mud house," which, in its finished form, proved cool in summer, warm in winter and quiet whatever the weather. Dr. Jackson's daughter and son-in-law assisted in forming the bricks, and later helped plaster the hospital's walls with a coating of lime and adobe.

Locals who called them the "Dirty 30's" found two more reasons

Edward (Ted) Craig
Brea's First Statesman

The son of Brea's pioneer derrick-builder-turned-building-contractor Isaac Craig, Edward (Ted) Craig grew up in Olinda and Brea, and served in World War I before returning home to become a contractor and town trustee.

The first son of a former trustee to be chosen as Brea's mayor, Craig took his political career far beyond local bounds. Voted into office five times as a California State Assemblyman, he was elected by his peers in 1935 to the prestigious post of Assembly Speaker.

Ted Craig

Following his retirement from the legislature, Craig served 28 years as a legislative advocate for Pacific Lighting Co. of Los Angeles, the parent company of today's Southern California Gas Co. His last years were spent as a lobbyist for the County of Orange, and while working in this capacity, he celebrated 50 years of service in Sacramento.

Craig chaired several important legislative committees, and once even filled in as acting governor—hosting President Herbert Hoover on a California tour while the state's governor and lieutenant governor were out of town. Lauded by his peers as "the grand old man of the third house" and "Orange County's favorite son," Craig divided his last years between Sacramento and his ranch house in southeastern Brea.

Ted Craig died in 1979 at the age of 83, and was buried at Fullerton's Loma Vista Cemetery. In appreciation of his many years of dedicated service, Orange County's Supervisors in 1972 dedicated Craig Regional Park in his honor.

House Humor

In a 1979 newspaper interview, Ted Craig shared a memorable story from his heyday in the statehouse:

"I just got through the eighth grade," Craig reminisced, "but as Speaker, I sat on the University of California Board of Regents with A.P. Giannini, the head of the Bank of America. I told him, 'You follow my vote.' He said, 'why?' And I told him, 'I only went through the eighth grade, but you only went through the seventh.'"

Glenn Curtis
Brea's Beloved "Country Doctor"

A transplanted Georgian known by Breans as a fine and caring physician, an avid collector, an enthusiastic student of politics, a dedicated supporter of the arts and an irascible practical joker, Dr. C. Glenn Curtis drew fame for his humanitarian acts, yet always referred to himself as a "simple country doctor."

Dr. C. Glenn Curtis

Establishing his local practice in 1927, "Doc" Curtis quickly became one of Brea's best-loved residents. "Hours or time of day meant nothing to him if his patients needed his attention," wrote Brea Progress editor Frank Hall. "This unselfish devotion to his profession helped more than anything to endear him in the hearts of those he served."

Though the hours he worked were long, Dr. Curtis found time for many interests. He was a celebrated coin collector, an enthusiastic amateur photographer and a supporter of numerous professional, social and political organizations. He served as president of the Orange County Medical Association and helped influence the building of St. Jude's Hospital. His work with the Institute of Inter-American Affairs under the U.S. Department of State brought him international acclaim when he helped avert an epidemic following a major earthquake in Ecuador.

Dr. Curtis died in 1959, and was buried in Memory Garden, where an inscription on his crypt eulogizes his " Life Dedicated to Humanity." In his honor, the Kiwanis dedicated a plaque and tree at the Brea Golf Course and the Lions planted a grove of flowering pear trees at Craig Regional Park. His greatest tribute, however, came in 1980, when the Brea Civic & Cultural Center's new performing arts center was christened the Curtis Theatre.

to think so as nature nurtured disaster in the winter of 1937-38. Though traditionally considered frost-free, the La Habra Valley had known scattered spells of bitter weather. Freezing temperatures were recorded locally in 1899, 1913 and 1922, but caused small damage, since most of the valley's cold-sensitive citrus had yet to be planted. But now the orchards were well established, and darkness was about to fall on Brea's coldest night.

Warned by radio broadcasts of drastically dropping temperatures, Southern California's citrus farmers fired their smudge pots early on the evening of Jan. 22, 1938, and hoped the clouds of choking, oil-fired smoke would keep in the heat—and keep out the cold—through the brittle-clear night ahead.

Well aware that any drop below 28 degrees would spell disaster, worried local growers watched helplessly as thermometers plunged in the pre-dawn hours, finally falling to a record low of 18 degrees. As the wind howled, the trees grew gradually colder and the citrus juices expanded, tearing the tender membranes and destroying the fragile fruit. Though a small part of the crop could be salvaged, the work of nearly a year was lost in the cold of a single bitter night.

A Local Legend
He made the city smile, as shown in this oft-printed 1940 photo. When Wendell Willkie lost the Presidency, *Brea Progress* owner Howard Bowers lost the bet—and paid off a debonair Curtis with a rickshaw ride around town.
Photos Courtesy Brea Historical Society

In less than a month, far greater devastation struck low-lying parts of the Southland basin. Set on a plateau at the county's highest elevation, the town of Brea always had enjoyed natural flood protection—a benefit clearly understood by the city's founders. Portions of nearby cities to the south and east, however, including Anaheim, Fullerton and Placentia, lay low in the Santa Ana Valley, where floodwaters pooled during storms. It was here in the days of late February, 1938, that disaster came calling again.

The cold that took the citrus crop in the winter of 1938 spread a heavy layer of snow in the San Gabriel Mountains. Though normal conditions would have seen this snowpack melt slowly, several days of warm spring rain quickened the process, and millions of gallons of water sped in swollen streams to the valleys below. There was no Prado Dam or Carbon Canyon Dam—nothing at all to hold the water back, and it rushed southward unimpeded to inundate the lowlands.

Calls for help again came out to Brea, and local citizens responded. Some, like Harry Winchel and Curtis Bush, rushed to the flooded areas with boats to rescue people trapped in their

homes. Many in the stricken cities had awakened to find water swirling several feet high through their darkened houses, and were forced to climb out windows or attics to save themselves from drowning. Even so, many people died in the flooding, and property damage was high. Bridges were washed out, and stores and

End of the Line
The once-thriving Pacific Electric station, abandoned and boarded up, closed its doors forever on July 23, 1938. It was demolished in 1950.
From the William Myers collection

The Great Flood of '38
Anaheim waded in water as the Santa Ana River overflowed, but Brea stayed dry on the highlands and helped care for those who were hurt. The widespread destruction soon inspired a series of regional flood-control projects.
Courtesy Anaheim Public Library

Nicknames and Kid Games
Growing Along with Brea

"Turkey" Stives, "Mush" Crabill and "Socko" Wall all had one thing in common—they were nicknamed by Perry Thayer. Nearly every boy in Brea's early years benefitted from one of young Thayer's witty gifts. For some—like Harry "Frog" Winchel and Leland "Toad" Kinsler, the labels lasted a lifetime.

But life then wasn't all puns and names. In the days before there was "nothing to do, Mom," Brea kids found adventure in everyday things.

Young people dug shells from hillsides, splashed in swimmin' holes and biked on back roads. Boys hunted rabbits and squirrels, jousted with frogs and snakes, and warily searched out the hidden haunts of huge and hairy tarantulas.

Handmade kites were flown, homemade boats took sail, and everyone joined in games: jacks and marbles, tag, "run sheep run," and "shinny"—field hockey with sticks and a milk can. Horses were ridden, picnics and weenie-roasts hosted and Saturday movies enjoyed. Quiet hours were spent playing Flinch and Rook, reading mystery books or savoring sweets: Snickers, Walnettos, licorice ropes and hard-candy "twofers," sold two to the penny.

Dad often took the kids along as he worked, and sometimes let them drive as well. Many boys manned the wheel by 12 on the unrestricted oil-lease roads.

Girls spent leisure time in similar ways, and in "ladylike" pursuits as well: shopping or baking with mother, sewing, embroidering and learning to knit. Many girls played the piano, and nearly all enjoyed paper dolls.

homes swept away or filled with water and mud. For the last time in the 1930's, Brea opened its doors to feed and shelter the needy.

Though the decade was nearly over, not all its blows had been dealt. The passenger rail service Brea had taken for granted stopped abruptly in 1938, when the financially strapped Pacific Electric abandoned service on its Whittier, Fullerton and Yorba Linda lines.

Flagging ridership had long plagued the system, as a losing battle with the automobile and its encroaching right-of-ways progressively weakened this once-vital regional railway. Amid local protest, the P.E. boarded up its Brea Station and announced a new system of passenger buses. Mail service declined and was later halted, but heavy shipping in both agriculture and oil allowed freight service to continue, with handling done though the local substation on North Orange Avenue.

As the decade drew to a close, the people of Brea suffered one last and lingering disappointment. With its hundreds of local wells, numerous tool shops and offices, and massive groves of citrus, Union Oil was, in the 1930's—and always had been—Brea's economic mainstay. The company rallied money and support for local causes, and its employees helped shape the town: serving as city trustees and school board members, chamber of commerce officers and service club leaders.

From the 1937 Brea Progress

In late 1939, Brea residents reeled from news that Union's pipeline offices soon would be transferred from Brea to Santa Fe Springs. Many of the town's leading citizens were lost in the coming move, and the oil company's long involvement in local affairs declined markedly.

After a string of difficult years, most of the worst seemed over by the end of 1939. Though little civic progress had been seen in the troubled decade, the struggling community had held itself together. Faced with dwindling funds and fading opportunities, many residents discovered unique ways of "making do." C.L. Smith of East Elm Street picked up a tidy profit crafting home-grown sweepers from broom corn, while K.L. Trendt took to the hills—collecting black walnut burls and shipping them east to be turned into furniture. Far more than ever before, local residents learned to use what they had, build what they could, patch what was broken and get by. Few would ever forget the experience.

Having suffered with little and gone without, the city took joy in small things. Just 14 and already a star, Judy Garland delighted local fans with a 1938 appearance at the Brea Theater. Shaffer Tool Works

and Chiksan proudly accepted invitations to exhibit inventions at the 1939 New York World's Fair, and local teenager Bill Griffith captured the town's imagination by racing away with top honors at Southern California's 1939 soap box derby. From a field of 1,128 entries, 14-year-old Griffith sped to success at the regional meet, stepping from his home-built *Spider Special* to accept a silver cup, a bicycle and a round-trip airplane ticket to the national derby finals in Akron, Ohio.

Led by local Lions, a caravan of Brea residents accompanied the soap box star to the airport, while his parents followed by car, arriving in Akron five days later. Though Griffith was nosed out at the finish line, his local fame remained, and for many years his victory picture graced promotions for the homespun sport of soap box racing.

For nearly all, the decade of the 1930's had been difficult, and few Breans would miss these troubled times in years to come. With little fanfare, the calendar turned, and a new decade brought fresh challenges.

"Home soon, don't worry!

WITH A TELEPHONE in your home, loved ones can talk to you any time from practically anywhere. That helps to keep the family circle close and does away with many an hour of anxiety.

SOUTHERN CALIFORNIA
TELEPHONE COMPANY

118 E. Birch St.   Brea 2

The Triumphs of Technology
Keeping in touch, 1930's style—a phone in every home. Note the number to call — just "2."
From the 1935 Brea Progress

Looking Ahead
Laurel School's students face the future with serious expressions, as seen in this 1938 photo. Teacher Margaret Culp stands in the back row, right.
Brea Historical Society

On the Line
Operators at Brea's telephone exchange fielded
disaster on more than one occasion, making criti-
cal connections in time of earthquake, fire and
flood. Among those answering the call to local
duty were (from left, standing) chief operator
Naomi Nash and Jessie Wilson, (seated) Hazel
Casparie, Evelyn Stephens, Ruth Moseley
(Calderwood) and Anna Hill.
From the Ruth Calderwood collection

CHAPTER 7

Generation of Growth

*T*hough much of the world was at war as the 1940's dawned, Brea seemed far from the struggle, and local life continued at its calm, familiar pace. Limping slowly out of the Depression, the community counted itself and found just 2,562 residents, a net loss of five from the census of 10 years before.

Young Brea sprinter Paul Moore got the decade off to a running start, setting a new world's record for the three-quarter-mile that spring on a Stanford track. A second local star shone a scant six months later, as hometown-tenor George Stinson, California-Highway-Patrolman-turned-San-Francisco-opera-sensation, returned to sing for a sell-out crowd at the BOHS auditorium.

Fresh from study in Italy and an enthusiastic debut in *Pagliacci*, Stinson vied for his audience's attention amid a cast of strong-men and acrobats, adagio dancers, vaudeville stars and the award-winning 70-piece BOHS band, clad in all-new green-and-white uniforms.

Rumors of a puzzling new citrus disease circulated widely that summer, and local growers anxiously watched their trees for signs of wilting. Concern turned to fear before fall, when word came that the stricken groves were infected by a virus now threatening the entire citrus industry. Saving the groves,

researchers advised, would require not only luck, but expensive and difficult grafting of disease-resistant varieties to the old citrus stock. Faced with this unexpected burden, Times-Mirror bowed out of its management role with Union Groves, and the extensive acreage was returned to oil-company control.

Local Motion
Innovative wind machines helped keep frost from the local groves. Powered by diesel engines, they were designed by Brean Fred Thaheld and built by Shaffer Tool Works.
Brea Historical Society

The pages of that season's *Brea Progress* revealed the federal deficit soaring to a high of $41 million and Mrs. Franklin Roosevelt setting an example for the nation by doing her holiday shopping early. Local notes found patrons gathered behind a carved mahogany bar at the remodeled Imperial Cafe, Laurel School awaiting the building of a new kindergarten and Brea Grammar posting profits of $185 from a carnival featuring games, assorted edibles and a flamboyant fortune-teller.

The year 1941 brought the town fresh shares of sadness and frustration, with the passing of a longtime local businessman and the winding down of a major area industry.

Neff Cox, Brea's popular black shoeshine-stand owner and operator, died in August after a local career of 16 years, and was mourned by many. In the racially restrictive climate of the times, Cox had commuted to work from Fullerton, and some would later speculate that an unwritten code prevented him from living in Brea or even remaining in town after dark.

Even so, Cox was acknowledged as one of the community's best-known and most-liked citizens, and the *Progress* eulogized him as one

who, "so lived that when he died, hundreds felt a real loss." More than 100 local residents contributed to a fund for Cox's widow and children, and many Breans helped fill the chapel for his funeral.

An ending of another kind began just three months later as Union Oil Vice-President Arthur "Cy" Rubel and Land and Lease Department Supervisor Hubert Ferry appeared in town for a visit that proved far from routine. Calling on Grove Manager Dean Millen to lead them on a tour of local holdings, Rubel dropped the "bombshell" that Union would cease its citrus operation and liquidate the entire acreage within two months. Millen, who had tended the thriving groves for six years, was instructed to order in machinery and phone the main office when bulldozing had begun.

While thousands of trees were pushed out, piled up and burned in the coming weeks, Millen and Union Citrus Supervisor Joe Neuls scrambled to save as many groves as they could. The avocados were leased to a group called Avocado Associates, while the surviving oranges, lemons and grapefruit were split among a variety of operations including Valley View Ranch (Leo West, manager), Deodara Orchards

(Neuls and C.E. Dunbar, owner-managers), Everett Reese (owner of the old Hualde property), RCB Ranch (Robinson-Curtis-Bergen, owners) and Brea Groves, Inc. (which later formed Arovista Mutual Water Company and further divided the property).

Though only two months were allowed to finalize these many transactions, the company's deadline was met. By Dec. 31, 1941, all 2,500 acres of the Union Citrus Orchards were gone: destroyed, sold or leased under new supervision. This sellout proved a portent for the future of local groves. In the days ahead, rising costs and the devastating disease commonly called "quick decline" would bring the destruction of ever greater numbers of trees. Within a few years, nearly all the waxy green groves would fall to housing tracts, and the perfume of blossoming citrus no longer would scent the springtime skies.

Back in town, a rare and daring daylight robbery took the Oilfields National Bank by surprise, as a lone gunman struck just before closing on an afternoon late in November. Hoping to foil the culprit, Banker Barnes stalled as he counted the money, but the robber escaped with $3,000, and the crime was never solved.

The nation's isolation came to an abrupt end just nine days later, and Breans forever remembered where they were when the shocking news came. Japan's Dec. 7, 1941 attack on Pearl Harbor brought the country into World War II, and residents once again took up the call to arms. More than 300 local men and a dozen women served abroad or stateside in the military, while those at home supported their efforts through work with the Red Cross and American Legion. Families and friends kept their radios tuned to news from the war's

Up on the Roof
Armed with aircraft handbooks, binoculars, telescopes and telephones, Army Air-Watch spotters atop Brea-Olinda High scan the sky for enemy invaders. In addition to this rooftop outpost, the school's gymnasium was readied to serve as an aerial-attack decontamination station.
From the Dorothy Mon collection

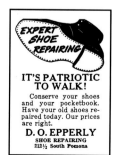

many fronts: far-off places with unknown names that became battle-fields for Brea's sons.

Brea Progress, Feb. 26, 1943

Concern for coastal defense led to California's designation as a military zone by 1942, with strict curfews set and emergency procedures adopted. Homes and businesses pulled blackout shades over windows as darkness fell, and cars cruised night-shrouded streets without their headlights. Air-raid instructions were printed in newspapers and posted in prominent buildings, and fear of attack ran high.

Anxiety over such raids escalated after a submarine strike off Goleta and a night of blazing anti-aircraft artillery-fire over Los Angeles, and Brea "armed" itself with an air-watch tower erected atop Brea-Olinda High. Schooled in the sighting and reporting of enemy planes, community spotting crews climbed a narrow ladder to the roof, where they manned telescopes and donned binoculars to scan the sky.

Many of the city's most prominent citizens lent their support to the effort, and a few spirited watchers like Edith Bennett, Madelyn West and Alice Whipp volunteered more than 500 hours.

Shifts at the post normally proved uneventful, though one crew did sight an errant plane. Lost and low on gas, an Army pilot destined for Riverside's March Field crashed in a local grove one Saturday afternoon in 1943. Though several orange trees were uprooted, the flier emerged from his P-38 almost unscathed, and both plane and pilot were soon scooped up by the military and shepherded back to base.

Wartime fervor combined with fear of enemy informants in 1942, reaching out to claim four Breans. The Hiroo Kitaoka family, a Japanese-American father, mother and two daughters, were displaced from their Ash Street home by federal order and relocated to internment facilities in the Southwest. The only known local residents among nearly 2,000 Orange County Japanese-Americans detained at such camps in the war years, the Kitaokas sold their car and stored their furnishings, and left Brea for the duration.

Accustomed to the deprivations of the Depression, Breans once again experienced a time of doing without as the nation channeled its energy overseas. Rationing combined with shortages to slow the pace of local life. Building stopped, shopping slackened, events were postponed

Fancy Footwork on the Front Lines

Brean Oliver (Andy) Ortega of West Date Street literally danced his way across Europe during World War II with a select group of "Jeep Show" entertainers. One of only 53 singers, musicians, magicians and others chosen to work in small troupes near the front, the Spanish dancer joined Mickey Rooney, Bobbie Breen and other famous names in bringing amusement to soldiers stationed in outlying combat zones.

Injured during a performance and later returned home for surgery, Ortega was awarded three battle stars for his contributions to the Allied war effort.

and people stayed home. The city hall and Laurel School became issue points for ration books, places where residents claimed entitlement stamps for items from coffee and butter to

Brea Progress, March 20, 1942

sugar and meat, gasoline and tires. Collection centers were established for salvage items, and even waste cooking fats were saved for use in making munitions.

Two Army battalions were quartered at Brea-Olinda High during the summer of 1942. The gymnasium, band room and several classrooms were used for housing, the cafeteria served as a mess hall and the commanding officer lodged in the Practice House bungalow. Opening day of the fall school term was delayed until October so the campus could be readied following the troops' departure.

In line with serious times, many of the high school's athletic competitions and extracurricular activities were suspended, and students instead turned their attention to the war effort. Campus clubs organized community-soldier dances, assisted with Red Cross work, planted "victory gardens," supervised salvage drives and

maintained the city's service flag, which hung in the school's main hallway. Students and teachers alike sold war bonds and stamps in spirited drives highlighted by contests, rallies and assemblies featuring military personnel.

"Care packages" went out from local residents to soldiers overseas, and letters arrived home from the war front. Veteran Brea firefighter Voloney Siebenthal, drafted to battle new blazes in Europe, wrote of his advance unit's part in the Allied Invasion of Normandy. Siebenthal would spend the next 28 months in the battlefields of Belgium, France and Germany, dodging buzz bombs and fighting fires with a Springfield rifle slung over his shoulder—a tour of duty that earned five silver stars.

Brea's oil wells churned out fuel for the conflict, and its industries re-tooled for battle. East of town at Union's Stearns site, the battalions formerly lodged at the high school found more permanent homes at "Camp Brea," where more than 500

Brea Progress, July 17, 1943

men were trained in the opening and operation of oil fields.

Under the command of Union Oil's Harry Eggers, local soldiers drilled wells, built bridges and roads, and otherwise prepared for the day when Japanese forces would be driven from Burma—opening the door for reactivation of this nation's strategic oil fields. Difficult terrain and shortages of troops and supplies hampered the Allied advance in the South Pacific, and—after 18 months of waiting—Brea's oil-drilling battalions were reassigned to other duties.

Brea Progress,
March 20, 1942

Down the slopes in town, Brea's industries geared for war. Shaffer Tool Works turned to the making of anchor chain for the Navy, while McGraw & Sons Foundry built lift gates for thousands of Allied landing craft. Chiksan and Enterprise Equipment swung into military production, and even the high school machine shop supported the cause, running contract jobs at night by special arrangement with Shaffer Tool Works.

With so much work to be done and so many men overseas, women entered the job force, joining their local male counterparts by taking defense work at aircraft factories and shipyards. Labor shortages in the fields led to the importation of Mexican Nationals and Jamaicans to pick the crops, and a small tent settlement was erected for the harvesters in La Habra. German prisoners of war later were brought in to pick local fruit, an experiment that backfired when two clever inmates stole a car and escaped over the border into Mexico.

The town took its final "solid-steel" shot at war glory in February of

"E" for Efficiency
The Chiksan company won Brea's first "E" Army-Navy award for war manufacturing, followed by Shaffer Tool Works (the presentation pictured) and the McGraw & Sons Foundry. Shaffer crafted enough anchor chain to stretch from Brea to San Diego, and McGraw built gates for more than 45,000 landing craft.
Brea Historical Society

1945, as the tanker *S.S. La Brea Hills* was launched at Sausalito in the presence of hometown dignitaries. Named in honor of Brea's prolific oil fields, the ship, "glided into San Francisco Bay," according to the *Brea Progress*, "its ample cargo space and bristling defensive guns jointly yet another symbol of the city's military role."

Arriving by "non-stop special city car," guests of honor for the launching included Brea Mayor Emil Carlson, Councilmen R.V. Monroe and L.A. Crowe, and *Progress* Associate Editor Martin Norins. In a happy coincidence, Bonnie Lookabaugh Gee, the wife of the ship's supervising builder, was discovered to have spent part of her childhood in Brea. It was Mrs. Gee who launched the ship, but not before

Mayor Carlson declared her an honorary Brean.

The 523-foot, 16,500-ton tanker *La Brea Hills* and her crew of 52 saw only four months of active duty, picking up a cargo of gasoline in Los Angeles and docking in San Francisco before entering the Pacific war zone late that May. She was grounded in Leyte, but continued undamaged to Utithi in the Caroline Islands and Enewetak in the Marshalls before turning home again at war's end.

For the second time in less than a quarter century, gold stars appeared on a service flag for local men lost in battle. The pages of the *Progress* revealed the names of several still missing, and 15 who wouldn't return. Residents Thomas Smith, William

Fred Thaheld
Flight Pioneer

He got his start in Austria, flying gliders off the roof of the family barn, and cast off the role of farmer for a career as an engineer. He worked as a stunt man in Vienna, and made his way to Hollywood jumping out of airplanes. Established in Brea by the early 1920's, he partnered with Bill Tremaine, laboring in a local garage to build a flying machine unlike all others.

In the biplane and triplane era of the 1920's, Fred Thaheld was the trail-blazing designer of the first low-winged monoplane ever flown in the United States. A "trim little single-seater" with a 42-horsepower motor, his Humming Bird clocked in at 140 miles an hour, and drew attention from the military for its tiny size and uncommon speed.

During World War II, Thaheld turned his talent to engine design, creating America's only air-cooled radial diesel, built by the Guiberson Company of Texas for use in airplanes, boats and tanks. His famous "pancake" diesel engine followed, again gaining widespread acclaim.

Returning to Brea at war's end, Thaheld took a job at Shaffer Tool Works, adapting his earlier designs for use in wind machines and experimental aircraft.

The inventor-designer's first Guiberson T-1020 engine today is displayed at the Smithsonian.

Top Flight
Brea inventor Fred Thaheld (second from right) joins (from left) Don Shaffer, Elvin Wilson and W.D. Shaffer at the test of a Stinson plane powered by a Thaheld engine.
Brea Historical Society

Murray, Allen Nolen and Tom Videnti were reported lost early in the war, as was Hal Fisher, who won the silver star. Conley Neal and Kenneth Fuller (son-in-law of City Clerk Grace May) died while serving in England, Robert Atkins (son of Police Chief William Atkins) fell in France, and Breans Bob Ball, Herman Carnine, Joe Gonzales, Horace Patterson and Clyde Rasmussen, as well as the namesake sons of former Assemblymen Joe Burke and Ted Craig, lost their lives in the Pacific.

Brea residents had drawn together through the four long years of war, caring for one another and supporting their servicemen overseas. Though much of the town's time and energy had been absorbed in efforts abroad, important events also had occurred on the home front.

Longtime School District Superintendent W.E. Fanning retired in 1942 after a 38-year local career, and his position was filled by former Brea Grammar School Principal Vincent Jaster. After nearly two decades and 500 births, the Brea Maternity Home closed its wards in 1942, and the old Randolph Schoolhouse (for many years used as an oil company office) fell in 1943, and its scrap lumber was salvaged for sheds built in Carbon Canyon.

With memories of the previous decade's flash floods still fresh in residents' minds, the town welcomed a series of federally funded flood-control projects in the early 1940's. The building of the Prado Dam (near Corona) was followed in 1941-42 by two smaller local controls: Brea Dam (located near Harbor Boulevard in the City of Fullerton) and Fullerton Dam (located near Associated Road just south of the City of Brea).

The landscape east of town took on a pastoral look in 1944, when the Brea Cattle Company leased 1,400 acres of the old Graham-Loftus oil land and stocked it with 500 steers. On the civic scene, the Brea Junior Woman's Club met for the first time with Marjorie Lacy presiding, and Emil Carlson, former airplane builder and road-race driver, was voted that fall to Brea's top elective job.

Lazy Day in Brea, 1942
City Hall Park had a fishing pond where anglers
whiled away their hours, and young Lynn Oliver
(left) took a lesson on lures from fishing friend
Bill Hodkins.
From the Dorothy Mon collection

Few residents took issue in 1945 when the *Brea Progress'* new masthead announced it served the "Finest Little City in California." Civic pride had continued strong through the war years, at the same time city size had stayed small. When a local boy got into trouble at school, he could count on his parents knowing long before he ever reached home. There was little crime, almost no one locked their doors, and a sense of camaraderie bound the town together. People took time to visit their friends, and made time to help their neighbors. Though many had cars, nearly everyone walked when they went downtown—and all could count on knowing almost everyone they met.

The post-war years ushered in changes for Brea's business district. Stores that had long stood vacant now opened their doors again, and new faces were noticed in town. Local manufacturing and industry diversified. Ceramics by Kirk moved its kilns north from Laguna, Winchel Manufacturing began building garage doors and hardware, Brea Oxide mixed bases for lipsticks and creams, and Brea Manufacturing built walk-in refrig-erators. Chiksan opened a large addition, and Hart Fruit Products started business in a plant built near the train tracks. Founded by Edwin G. Hart, the son of a pioneer resident, Hart Fruit began as a small operation marketing citrus peel, but soon expanded to the production of far more popular and profitable products—reportedly shipping New York City its first carload of California frozen orange juice.

The year 1946 saw a transition in BOHS leadership as Carl Harvey left his longtime post to become Orange County Assistant Superintendent of

To Still the Waters
Built closer to town than the dam that bears
Brea's name, Fullerton Dam has been a vital link
in the county flood-control system since the
early 1940's. Craig Regional Park was built in
this facility's northern spreading basin in 1972.
Brea Historical Society

Family Act, 1949
Young Sharon Alexander (Dean) considers a purchase suggestion made by her father, market-owner Dayton Alexander. Alexander's Super Market (northwest corner, today's Brea at Birch) brought increased variety to Brea buyers.
Photo by Archie Logsdon, from the Sharon Dean collection

Schools. Brea math teacher Frank O. Hopkins signed on as the school's new principal, serving in this position for the next 15 years. And sadness spread swiftly through town as two of Brea's leading citizens, W.D. Shaffer and his wife, Edna, died within weeks of one another.

Mourning the prominent couple's passing, residents quickly began planning a memorial in their honor. Efforts led by employees at Shaffer Tool Works saw success in 1948, when Mayor Charles McCart dedicated the Shaffer Memorial Fountain at City Hall Park. The Shaffer Fountain quickly became a local landmark, its cool dancing waters welcoming passersby to stop and watch a while, and its colorful night-lighted displays always a favorite with cruising drivers. Chronic plumbing problems necessitated the fountain's destruction in the late-1960's, and its site later was rededicated as the Brea Memorial Rose Garden.

The late 1940's proved an era of connections for Southern California, and Brea hooked up and joined in. Linked in 1947 to Texas by "The Biggest Inch," a pipeline running a thousand miles from the natural-gas fields of the Lone Star State to the cities of the Southland, Brea that year also cast its eyes on eastern waters, and vied to tie into the Colorado's flow.

The mighty Hoover (Boulder) Dam had been finished in 1936, followed by a lesser dam and channels leading the Colorado's waters nearly 400 miles southwest to the thirsty Los Angeles basin. Formed in 1928 to fund and tap this flow, the Metropolitan Water District (MWD) took on a bonded indebtedness of $220 million to finance the project, and offered connections to all communities that could afford them.

Small towns like Brea were left high and dry in the early years, unable to muster enough revenue to even come close to qualifying. Though the city tried several times to form a partnership with neighboring towns, no one cared to share the burden, and Brea went without. The

W.D. Shaffer
Brea's "First Citizen"

Businessman, inventor, civic leader and philanthropist, William "W.D." Shaffer played many parts during his quarter-century of local service. Founder of Shaffer Tool Works (for many years the town's largest employer), Shaffer was Brea's foremost civic leader in the years between 1923 and 1946, elected to the high-school district's first board of trustees and serving eight years as Brea's mayor.

An engineer, Shaffer invented tools to make oil work easier and safer, designing and patenting the "flow bean" and "control gate" to regulate high-pressure drilling. The impressive (yet costly and often dangerous) gusher became a thing of the past with the introduction of Shaffer tools, and the company's name became internationally synonymous with devices for wellhead control.

Though Shaffer Tool Works grew into an international business, W.D. Shaffer's employees remembered him as a "shy tycoon" and "a man with heart" who threw big company picnics and displayed a "father-like caring for his workers"...a man who wore a suit, yet often would drop down with a piece of chalk and sketch out ideas on the tool-shop floor.

William "W.D." Shaffer

A Mason and a Shriner, Shaffer was also a strong supporter of Brea's Congregational Church. The pipe organ still used in its sanctuary was donated in memory of his son, and W.D. played it at worship services each Sunday until his death.

Shaffer Tool Works, 1954
Following W.D. Shaffer's death, the business passed into the hands of his son, Donald, and later was sold to the Rucker Company. Located on Redwood at Birch, the plant was demolished in the early 1980's to make way for new development.
Brea Historical Society

community's repeated inability to enter the project proved both galling and ironic, for the water system's huge Orange County Reservoir lay right in Brea's backyard, atop the hills to the north of town at the end of today's Balsa Street.

Help from an unlikely source—the Laguna Beach-based South Coast Municipal Water District—finally aided Brea in joining the MWD, and six years after work had begun on the nearby reservoir, the city tapped into the system. Local and MWD dignitaries joined in a brief ceremony near the front of BOHS, where Mayor Carlson descended a manhole

on the main line and drew off the first glass of water. The mayor smiled for pictures and congratulated those attending, and few took note when he failed to tip the glass. While no one was looking, he threw out the "filthy" water, and quickly climbed up from the hole.

The Colorado River Project gave Brea and communities like it a dependable future source of both water and hydroelectric power, permitting almost unhampered growth in these otherwise arid zones. With its new water wealth, Southern California gained what seemed free rein to build as expansively as it

Awash in Sentiment

In 1964, former Mayor Carlson related for the *Brea Progress* the inside story on the city's MWD water success:

"We went to a final meeting with (South Coast Water District) and fully expected to thank them for their trouble and give the whole thing up. Just as a parting shot, I told the board that this was like the story about the little boy who wanted a drink out of a water fountain, but he was too short. The old man came by and lifted the little boy up and gave him a drink. I told the board that we were the little boy and they were the old man. They burst out laughing and voted to give us the necessary assistance, and we joined Metropolitan Water."

The Fourth Estate
Kansas newsman Frank Hall (above right) became *Brea Progress* owner-publisher in 1947, when the paper's office was located in the Oilfields National Bank building. The *Progress* built its own Brea Boulevard office in the early 1950's.
From the Roberta Hall Fox collection

chose, and the coming years saw the start of an era marked by mammoth development.

First word of the transportation tie that would one day transform the town came in 1947, when the *Progress* profiled the state highway department's proposal to build not one, but two freeways through Brea. Though plans for both north-south and east-west routes were revealed, progress on both byways was thwarted. Funding for many years was concentrated in more populous areas, and isolated Brea waited a full quarter-century for its multi-lane link to the larger world.

An idea born in Brea won statewide acceptance in 1947, when a new law designed to enhance highway safety was enacted in Sacramento. Inspired by an article concerning the hazards of under-trained drivers, Chiksan employee Frank Burrill teamed with CHP Officer R.I. Morris to promote compulsory driver education and training courses for all 16-year-olds seeking a license.

Gaining assistance from Assembly Speaker Sam Collins (a neighbor from nearby Fullerton), Burrill and Morris drafted a bill later brought to the legislature by Assemblyman Earl W. Stanley. Months of letter writing, lobbying and hearings finally yielded success, and the bill was signed into law in June of 1947.

Brea-Olinda and Fullerton became the first school districts in the state to implement the new curriculum, which mandated both classroom study and behind-the-wheel time in specially equipped training cars. Other states followed California's lead, and similar laws were enacted widely within a few years.

Burrill and Morris were honored for their contributions to highway safety by the California State Senate in 1969. The state-wide course of instruction the pair had championed continued until 1990, when altered governmental agendas and beleaguered legislative budgets brought driver training to a stop in California's schools.

Brea's police department enhanced its image in the years of the 1940's. James Pearson was selected chief as the decade turned, and soon led his three-man team in the purchase of a .38-caliber pistol, two pairs of handcuffs and a 1941 Ford. William Atkins began his 15-year career as chief in 1946, and quickly took steps to improve safety (setting up bus stops and restricting curb parking), communication (starting two-way radio contact with the county), equipment (buying tear-gas equipment and a '47 Chevy) and standards (mandating uniforms, and forming the city's first reserve force).

Dial service came to the town's telephones in 1948, and Brea bid farewell to both its friendly switchboard opera-tors and its outdated local exchange. City phones took the prefix JAsper, and by 1950, local listings soared to 944.

By the late 1940's, the pent-up demand for housing found building begun on several fronts. Early post-war subdivisions took shape to the town's southeast and in the area just north of the high school, and homes at both

ABOVE: The Mod Squad
Brea's police fleet in the late 1940's. The department's original patrol car (a 1929 four-door sedan) is surpassed by more up-to-date additions. Police headquarters in these years was at the all-in-one city hall.
Courtesy Brea Police Department

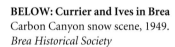

BELOW: Currier and Ives in Brea
Carbon Canyon snow scene, 1949.
Brea Historical Society

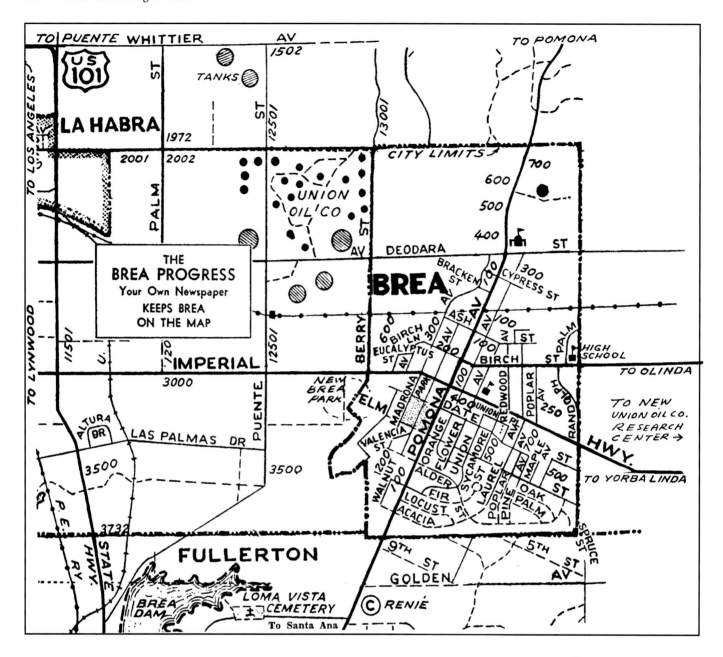

Brea, 1950
Thirty-three years after incorporation, the town hadn't grown much at all. Though a few new streets spread out to the south and east, the city limits had hardly expanded.
Brea Chamber of Commerce

sites sold almost as soon as they were finished. Though builders sought additional property for development, the oil companies held onto their investments, and, for a time, further construction was stalled by a lack of available land.

Breans were surprised for the first time in the town's history to awaken on Jan. 11, 1949 and find their streets frosted with fallen snow. "Old and young alike scampered onto the lawns and through the fields," wrote an amused *Brea Progress* reporter, "playing in the snow that lasted until the noon sun

melted it away." Though nearby drifts disappeared far too soon for the taste of local children, Carbon Canyon's fields stayed white through the following day.

New industry found a foothold in Brea as the decade drew to its close. Los Angeles manufacturer T. Kirk Hill instantly became the town's biggest businessman when he bought a plot of land from rancher E.M. Reese and announced he would relocate his large, lucrative Kirkhill Rubber Company to 300 E. Cypress. Opened by 1951, Kirkhill became the town's first non-oil-related industry

High Style for a New Decade
Updated and ready to roll, the Brea Theater welcomes film fans. Though it opened and closed
many times, the Brea Theater was "the only show in town" until the late 1970's.
Brea Historical Society

and the area's top employer, later
numbering, at peak production, as
many as 1,000 among its work force.

The town's oldest company soon
announced its own new development. A pioneer in petroleum
research, Union Oil unveiled plans to
relocate its laboratories to Brea,
building an innovative facility that
became the first large industrial
complex on the town's east side.
Nearly 300 employees worked here
by 1951, conducting petrochemical
research leading to new uses for oil
and natural gas.

Brea's eastern skyline took on a
new look the following year as Union
raised the towers of Brea Chemicals,
a facility to manufacture and market
the petroleum byproducts ammo-
nium nitrate and liquid ammonia
fertilizer. A 1957 merger of this
company with R. T. Collier yielded
Collier Carbon and Chemical Company, soon the West Coast's largest
supplier of nitrogen fertilizers.

The year 1949 saw local schools
improved, as bonds were passed for
the building of classrooms and a
cafeteria at Laurel, and classrooms,
tennis courts, shower facilities and a
long-delayed, 350-seat "ultra-mod-
ern" auditorium at Brea Grammar.
After lengthy consideration and
several false starts, the same season
brought Brea's inclusion in the new
Orange County Outfall Sewer
System, a move which marked the
community's last vital link to the
region's infrastructure.

The 1950 census found the town's
population had grown to just 3,208, a
still-slow gain of 646 in a period of 10
full years. As the decade turned, the
Baptist Church rebuilt on a larger lot
at Date and Flower, the long boarded-
up Pacific Electric train station was
torn down, 20 acres east of BOHS was
turned into a barnyard home for
animals from the school's new
agriculture department, and Chamber
of Commerce Secretary Purl Harding

began penning a city history that
would serve for 40 years.

A controversial decision by
leaders of the elementary-school
district made headlines in the first
years of the 1950's, when supply
funds were used to buy a citrus
grove east of the BOHS farm. Purchased as the site of a proposed (but
never built) elementary, the 13-acre
property was bought for $20,000, but
earned the schools a smart profit
when it sold in the early 1980's at a
price tag of $2.5 million.

Progress editor Frank Hall
chaired the city's March of Dimes
drive in 1951, and Brea shoppers
dropped coins into collection boxes
patterned in the shape of iron lungs.
Local response to the nationwide
polio epidemic had been noted as
early as 1943, when the city-park
pool had been closed for the summer
due to escalating fears of contagion.
Not until 1955 did anxious local
children and their grateful parents
line up for shots of the new Salk anti-
polio vaccine.

Brea's 1951 social scene marked
the entrance of a Kiwanis Club led by
Claude Hellman, while 1952 saw
Lieutenant Governor Goodwin
Knight look on as Master Vincent
Jaster broke ground for a Masonic
Lodge on Imperial at Sycamore.

That year found action on
Pomona Avenue (Brea Boulevard) as
the King Professional (medical)
Building went up on the south, the
post office moved in on the north
and "Doc" Curtis paid off an election
bet by marching through town
dressed up in pajamas and an old-
fashioned nightcap. The pages of the
Progress noted the wreckage of a
missing hospital plane had been
found in Carbon Canyon, and
marked the passing of Army Medical
Corpsman John Atencio, a Brean
killed in action in Korea.

Brea kept up its busy pace in the
remaining months of 1952. The Rev.
Loren Wood and his two-year-old
congregation celebrated the dedication of the Brea Foursquare Church,
the local Woman's Club reaped the
rewards of good taste by publishing

What's Cooking in Brea, the county branch library moved to a novel site on Date Street and nearly 4,000 spectators packed the stands for the first Lions' Brea Rodeo.

A neighboring notable stumped through town that summer on his rocky road to the White House. Hardly a stranger to Brea, Yorba Linda-born Richard Nixon had traveled through the city countless times as a youth, a Whittier College student and a La Habra lawyer, and garnered strong local support in his bid as Dwight D. Eisenhower's Republican running mate.

The year 1952 marked the end to a familiar aspect of local life, as statewide judicial reorganization closed the case on city court. In its last years, local sessions convened in city hall under the gavel of Judge Harvey Moore, a Brean who drew widespread notice as a formidable, fine-levying foe of drunk drivers. Following the local court's closure, Brea cases instead were heard in Santa Ana.

On His Way to the Top
Seventeen years later he would become President, but in 1952 Richard Nixon had just begun to run for the country's second highest office. Brea gave the candidate a warm welcome when he took the stage at City Hall Park, flanked by his wife, Pat, and local political pundit Dr. C. Glenn Curtis. Eisenhower and Nixon "swept Brea like a new broom" in the coming election.
Brea Historical Society

The long-awaited beginnings of population growth reached out at last to Orange County, and its cities looked with increasing interest at the unincorporated lands beyond their borders. Attempting to forestall possible annexation conflicts, groups representing Brea,

Fullerton and La Habra gathered for discussions in 1953, but tempers flared and Brea's delegation headed home when word leaked out that Fullerton had indulged in "giant, secret land grabs" while the talks progressed. Though Fullerton gained valuable acreage north of Imperial

The Middle Ages
Brea Boulevard (then Pomona Avenue) in the early 1950's was the only commercial district in town, a four-block stretch of shops with parking slots on the street.
Brea Historical Society

ABOVE: Uptown Drop
The often-moved local post office finds a more permanent home on (today's) southwest Brea Boulevard at Ash. Postal service had come a long way from the early days, when residents waited on muddy corners hoping to catch the mailman on one of his infrequent trips from Fullerton.
Brea Historical Society

RIGHT: Bar None
His luck is running out and there's a knotty necktie over his head, but this unknown inmate keeps smiling as Lion John Daugherty makes his stand. The Lions' annual fest of riding, racing and roping was a popular part of Brea life in the 1950's.
Brea Historical Society

Jack Armstrong
Hometown Hero

Major Jack Armstrong
From the Ella Armstrong Post collection

He grew up on the oil leases of Olinda, graduated from Brea-Olinda High School and fought his battles in World War II's air war over Europe. A pilot stationed with the 8th Air Force in England, combat squadron leader Major Jack "Jake" Armstrong was shot down over Germany, and spent the war's last years in a prison camp near the Baltic Sea.

Pursuing his career as a military pilot, Major Armstrong graduated from Edwards Air Force Base and was assigned to Wright-Patterson Field in Dayton, Ohio, where he set the world's closed-course speed record at a 1954 Labor Day air show. He lost his life the following day in an attempt to better this record.

A stand of pepper, pine and cypress trees in Carbon Canyon Regional Park marks the site of Armstrong's boyhood home, and this quiet place has been dedicated as the Major Jack Armstrong Grove.

and east of Harbor in this and allied annexations of the 1950's, Brea learned a lesson that led to far greater gains in the future.

Brea's firefighters took delivery of a new truck in 1954, and belatedly learned it was too large to fit through the arched doors at city-hall station. Remodeling began in short order.

Word that a Brean was working with the House Un-American Activities Committee made the papers that year, and articles described the agent's work in the investigation of Hollywood stars. Summer's end saw the community mourn a hometown hero, when Olinda-born Major Jack Armstrong, war hero and flight pioneer, was killed at a Labor Day air show.

Through more than four decades, Brea had suffered growing problems of access. By the mid-1950's, east-west commuters moved at a steady clip along three routes: Central, Brea-Olinda (Birch) and

Imperial, while only one street (today's Brea Boulevard), ran north-south, and each year carried an increasing tide of both local and regional traffic.

As early as 1923, plans had been laid to extend Orange Avenue across the train tracks, but railroad opposition and a high price tag left the job undone. Growing traffic and safety concerns led to the consideration of Poplar Avenue as a crossing site in 1954, but costs again proved prohibitive. Downtown never did get its second rail crossing, though the building of State College Boulevard and the Orange (57) Freeway helped divert non-local traffic from Brea Boulevard in later years.

The city's first commercial district built apart from the downtown area arrived in 1954, when Cursi and Turner began development of Brea Heights Shopping Center (today's Brea at Alder). Mayor Charles Russell turned the first spade

Whimsical Window
Un upside-down dummy gets a lot more notice than one that's right side up, a fact not lost on the owners of Haddad's Haberdashery. One of only a few clothing stores in town during the 1950's, Haddad's was headquarters for the fashionable.
From the Esther Haddad Fieldhouse collection

Uptown, Downtown
Brea had two business districts by the late 1950's—the North Boulevard and the Heights. Even so, more and more shopping dollars kept flowing out of town.

of earth for Bob's Super Market, a 15,000-foot food emporium featuring air conditioning and ample parking. The opening of drug and variety stores followed, and Breans soon streamed in to enjoy the new "one-stop-shopping" trend. Downtown shopkeepers watched...and worried.

Main-street Brea in the 1950's still seemed much like a Midwestern town. Though most of the 30 and 40-year-old storefronts sported facelifts of plaster or paint, the goods they sold remained simple, with little floor space left over for frills. Mom-and-pop markets rubbed elbows with a smattering of drug and dime stores, a handful of clothing shops and a few small cafes. The old Brea Hardware shared its sidewalk with the new Brea Bowl, and the Trojan Cafe made way for the Tastee-Freez.

Ten miles to the south, a new breed of amusement park opened to rave reviews in 1955, bringing obscure Orange County into the national spotlight. On the heels of Disneyland's debut, a troupe of businessmen headed by Beckman

Instruments-founder Dr. Arnold O. Beckman, Brea Mayor Russell and City Administrator A. W. Studebaker traveled east to promote Orange County industry.

Meeting with political leaders in Washington and American Industrial Development Council members in New York, this early delegation launched a program of business recruitment that became the pattern for future years.

The mid-1950's saw a marked upturn in local growth, as former citrus land to the town's southwest was subdivided. Families moved in, children headed to school,

and the buildings of a new elementary—the city's first in 35 years—took shape on Eadington at Arovista. A small and exclusive tract of custom homes, called Briarwood, soon was begun nearby, as was the first subdivision north of Central, a tract of custom-built, ranch-style homes that took the name Pleasant Hills.

Oilfields National Bank, the town's only financial institution, became the county's first branch of the California Bank (later United California and now First Interstate) in 1955. The following year saw the Brea Mounted Posse formed at El Rodeo Riding Club, more new homes built north of the high school, Brea Grammar School reopened as Brea Junior High, the town's first stoplight turned on at the intersection of (today's) Imperial and Brea Boulevard, and BOHS's varsity grid squad blocked only inches from victory in a CIF battle with Claremont.

Responding to the growing population's need for expanded parklands, town leaders acquired 22 acres adjacent to a southwest wash, passed over the names "Baranca" and "Memorial," and tagged the new site "Arovista." The nine-hole, 30-acre Brea Municipal Golf Course opened on the park's south side

Arovista School
The site was once covered with citrus irrigated by Arovista Mutual Water, and the name came from a landowner's beach house (Arrow-Vista) known for its excellent view. Fourteen acres of the old Loma Ranch sprouted classrooms and opened to elementary students in September of 1956.
Brea Historical Society

three years later, with Mayor Leo West teeing off with a tailor-made golden club.

The Cold War heated up, and a Nike Air-Defense Base was built in Brea's hills. One of 16 such units set up to defend the Los Angeles area from air attack, the Brea-La Habra Battery was situated near the top of today's Site Drive and stocked with an arsenal of Ajax and (later) Hercules anti-aircraft missiles. Army troops often numbering more than 100 remained on alert at the hilltop site, where radar units constantly scanned the sky. Volatile fuels and explosive missiles were housed in underground structures, linked by an elevator to launching pads on the surface.

Though the missiles stored here were frequently reported in local newspapers as "deadly defensive," the community accepted their presence as a sign of security in troubled times. Scout troops and civic organizations often toured the Nike site, and the general public dropped by when the base hosted an open house. The rising tension of this era was reflected in the pages of the *Brea Progress*, which noted that plans for backyard bomb-shelters were available at all city building departments in the county.

Brea's Catholic population, for many years lacking a local church, celebrated St. Patrick's Day, 1957 with the dedication of St. Mary's

An Ominous Presence
A fleet of Ajax missiles (pictured) drew Cold War duty at Brea's Nike Base 29, stored in underground silos for defense against enemy attack. Larger, atomic-capable Hercules missiles replaced the Ajax in the early 1960's, and a stockpile of nuclear warheads waited in readiness at the site.
Courtesy Air Defense Artillery Museum

Mission, an outreach of the long-established Fullerton church. James Francis Cardinal McIntyre, Archbishop of Los Angeles, was present for the formal opening of a small structure on Walnut at Elm, the first step in a long-range building program that grew into St. Angela Merici Church and School. The north county's first major hospital, St. Jude's, opened to patients that May, its construction aided by contributions from Brea residents and businesses.

Orange County's population topped the half million mark for the first time in 1957. The Brea Welfare Council (later Brea Community Emergency Council) was formed, Memory Garden opened with a concert of its Schulmerich Carillons, the Diamond Bar Ranch began development on the first of its 8,000 acres and the local Optimist Club opened a track for midget racers on Birch Street east of the high school.

Puente Street was paved from Central to Imperial, opening up a 700-acre industrial park that quickly drew companies like Amercoat (now Ameron) and Tretolite to town. Shaffer Tool Works moved its offices west to this new site, and Chiksan, recently merged with Food Machinery Corporation (FMC), transplanted its manufacturing facilities here.

Major regional construction literally moved mountains in the late years of the 1950's. The Army Corps of Engineers began work on the $5-million Carbon Canyon Dam, an extensive project that erased almost all traces of old Olinda. In the years between 1958 and 1960, nearly every remaining structure in the once-booming town was moved out or destroyed. Rose Drive and Carbon Canyon Road were relocated, and a towering earthen dam took shape in the pass where Olinda Creek flowed through to the lowlands below.

This massive construction project cleared the way for $43 million in county flood-control improvements, including the local building of two concrete channels (Brea Canyon and Loftus) and new

Eclectic Electric
Consumer goods galore tempted Brea Electric patrons in the 1950's. Founded
in the town's first years and owned since 1932 by the Holly Family, Brea Electric
today is the city's oldest continuously operating local business.
Brea Historical Society

bridges over the Brea Channel at Lambert and Imperial.

The year 1958 saw the Brea Rotary Club started with Richard J. Wilcox as president and the Brea police detective bureau begun with William Hobbs as investigating officer. Sixteen-year-old local resident Shirley Nipp was crowned queen of the Orange County Fair, and two annexation issues grabbed banner headlines in the *Progress*.

A surprise move by Yorba Linda leaders to annex their unincorpo-

rated town to Brea dominated newspapers for several weeks in the summer of 1958. Public meetings were held and petitions circulated, but in the end no merger ensued. In the midst of discussions, Fullerton approached Yorba Linda with enticements to enter its boundaries instead, and negotiations broke down in confusion. Yorba Linda remained independent, waiting until 1967 to incorporate on its own.

Brea laid claim to its greatest land victory only a few weeks later

when secret negotiations led to approval of the Robinson Annex, a narrow strip of land stretching from the city's former boundary at Randolph Avenue 3.7 miles east to the mouth of Carbon Canyon. Though a gain of only 380 acres, the annexation increased the city's size by nearly a fifth, and shut the door on neighboring cities hard at work on acquisitions in this area.

The crucial backing of Union Oil, major area landowner, helped speed the annexation's approval, and a

Brea Progress, Aug. 15, 1957

Fullerton bid to cut Brea off on the east was defeated by a matter of days. Brea now had the potential to grow northward from its new borders unobstructed, a boon Mayor Leo West recognized by calling the Robinson Annexation, "the most important step made since the city's inception."

Plans for a "Brea Canyon Freeway" surfaced again in 1958, when the California Chamber of Commerce urged allocation of state funds for surveying and design. This era's master plan for freeways shows not two, but three freeways ultimately converging in Brea, the "Brea Canyon" from Santa Ana to Pomona, the "Imperial" from Los Angeles airport east through Brea (along Imperial, or the alternate Lambert toward Riverside), and an unnamed roadway

linking Brea through Yorba Linda to the Riverside Freeway.

A bronze plaque was unveiled in 1959 at Vice-President Richard Nixon's Yorba Linda birthplace, the Republican Women of Brea organized and the Brea Lions sponsored Orange County's first North-South All-Star Football Game. The Tap Toes Dance Studio shuffled into the spotlight, Elissa Walt became the city's second queen of the Orange County Fair and *Progress* editor Tom Gillespie wondered in print if the Stanley Steamer shouldn't be reintroduced to help stamp out Los Angeles smog.

Brea adopted the California Pepper as its official tree, North county marked the founding of its first four-year institution of higher learning as California State College (later University), Fullerton opened its doors, and Brea-Olinda High School expanded with a new pool and boys gymnasium.

The county approved matching funds that year to improve two local streets, tying them together as a single, regional roadway. Gasoline-tax dollars went to work on Deodara to the east and Ocean to the west, and a plan was formed to link the streets together through the old Union Oil tank farm between Berry and Puente. By the mid-1960's, a new street named Lambert would extend unimpeded westward to La Habra and beyond.

The town perked up and took notice in the fall of 1959 when two out-of-town businessmen filed a permit for a coffeehouse featuring live folk and jazz entertainment. Local youth expressed approval, while their elders found grounds for concern, and an overflow crowd caused quite a stir when councilmen let the motion cool for lack of a second. Within a few weeks, service clubs had begun a local youth club, whose members posed for the *Progress*, coffeepot in

hand, announcing a Halloween "Beatnik Ball."

Nearly 4,000 spectators packed the BOHS bleachers six weeks later as Brea's varsity football team took on Beaumont for the Southern-Section CIF championship. "Always a bridesmaid, never a bride," Coach Dick Tucker reminded his crew, firing players up over past titles lost and urging them on to a win. It was a chilly night in Brea, but cheering fans soon warmed up the stands. Led by the "great left arm" of quarterback Gary Holman, the Wildcats trounced the Cougars 47-21, bringing Brea's 32-year-old grid team its very first CIF victory. When the gun went off, the *Progress* wrote, "elated players carried Tucker from the field...dumping him into the swimming pool to the great enjoyment of fans."

For Brea, the decade of the 1950's marked a turning point from the slow, steady tempo of the past to the quickening pace of a new day. Its needs for water, power and other vital services at last met through the regional infrastructure, the city turned its attention to planning and growth—annexing land, improving roads, building homes and attracting vital new industries.

Brea Progress, Dec. 10, 1959

SPECIAL VICTORY EDITION

The Wildcat

VOL. XXVIII NO. 6   Brea-Olinda High School, Brea, Calif.   December 18, 1959

C.I.F. Championship!

Producing by far the supreme football game in the colorful history of the school, the Brea-Olinda Wildcats overwhelmed a game but bewildered Beaumont eleven, 47 to 21, last Friday, Dec. 11, to win the coveted C.I.F. "A" Championship for 1959.

Never before has a team from Brea done so well before so many at such an opportune time! Quarterback Gary Holman led the parade of outstanding athletes as he turned in the top effort of a southern California high school player this season. He called signals and led his squad to 47 points and the C.I.F. champoinship; he passed for a phenominal 350 net yards during the evening, completing 18 of 27 attempts, for an average of 20 yards per toss; he threw four touchdown passes, two to Jim Williamson for 60 and 9 yards, and two to Lyndell Emrick for 30 and 42 yards. In addition he booted four extra points, and passed to Williamson for another.

Equally outstanding were the performances of Fullback Dick Cooke, who caught one pass for 14 yards, carried the ball nine times for 79 more and one touhdown; and Left Halfback and Co-Captain Bob Coons, who also tallied one t.d., while carrying for four times for 83 yards and a 20.8 average. He also caught two passes good for 39 yards.

Both first string ends scored twice during the contest. Williamson caught nine of Holman's aerials for 186 yards and Emrick gathered in six for 111 yards.

Coach Dick Tucker was also pleased with the line play of his all-league tackles, Co-Captain Jim Mascaro and Rich Amon, as well as Steve Johnson and Gary Garfield, for their excellent work on defense and the protection they gave Holman on his passing.

Although they trailed in the scoring twice in the early stages of the game, the Wildcats

DICK COOKE (#37) eludes a would-be tackler late in the Beaumont game as Jerry Hale (#47) comes up fast to help out.

proved too strong for their opponents as they scored seven touchdowns in all, their seasonal high.

Cooke bulled his way over from the one-yard line for the first tally, culminating a drive that started from the Brea-Olinda 41.

The Green and Gold's second score followed a blocked punt by Bob Jackson and Mascaro on the Cougar 30, with Emrick taking a Holman pass over from there.

Following a Beaumont score in the second quarter Right Halfback Larry Montgomery returned the kickoff to his own 40, and on the first play from scrimmage, Holman zeroed in on Williamson on the Cougar 30 and Willy went the distance.

Gary Holman
An all-around athlete, the BOHS gridiron great later played baseball for the Washington Senators.
Gusher, 1960

A Night To Remember
Brea Comes in a Winner.

A 1959 report card for Brea would have shown both good marks and bad. Taxes were low and schools were good, and community hopes remained high. The population was growing and industry had boomed, and change was both popular and planned. But there were problems, too. Residents complained there was nowhere to shop, and increasingly bought goods out of town. Longtime owners held on to their land, leaving too little room for expansion. And the oft-promised freeway had yet to be built, and commuters were growing weary.

As the end of its fourth decade came, Brea held onto the spirit of simpler times. Huge crowds turned out for football games, Public Schools Week, rodeos and the annual fair, and the Community Fund drive exceeded its quota in every year. Though change had begun to take root, the city was still, in the words of then-Mayor Charles Russell, "a small, prosperous, friendly community surrounded by orange groves and oil fields."

Fast Lane to High Finance
The coming of the 57 Freeway opened the city's
doors to a rush of commerce and industry never
possible in the past. With access, the city's central-
ized regional location became its greatest asset.
Brea Historical Society

CHAPTER 8

Access and Opportunity

$\mathcal{F}$rom the first, and for almost two centuries, Los Angeles had been the Southland's only world-class city, the center of business and arbiter of culture for a hundred lesser-known suburbs. But by the 1950's, Orange County had begun its own run for a place in the Southern California sun. The opening of the Santa Ana Freeway tied the county into the transit system, Disneyland put it on the map, and thousands of acres of farmland were plowed into shopping centers and housing tracts.

Businesses long based in the metropolis cast their lots on southeastern lands, and industry relocated to acres that once had spawned only oranges. Education and culture followed, and within a short score of years, Orange County emerged with a strong identity all its own.

To the county's extreme north, in Brea, the same scene unfolded more slowly and on a far smaller scale. By 1960, Brea had been transformed from an oil and agriculture town into a growing industrial center. Population and land area, near-stagnant for 30 years, had more than doubled in a decade, and a rallying economy fed the growing trend. Noting the town's regional location, rail link and proximity to planned freeways, *Brea Progress* Editor Tom Gillespie accurately assessed the city's place in the

evolving county order, noting that Brea was "sitting on a gold mine, as far as taxes go."

Efforts to effectively channel anticipated growth arrived early in the new decade. Though the city's first planning commission had convened more than 10 years before, a formal planning study remained unwritten until 1960. Prepared that year without the assistance of outside consultants (some claimed it was framed over one commissioner's kitchen table), the homegrown effort focused on revised standards for land use and annexation, improvement of highway ordinances, and the acquisition of property and beginning of work on new schools, new parks and a new civic center.

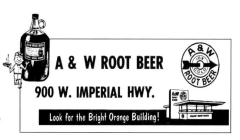

Landmark Stand
Jerry's A & W Root Beer made its bright-orange entrance on Imperial Highway in 1960. Though Imperial was still a two-lane road stretching through acres of orange groves, it remained for a dozen more years the main byway to Los Angeles.
Brea Progress, Nov. 10, 1960

'PICNIC AT HOME WITH DICK'

Plan to attend this old-fashioned family picnic honoring a great American, Richard M. Nixon, when he visits his home county.

WEDNESDAY, OCTOBER 12
at KNOTT'S BERRY FARM
BUENA PARK
MAJOR TELEVISION ADDRESS, AT THE PICNIC,
BY VICE PRESIDENT NIXON AT 8:00 P.M.

*   box lunch   *
gates open at 5:00 p.m.
entertainment 'til 8:00
OLD-FASHIONED TORCHLIGHT PARADE
booths—fun for everyone

ALL FOR ONLY
$5.00 PER PERSON
GET TICKETS NOW AT:

CHARLES RUSSELL
JAsper 9-2121
BREA REPUBLICAN HEADQUARTERS
132½ BREA BLVD.—JA 9-3979 OR JA 9-3970

Neighbor in the News
Breans came out to support Richard Nixon's 1960 run for the White House, but the Yorba Lindan lost to John Kennedy in one of the nation's closest elections.
Brea Progress, Oct. 6, 1960

Brea's long commitment to balanced growth for a strong tax base was solidified in this early study. Unlike a number of nearby cities which had shunned industry and become almost entirely residential, Brea had zoned large parcels of level land with good access "industrial," and held out, often under pressure from residential builders, for such development. In the days before the Brown Act formalized government's activities, early councils often gathered at downtown's Hub Cafe

for a coffee klatsch, laying out maps on the tables to sketch the face of future Brea. Clear delineation between the city's industrial, commercial and residential areas was, from the start, a high priority, and the release of land from the oil companies—done slowly and in large parcels, allowed time for careful planning and avoided piecemeal development.

Though much had been done by 1960 and the future held certain promise, Brea still traveled a bumpy road toward progress. Residents who moved to town in the 1950's thinking freeways would quickly follow were disappointed as months of waiting stretched instead into years. Dozens made the 25-mile drive to work in Los Angeles on surface streets—an hour a day each way—while others who might have moved to town found Brea's isolation unacceptable. Industries which could have created jobs close to home were kept from building by a lack of available land, and Brea sat back for a time and played a waiting game.

The 1960 census brought Brea's population to 8,487, nearly triple the number of residents counted just 10 years before. Though residential and industrial construction showed strong gains, commercial building lagged, and new shopping centers in nearby cities eagerly welcomed Brea buyers.

The old downtown had reached a sorry state by 1960. The *Progress* decried it as "the corpse of Brea," taking aim at the "sluggish" chamber of commerce, challenging out-of-town investors to modernize the "aging antiquity" of the buildings, and warning that quick steps might, "make the complete exodus of business enterprise from downtown a remote possibility and not a probability." Though many agreed with the assessment, few improvements followed, and by the time a real plan emerged, downtown lay in the looming shadow of a vital new retailing giant.

Frank Schweitzer, Jr., the son of a longtime councilman, was elected mayor in 1960, and wrote a glowing

state-of-the-city report for the *Progress* late that year. Building permits, he noted, had doubled in 12 months, with more than 300 homes added in six new subdivisions. There were new stores in Brea Heights, a new United California Bank on (today's) Brea at Fir, and a new rock-and-gravel plant on main street just south of the train tracks. With local taxes lowered for the fifth straight year, the city maintained its fiscal fame, boasting one of the county's lowest tax rates. The town had selected the red rose as its official flower, and—at long last—asserted its local identity, renaming Pomona Avenue "Brea Boulevard" in Council Resolution 862. The year's end saw the reactivated chamber of commerce improve its downtown Christmas decorations, and 100 baskets of food delivered to needy local families.

Long under construction, Carbon Canyon Dam was finished in 1960, providing a last link in the north county's flood-control system. The few remaining residents of Olinda were forced to leave their homes in the wake of the dam's completion, and most of the remaining structures were moved out or destroyed.

The old school and an adjacent building were trucked into Brea, the

Banking on Local Prospects
United California Bank (the former California and later First Interstate) moved south from its old site on Brea Boulevard and Birch in 1960. Bank Manager Clarence Schwartz played a key role in bringing new industry to Brea.
Brea Historical Society

Friendly Persuasion
Brea welcomed in a wealth of new land in annexations of the 1950's and 60's, its limits stretching in a stair-step pattern to the San Bernardino County line. Though the town's altered profile prevented nearby cities from surrounding it, most of the newly annexed acres remained undeveloped, as seen in this Imperial at Valencia intersection.
Brea Historical Society

school taking its place on Elm at Sievers as a youth center, and the smaller structure set up in Arovista Park for scout activities. The few east-side students who would have continued at Olinda School instead attended classes at the district-leased El Rodeo Riding Academy, and the bell that had hung at the old school was stored for use at a new facility built farther east in the canyon.

The Carbon Canyon Annexation of 1960 for the first time brought Brea's boundaries to the border of San Bernardino County, encompassing lands to the northeast including the site of old Olinda. Already a boomtown when Brea was just beginning, Olinda had always been visible from the southwest, but the building of the dam obscured the former townsite, shutting it off from

view just as it was absorbed by its one-time rival.

In the 1760-acre Carbon Canyon annexation, Brea defeated other cities working to cut off its eastward growth, gaining not only the dam, valuable residential acreage and land for a large regional park, but the promise of future expansion north to the Los Angeles County line. When the annexation ink was dry, Brea had gained the potential to become one of Orange County's largest cities, and had turned back the pages of its history two decades to encompass Olinda's past.

The early years of the 1960's saw growth continue both "in" and "out" of town. Long a landmark on Valencia at Birch, El Rodeo Riding Academy relocated to a new site near the mouth of Carbon Canyon in 1963.

Inspiration Point
A quiet place with a sweeping view of Carbon Canyon's grandeur, Wayside Chapel still
draws its share of passing travelers, and was joined in 1992 by the new Living Faith Church.
Photo by Susan Gaede

and the first custom homes were begun in Olinda Village, land north of the canyon road that once was the bramble-rimmed border of Ed Gaines' Flying Cow Ranch.

Newcomer Syd Sybrandy set his sights on property south of the road, building a small "Wayside Chapel" with a wide window overlooking the canyon. Sybrandy soon opened Edendale, a Christian retreat, but this short-lived operation later became Hollydale Mobile Home Park. The chapel remains today as a canyon landmark, joined by the new Olinda School, built north of the road in 1964 at 109 Lilac Lane.

Church happenings dominated the news in the 1960's. St. Mary's Mission formally became St. Angela

Merici Parish in 1962, with Msgr. Emmett McCarthy as first pastor. St. Angela School opened in 1964, and mass was first celebrated in the new church sanctuary on Easter, 1969.

Christ Lutheran Church rose on the southeast side of Imperial at Arovista in 1962 (followed by a preschool in 1967 and an elementary in 1979). Emanuel Lutheran (now of La Habra) held its first services in the mid-60's at Neels Brea Mortuary. The Christian Church gave up its site on West Ash in 1962 to build the new Lark Ellen Christian Church in North Fullerton, and this congregation's former church became home to the new Brea Missionary Baptist.

Richard Baugh was named Brea's chief of police in 1964, and

Thomas Speer was sworn in as the city's mayor. Fire and firefighting dominated the news in the months to come as Kenneth Staggs began his 15-year career as fire chief, a second fire station was opened (on Berry Street), the department's 1923 Seagrave pumper (*Old Susie*) took her final run, and the landmark Hualde House was swept by a spectacular blaze as hundreds of football fans watched from the BOHS bleachers.

Orange County adopted an ambitious, 20-year Master Plan for Regional Parks in 1963, and two years later chose the 114-acre Carbon Canyon flood basin as a future recreational center. Celebrating the welcome news on Arbor Day, 1965, Breans bought 200 coastal redwood

Olinda School

Though the modern school bears little resemblance to the structure it replaced, the new Olinda School carries the name and houses the bell that belonged to its predecessor. Built by the Army Corps of Engineers and led for many years by now-retired principal Joan Lewis, the school today serves students from Olinda Village and Eagle Hills.
Brea Historical Society

Mariposa School

Built under the guidance of longtime district administrator Leonard MacKain and led for 26 years by Principal Howard Bryden, Mariposa School has won three Freedoms Foundation of Valley Forge awards and earned fame in the community for its patriotic programs.
Brea Historical Society

seedlings and donated them for later planting. A wait for funding delayed work several years, but by the mid-1970's, construction had begun at the scenic canyon site.

The California National Guard assumed control of Brea's hilltop Nike Base in 1964, relieving the Army to meet its growing commitment in Indochina. Battery C of the Fourth Battalion, a division of the 251st Artillery Brigade, took command of the nearby post, its borders patrolled by guard dogs and its facilities manned by a full-time staff numbering more than 90.

A countywide educational reform movement in the mid-1960's promoted the unification of small school districts, and several north county candidates were named for consolidation. Though local schools rejected unification with Yorba Linda, consolidation did come for the

three districts operating within Brea's borders.

Brea elementary (three schools), Olinda elementary (one school) and Brea-Olinda Union High (one school) merged to become the Brea-Olinda Unified School District, and an election saw the naming of its first board, with Leo Piantoni as president. Longtime Brea (elementary) Superintendent Vincent Jaster retired in 1966 at the time of unification, and was replaced by Dr. Paul Bolie, first superintendent of the unified district. Mariposa School opened later that year in a new subdivision north of Central at 1111 Mariposa Drive.

Orange County's population topped the one million mark for the first time in 1966. Anaheim Stadium opened to enthusiastic crowds, and Brea logged its greatest of all growth surges. The earliest subdivisions in North Hills and along an eastern extension of Central Avenue later renamed State College Boulevard quickly drew buyers, and a large parcel of Union Oil land a quarter-mile southeast of the high school was annexed and subdivided by a company called Macco. Where lemon groves had stretched out in all directions, Glenbrook Homes soon took root, and the city's population shot up to an estimated 14,000.

The *Brea Progress* lost its familiar local title in 1966, having previously been sold to the *La Habra Star*, and then bought (along with the *Star*) by the nationwide chain, Freedom Newspapers. The two community tri-weeklies were consolidated into the *Daily Star-Progress*, with offices on Palm Street, just west of the Brea-La Habra border. A 1992 reorganization shifted the local papers' base of operation to Anaheim, and publication came full circle as the *Brea Progress* re-emerged as a branch of the *North County News*, distributed weekly by the *Orange County Register*.

Shopping options expanded in 1967, as South Coast Plaza opened as the county's first enclosed regional mall. Led by Cleta Harder, the Brea Junior Woman's Club that year took on the challenge of working with disabled children, beginning an effort which would grow into the highly regarded organization, Help for

Brain-Injured Children. The congregation of Brea's United Methodist Church moved to growing quarters on the northeast corner of Central (State College) at Lambert, and shortly opened a preschool now popularly known as "BUMPS."

The city's 1967 Golden Jubilee celebration brought Brea a nine-day extravaganza of events including a golf tournament, costume ball, community worship service, carnival, service-club luncheon, ladies' baking contest, luncheon and style show, old settlers' picnic, "small-fry" parade, historic parade, barbecue, parking lot dance and professional stage-show spectacular. A 90-minute pageant of history featuring a cast of 462, *The Brea Story* was enacted on a specially constructed stage at the BOHS football field, and ran nightly for five performances.

On the more frivolous front, Golden Jubilee events included ample

amounts of music and fireworks, square dancing, cake tasting, greased-pig chasing and tricycle racing, as well as judging for the "Brothers of the Brush" beard, mustache and sideburn-growing contest.

A Jubilee Hospitality Center was manned daily in the American Legion Building, and a full staff headed by chairman Frank Schweitzer (Jr.) directed the myriad events. Capping the week was a

And a Cast of Hundreds...
The Brea Story, staged on a massive set at BOHS, drew good reviews, but a disappointing crowd. When the Jubilee books were balanced, the city remained in the red.
Brea Historical Society

RIGHT: Celebration Staff
All dressed up and ready for the city Jubilee are (left to right, standing) Doug Barnes, Bevann Moisi, Jim and Jerrie Unger, George Stringer, Ruth Schweitzer, Jerry McDowell, Rosalie Williams, Alan West, Al Martinez, and (kneeling) Rick Unger, Jeffrey Lanyon, Ken Gordon and Myrle Calderwood.
Brea Historical Society

BELOW: For the Future
Tex Yarborough (left) and Brea Public Works Director Gene Mills lower the Golden Jubilee Time Capsule into the ground in front of old city hall, July 16, 1967. Well-worn by its quarter century underground, the vault was removed and its contents displayed during the 1992 Diamond Jubilee.
Brea Historical Society

Queen Beverly
A town newcomer, Beverly Heeney (Cary) was chosen Jubilee Queen based on ticket sales for the pageant, and won a trip to Hawaii awarded by Mayor Robert Clark.
Brea Historical Society

ceremony in front of old City Hall, where an aluminum vault containing anniversary items was lowered into the ground and buried until the far-off future year of 1992.

Major news hit the headlines in 1967, as start-up funds were received for local portions of the long-anticipated Orange Freeway. Disagreements between the state transportation department and Northern California communities over a freeway near San Francisco actually brought funding to the local route earlier than anticipated, but Brea and other nearby cities were well prepared to move ahead. Community leaders consistently had lobbied for

LEFT: Together in Time
One picture tells two stories as bulldozers cut a path for the 57 Freeway on one side of the hills and the distinctive pods of Fanning Elementary School await completion on the other. Fanning opened at 650 Apricot in the fall of 1970; the freeway followed in 1972.
Brea Historical Society

BELOW: Fanning School
This unique, open-plan structure was built under the supervision of Leonard MacKain, who served for 13 years as its principal. Fanning was first in Brea to win the California Distinguished School award, presented in 1990 to Principal Tim Harvey and staff.
Brea Historical Society

the start of construction, and joined with the state to help trace the roadway's course. Now, with funding assured, cities that had long lacked a transportation link eagerly awaited the ribbon of pavement that would bring the world to their doorsteps.

Yorba Linda native Richard Nixon was voted to the nation's top job in 1968, and sworn in three months laters as the country's 37th President. Brea celebrated its first Bonanza Days with a pancake breakfast, picnic and carnival and adopted, several years before state mandate, its General Plan—providing, for the first time, this comprehensive "road map to the future." Council members approved a change from the city-administrator to city-manager form of government, and the reins of civic administration were taken up by hometown-son Wayne D. Wedin.

The last year of the decade saw major improvements at BOHS, as the Main, Fine Arts and Industrial Arts buildings were refurbished, and a second story of classrooms added above the auditorium. The city's parks and recreation commission (later expanded to include human services) was formed, and Breans got their first taste of television's new

Second-Generation Schweitzer

Frank Schweitzer, Jr.

A lifelong resident of Olinda and Brea, Frank Schweitzer, Jr., was born in 1911, the son of pioneer-resident Frank Schweitzer and his wife, Julia. A graduate of BOHS, Fullerton (Junior) College and the University of California at Berkeley, Schweitzer was employed at Brea's Shaffer Tool Works, where he headed the engineering department.

A second-generation Brea councilman, Schweitzer was first elected to the city council in 1950, and continued in this post a dozen years. He served as mayor from 1960-62, was selected general chairman for both the city's Golden Jubilee celebration and U.S. Bicentennial recognition, and co-founded (with LaVeta Daetweiler) both Brea Bonanza Days (later the Country Fair) and the Brea Historical Society.

A past president of the Brea YMCA, Red Cross and Lions Club, Schweitzer chaired the Lions' North-South All-Star Football Game, and was awarded Lions International's highest honor, the Melvin Jones Fellow.

A Gift from New Amigos
Hermandad ("Brotherhood") by artist Carlos Terres came to Brea from the people of Lagos de Moreno in the Mexican state of Jalisco. "Lagos" became Brea's first sister city in 1969.
Brea Historical Society

options as CableCom General (later Century Cable) opened on Alder. The earliest stage of the Orange Freeway project was finished by the spring of 1970, and traffic flowed north as far as Nutwood. By midsummer, crews were at work reforming the local landscape, and Breans noted the project's progress as bulldozers ground ever closer toward the hills.

September saw the opening of Union Oil's Imperial Golf Course, an 18-hole leased landscape dotted with pumping "grasshoppers," while November found the school district's fifth elementary, Fanning, dedicated with its namesake honoree in attendance. Retired for 28 years, former (elementary) Superintendent William E. Fanning proudly joined in opening ceremonies for the district's first and only "school without walls."

The decade of the 1970's arrived with startling new population figures confirming what many had guessed. Census records revealed 18,447 people residing within Brea's borders, a net growth of nearly 10,000 in only a decade. Though population expansion had altered the local landscape, the community still

retained much of its small-town spirit. Events like Bonanza Days consistently drew a crowd, and support remained strong at schools and churches. Pharmacist Sam Magnus was elected mayor as the new decade turned, and residents took time to sound him out on public policy when they patronized his downtown drugstore.

The 1970 widening of Brea Boulevard brought an end to "pepper-tree lane," sparing only sparse reminders of the leafy green canopy that once stretched unbroken from the junior high north to the foothills. Highway construction in the late-60's and early-70's altered access on other fronts as well. Central Avenue was

widened, Imperial expanded to four lanes, and Deodora and Ocean connected through the old Union Oil tank farm and given the new name "Lambert."

Yet even at this late date, many now-familiar streets were missing. Angling upwards toward Brea from Fullerton, State College Boulevard dead-ended at Rolling Hills, picking up again for a short stretch north of the train tracks as Central Avenue. Newly named Lambert ended on the east at Kraemer (recently renamed from Carolina), and not one other street crossed north over Birch all the way between Randolph and Valencia.

The biggest of all transportation stories continued to unfold as the new decade opened, and Brea's long-awaited local freeway link was completed by early spring. The city celebrated the freeway's coming with ceremonies featuring old-fashioned fun, as residents raced over the roadway on bicycles built for two. Before the first car had even entered a local on-ramp, Brea was at work using the new highway to advan-

Modern Medicine
Brea Community Hospital opened in 1972 as the town's first general acute-care facility. Major expansion and the purchase of adjoining properties have more than doubled the size of this hospital, which celebrated its twentieth anniversary in 1992 with the dedication of an interfaith chapel.
Brea Historical Society

tage. Marketing efforts reached out to warehousing and distribution giants like Albertson's, and serious negotiations began for the building of a regional mall.

The town's secure financial position allowed it to assist a neighbor later that year, as Yorba Linda signed on for a unique shared-police arrangement. An agreement so unprecedented it required special state legislation, the plan allowed Brea's police department to serve Yorba Linda, a measure that today still minimizes costs to both towns.

Local law enforcement virtually had been redefined in the decade since 1960. Under the leadership of Chief Richard Baugh, Brea's police department upgraded its standards: adopting a regulatory manual, devising an improved system of report and record keeping, linking up to the Law Enforcement Teletype network and organizing the Brea Police Explorers. Improvements in technology followed as the new decade opened, and Brea soon joined other cities benefitting from a new multi-million-dollar coordinated countywide communication system.

Brea's rural past still was very much present in the earliest years of the 1970's—particularly "out east" at the 65-acre BOHS farm. More than just a little bit country, this small, student-run operation had grown by the mid-1960's into a barnyard home for 28 hogs, 35 beef cattle, 10 lambs and 500 chickens, and also included classrooms, animal units, a small orchard and greenhouse, a utility shed and equipment garage.

Students enrolled in the high school's "Ag" program chose from an extensive list of courses—from horticulture and farm management to accounts and bookkeeping, nutrition and flower arranging. In-class time was further enhanced for many by membership in the school's Future Farmers of America club.

A source of down-home delight, the BOHS farm would linger only a few years longer, its acreage steadily shrinking as new development closed in on all sides. An early 1970's

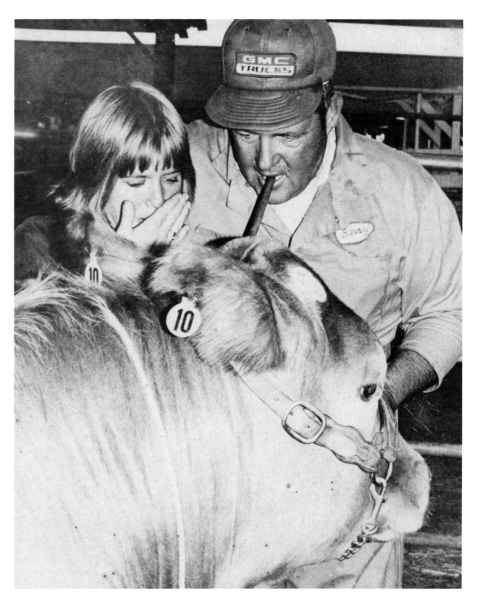

Down on the Farm
Members of BOHS' Future Farmers club owned and raised their own animals, exhibiting them at regional shows and frequently taking top honors. Selling a familiar friend was more difficult, as seen in this county fair photo. An unknown BOHS student is counseled by vocational agriculture instructor Barney Horan, whose father (Mike) built early Brea's first sidewalks.
Photo by Susan Gaede

easement through the farm allowed State College Boulevard's extension north of Birch, and massive construction began to the south before the decade's end.

Though cows could still be seen on the corner of Birch and State College as late as the mid-1980's, their grazing land each year became a more valuable piece of pasture. The development of Brea Corporate Place and the Marketplace eventually brought an end to Brea's hay

day, and the high school itself found a new home in the hills within just a few years.

The Brea Redevelopment Agency was formed in 1970, with the city council as agency members and the city manager as executive director. Hit by a citizen backlash in its first redevelopment proposal (a downtown project defeated in a 1971 advisory referendum), the agency embarked the following year on a new course for local improvement, adopting plans set forth by a citizen-advisory committee and earmarking two industrial/commercial areas for redevelopment.

In the coming years, redevelopment would provide the fiscal tools for massive local change. By the late 1970's, Brea had become a leader in this new form of civic improvement, eventually encompassing more than a third of its local area in one of three redevelopment districts, and pioneering in creative linkages between city government, the local schools and the private sector.

Brea's Nike Base was deactivated in 1971, bringing an end to days of guard dogs and hilltop troops, missile displays and combat drills. Edward Jackson became mayor, the Brea Historical Society was founded by LaVeta Daetweiler and Frank Schweitzer, the Brea Art Association met for the first time with Kay King as president and construction crews set to work on the Orange Freeway's final link.

The following year saw State Route 57 push its way north from Brea, struggling through rugged terrain toward an interchange with the Pomona. Drivers on Brea Canyon Road took note as the new highway stretched toward Diamond Bar, watching as huge cuts were drilled from the hillside and a dramatic 1,000-foot bridge arched out to span Tonner Canyon.

The opening of the freeway marked a watershed in Brea's history. Just as the county had learned to

speak of its past in terms of "before Disneyland" or "after Disneyland," the impact of this local transit tie now would divide all Brea history into "before or after" the freeway...and make possible the later addition of "before or after" the mall.

Like all freeway projects, the 57 was a mammoth engineering effort. Nearly a million yards of decomposed granite were trucked in to build local portions of the elevated roadbed—a dirty, noisy job that jangled nerves and kept residents busy dusting what they'd cleaned

A Soldier's Send-off
Marines en route to tours of duty in Indochina make a last stateside stop in Brea, enjoying brief stays in local homes as part of the city's "weekend welcome" program.
Courtesy Marine Corps Base, Camp Pendleton

just the day before. But the freeway's benefits far outweighed its inconveniences. Land values soared as easy access became a reality, and once-isolated Brea became the center of a vast regional transportation and commerce network.

Phase one of a new county park opened in October of 1972, as a lake, picnic sites, sports and recreation facilities, bicycle and equestrian trails were dedicated in honor of local politician Edward (Ted) Craig, whose ranch house once stood near the western edge of this 100-acre "Craig Regional Park."

Although half a world away, the war in Vietnam touched Brea in the years of the late 1960's and early 70's. At least four local soldiers (Kenneth Lawrence Dulley, Martin Guard, George Stephen Hadzega and Scott Miles) lost their lives in the conflict, while Marine Pilot Stephen Hanson was listed among the missing. Focusing its energies on Captain Hanson

A County Remembers
Longtime politician Ted Craig (center) is flanked by Leonard MacKain (left), Don Fox and his granddaughter, Jane Craig, at the 1972 opening of Craig Regional Park.
Brea Historical Society

and the POW/MIA (Prisoner of War/Mission in Action) issue, the community "adopted" Hanson by council resolution, and organized events on behalf of all soldiers missing or imprisoned. Spearheaded by Susan Gaede, local letter-writing efforts were followed by a fund-raising swim meet, and 450 students joined in a BOHS-sponsored walkathon to Knott's Berry Farm.

As the conflict escalated, local families opened their homes to Marines en route to combat missions overseas, and a national POW/MIA remembrance-bracelet campaign kicked off in Brea, with Captain Hanson's wife, Carole (chairman of the National League of Families), and young son, Todd, in attendance. Local residents joined John Wayne, Ronald Reagan and other prominent citizens wearing the symbolic bands, and actor Patrick Wayne appeared at BOHS for the campaign's opening ceremonies. Captain Hanson later was declared killed in action, and the bracelets bearing his name were gathered together, melted down into wings and placed on a commemorative plaque. A continuing BOHS scholarship was established in his name, and won in later years by his son.

Two years unused, the old Nike Base was declared government

Friendship Afloat
Landlocked and located in an arid zone, Brea nevertheless "adopted" a cruise ship in the 1970's, and crewmen of the P&O line soon steered a straight course toward town. *From the Leonard MacKain collection*

surplus in 1973, and a movement led by Girl Scout Daphne Wolfert prompted the city to seek this free land for a park. Though located outside the local border and over the Los Angeles County line, the oil-company owned, government-leased site had access routes only through Brea, and negotiations with Washington brought it under the city's control. Cal State Fullerton and Beckman Instruments joined in efforts to develop the park, and extensive plans were laid for use of its 32 acres and 27 structures, including a barracks, observation platform and several large missile silos.

The community read with growing interest stories of proposed park development. Accessed by trams ascending to the 1,400-foot summit—where Alpine-themed landscaping and structures overlooked 360-degree vistas—the planned park included a variety of recreational features on its lower slopes, and was crowned by a commercial area tailored to cover all operational costs. A "European Village" of restaurants and shops, plus picnic and campfire areas, overnight shelters, amphitheater, nature center, skating rink, pistol and archery ranges, and even an observatory were planned, but not even one pine tree was planted.

A wide stretch of producing oil field separated Brea from the site, and lingering unresolved issues of access, liability and financing finally put an end to hopes for the park. A last-ditch alliance formed with Los Angeles County failed to save the project, and 12 years after the property was acquired, Brea's city council quietly relinquished its claim on the land. Today little is left of the old Nike Base, and only the street name "Site Drive" commemorates the Cold War years when soldiers and guided missiles stood guard in Brea's hills.

Local businesswomen formed the Brea Soroptimist Club in 1973,

One Last Look
Observation Platform, Nike Site 29, 1976. Squads of Navy Seabees cleared this vandalized and weather-damaged site in the late 1970's, destroying the above-ground structures and sealing the underground silos. *Brea Historical Society*

choosing Bonnie Culbertson as president of this newest in civic service organizations. Brea celebrated "Claude Osteen Day" in the fall of that year, honoring the famed local pitcher with ceremonies at Dodger Stadium and Arovista Park.

School district administrator Leonard MacKain became mayor in 1974, the Brea-Olinda Friends Church was dedicated on Birch at Associated (followed by an elementary school in the early 1980's), Birch Hills Executive Golf Course opened on Union Oil acreage at Birch and Kraemer, and a Tokyo corporation purchased La Vida Hot Springs and announced plans for a new hotel and Japanese bath houses.

Cruising in a new direction, the city "adopted" the British P&O liner *Spirit of London*, soon to be known as the *Sun Princess*. Begun as a cultural exchange program, the unusual city-ship relationship brought crew members to Brea for visits in homes and appearances before student and service groups.

Brea residents toured the ship when it came into port, and crew members assisted with local civic events and charitable drives. Cast as the original "Love Boat" in the

feature film of the same name, the *Sun Princess* and its sister ship, the *Pacific Princess*, achieved fame in the sailing world, and several of the line's captains formed long-lasting friendships with Brea residents.

For Kids Sake, the award-winning, nationally known child-

Going Up
East-side homes rise in 1975 at the Country Hills corner of Lambert and Sunrise, the setting for Harold Pastorius' award-winning sculpture *Wall Warp*. More than 20 buyers camped out for two nights outside this development's sales office, waiting to make a down payment on their share of "The Brea Dream."
Brea Historical Society

The Shape of Things to Come
Prefabricated fireplaces watch over a new northwest neighborhood in the mid-1970's. The stone sentinels stand at today's corner of Northwood Avenue and San Juan Drive.
Brea Historical Society

abuse-prevention organization, got its start locally in 1974 when residents Jim and Pat Mead began a hotline at Brea Community Hospital. Seeking a wider audience for its child-protection program, the budding organization soon published *The Battered Child Identification Guide*, a handbook widely distributed to the nation's educators.

Brea residents and organizations rallied around this local group's early efforts to identify and protect young people in peril. The Brea Woman's, Kiwanis and Rotary clubs, as well as the students of Sonora High, became involved in the program, raising funds for pamphlet publication and otherwise advancing For Kids Sake's goals.

Future Brea Mayor Carrey Nelson launched the non-profit organization's fund-raising campaign, while developer Don McBride and builder Lyle Parks, Jr., made office space available as the

group's activities expanded. In ensuing years, Brea-based For Kids Sake would become one of the nation's leading child-abuse-prevention organizations, honored for its service to youth by six Disneyland Community Service Awards and special recognition from former President Ronald Reagan.

A campaign by local officials resulted in the upgrading of Brea's bond rating in 1974, a move that reduced municipal interest payments and incurred significant long-term savings. An innovative idea destined to bring the city fame took form that year as well, when King

Breans a decade before became Southern California's largest grove of redwoods. Late-August dedication ceremonies brought Breans together with canyon old-timers, all sharing memories of the place that once was Olinda.

The year 1975 saw a familiar Brea landmark moved to a new locale. Built on North Madrona in 1923 for Boy Scout activities and earlier relocated to (today's) Brea Boulevard for use by the Woman's and Lions Clubs, the long, narrow structure again was moved, this time to Elm and Sievers, where it was refurbished, renamed "Pioneer Hall"

LEFT:
Bicentennial Couple
Longtime Brea residents Dyer and Edith Bennett, grand marshals of the Bicentennial Bonanza Days Parade.
Photo by Susan Gaede

BELOW LEFT:
Brea Patriots
David and Julie Lane share a Bicentennial moment at the city's 1976 liberty bell.
Photo by Susan Gaede

Zimmerman's *The Birds* was unveiled at Lambert and Associated as the premiere sculpture in Brea's Art in Public Places Program—California's first privately funded outdoor collection of civic art.

Fifteen years after completion of the dam and a decade after plans were laid for recreational use, Carbon Canyon Regional Park opened in 1975. A new lake stood near the site of old Olinda School, a nature trail rimmed the canyon and the patch of trees given by

and set to work as a community meeting center.

The United States' Bicentennial celebration in 1976 brought Brea two of its most familiar modern landmarks: the gazebo in City Hall Park, dedicated on July 3 by the Brea Soroptimist Club, and the Brea Liberty Bell at the Civic & Cultural Center, a half-sized replica of the famous Philadelphia bell, inspired by the efforts of Phil Campbell and Frank Schweitzer (Jr.), funded by private donation, cast by the McGraw & Sons Foundry and dedicated July 4. Carol Weddle

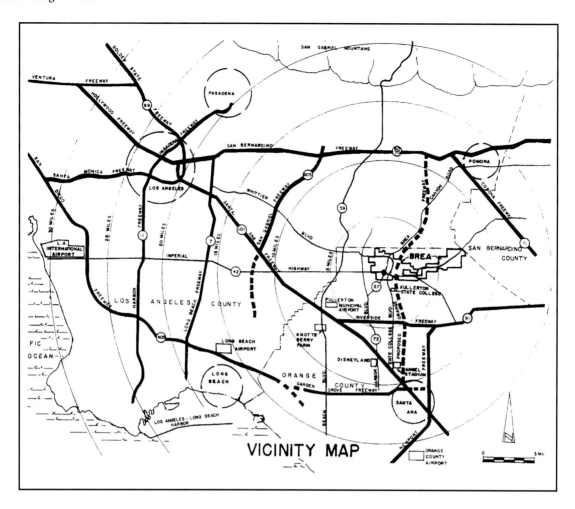

VICINITY MAP

served as mayor during the Bicentennial, which was highlighted by a Bonanza Days Parade.

Native-son Don Forkus signed on in 1976 as Brea's new chief of police, while the following year brought first-phase opening of Tri-City Park, a recreational venture funded jointly by Brea, Placentia and Fullerton. Once the site of a popular "old swimmin' hole"—Stone's Reservoir, the 39 acres surrounding "Lake Placentia" became home to picnic facilities, playground equipment and the region's last public flock of ducks. Alpha-Beta drove its Clydesdale-drawn wagon through town that year for a commercial filmed on Brea Boulevard, and Brea Plaza opened on Imperial at Associated with large food and drug stores, smaller specialty shops and the town's first operating theaters in more than a decade.

To the west, on a fallow one-time barley field, a massive construction

project stretched out across the landscape. A brilliant risk with a rich reward, the building of the mall brought Brea to bat in the "big leagues," and served up success to a tough one-time oil town willing to work for its promise.

As early as 1960, *Progress* editor Tom Gillespie had recognized Brea's strategic location, suggesting the city might one day become a "commercial hub." "We have," he wrote, "all the ingredients for a fine commercial cake, but we haven't got a cook to mix up the dough."

By the late 1960's, Gillespie's cooks were hard a work in Brea's kitchen. Hired by a council that assigned the project high priority, new City Manager Wayne Wedin tackled the task of marshaling city staff and resources, leading an effort that would bring some of America's largest businesses to a virtually unknown North Orange County town.

Building a Mall, Brea Style

First, you draw some circles...How many people live nearby? How high is their income and what are their shopping habits? How strong is the retail competition, and which areas remain unserved? Brea scored high on such data, but could easily have been passed by. Regional centers were planned in both Fullerton and Diamond Bar—and if either had broken ground first, there never would have been a Brea Mall...

With a "blueprint" provided by an executive at Sears, then one of the country's most successful retailers, Brea went to work "putting its house in order"—building streets and water lines to make its proposed mall site more attractive. Meanwhile, city staff compiled data detailing Brea's potential as a regional retailing center. Armed with facts and figures, the team took its findings and knocked on the door of Homart,

Barley Field to Brea Mall
A signpost heralds the coming of regional retail dominance and long-term economic security. Located at the heart of the Los Angeles-San Bernardino-Orange-Riverside metropolitan region, the completed mall would be within 15 freeway minutes of nearly a million people by 1980.
Photo by Susan Gaede

land development arm of Sears, one of the nation's largest mall builders.

In a series of discussions in Chicago and Los Angeles, Brea and Homart came together to learn more about one another. Union Oil, owner of the proposed mall site, entered the talks as well, and negotiations reached their final stages. On a bridge in Schaumburg, Illinois, the Brea bargain was sealed with a handshake between city Mayor Don Fox and Homart President Don Veman. Months of intense work had culminated in success, but the battle was still far from won. Town leaders flew back from Chicago with a long list of required site improvements, wondering where the money would come from to finance this costly work.

Though the mall site had never been developed, a major Metropolitan Water District line running below it would need to be moved. Heavy costs here were compounded by problems with State College Boulevard, built (in a straight line) to attract the mall, and then targeted for rerouting (to its present curved course) to make way for a fourth anchor store. The bill for these changes, plus costs for sewers and storm drains, curbs, gutters and sidewalks, streetlights and a high-pressure industrial fire line far outstripped the city's budget, but a

new avenue of funding—redevelopment—posed promise.

Redevelopment District B was formed in 1972, and a loan on the "blighted" barley-field site was arranged by banker Clarence Schwartz. Improvements worth $5.6 million finally brought the land in line, and Brea eagerly awaited the day when stores would start to rise.

Staff members had made it their business to "learn the language" of mall building, studying what made

Something to Smile About
The men behind the mall gather for ground-breaking ceremonies, April 18, 1974. From left (front) Councilman Carol Weddle, Mayor Leonard MacKain, Homart President Bill Lewis, Councilman Don Symmes; (back) Councilman Sam Cooper, Broadway President Jerome Lipp, Broadway Vice-president Jan Whetzel and Councilman Donald Fox. The all-American mall celebration featured apple pie and music by the BOHS band.
From the Leonard MacKain collection

LEFT: From a Distance
Viewed by air from the northwest, the emerging shopping center—Brea's most massive building project—spreads out across the landscape. Though work has yet to begin on any of the mall's anchor stores, the inner court's bottom floor is complete, and structural steel supports await the second story.
Brea Historical Society

BELOW: Opening Remarks
Mayor Rex Gaede addresses project dignitaries and enthusiastic shoppers at the mall's 1977 debut.
From the Rex Gaede collection

*Homart Development Co.
celebrates the Grand Opening of
Brea Mall
Orange Freeway and Imperial Highway
Brea, California.*

*We request the pleasure of your company at a
Champagne Preview Party
Tuesday, September 27, 1977
6:00 - 8:00 p.m.*

and

*Grand Opening Ceremonies
Wednesday, September 28, 1977
9:30 a.m.
Central Court
Brea Mall*

one regional center succeed while another failed. Nationwide shopper surveys helped finalize local design: Brea's mall would be carpeted (because Indiana housewives said carpeting kept their legs from feeling tired), would boast blooming plants (because landscapers claimed flowers brightened shoppers' moods) and would include an ice-skating rink (an attraction in itself, as well as a handy "kidsitter").

The recession of the 1970's deepened as site preparatory work reached its end, and local anxiety mounted as time passed without signs of further construction. Homart executives finally indicated the economic downturn had hurt their prospects, forcing cancellation of at least two malls and, "putting the Brea project on hold." Faced with several years of waiting and the probable loss of committed anchor stores, City Manager Wedin flew to Chicago to win back Brea's mall,

What Price Success?

A growing stream of mall revenue has flowed into Brea's bank accounts since 1977, the 15-year total in sales tax receipts in excess of $24 million. Following extensive late-1980's expansion, Brea Mall ranks in size as the county's second largest regional shopping center, its gross 1991 sales an estimated $300 million.

and—in the words of developer Don McBride—"pulled it out of his hat."

Concessions made in the last round of bargaining changed the scope of Brea Mall's design. Unexercised land options might have extended the site west to Poplar, but revised property lines ended instead at Randolph. A smaller mall, project leaders reasoned, was better than no mall at all, and proper planning would allow for later expansion.

Ground-breaking ceremonies for the 100-acre, 1.1-million-square-foot structure were held in April of 1974, and work began quickly on Sears, May Co. and 125 specialty shops. The climate-controlled, contemporary-designed center would, at the end of its first building phase, feature a third anchor store (the Broadway), theaters, restaurants and an Ice Capades Chalet. Nordstrom, phase-one's final anchor store, would follow in 1979. Opening-week festivities Aug. 17-21, 1977, brought

Waterworks
A new holding tank—this time for water—rises on the site of the old Union Oil tank farm. The completed reservoir is home port to the "Brea Navy," a single rowboat regularly launched to determine the tank's water depth. Brea's modern water needs are served by ground sources (California Domestic Water Co.) and imported water from Northern California and the Colorado River. The MWD's Weymouth and Diemer filtration plants monitor water quality, and storage is provided at Orange County's huge reservoir in the Brea hills.
Brea Historical Society

Wayne Wedin
Architect of Today's Brea

From student body president to city manager, councilman and mayor, few residents—if any—have influenced Brea more than Wayne D. Wedin.

**BOHS ASB President
Wayne Wedin
1957**

A Minnesota native, Wedin moved to Brea as a teenager and enrolled at BOHS in his sophomore year. He played football, and was part of the first Brea varsity grid squad ever to reach CIF. Named Orange All-League tackle, he was voted BOHS' "Most Inspiring Player," and found time off the field to serve as student body president and be named 1957's Boy of the Year.

Wedin attended Fullerton (Junior) College, where he also served as student body president. He graduated from the University of Southern California with bachelor's and master's degrees in public administration, and returned to Brea to make his home in the early 1960's.

Starting his career in Santa Fe Springs, Wedin served in a succession of positions from administrative intern to assistant city manager. Hired to Brea's top city job in 1968, he held this post 13 years, a period which would be—by far—the most dynamic in city history.

Working closely with council and staff, Wedin strove to bring balanced development and a stable economic base to Brea. Astutely assessing the city's redevelopment potential, he persisted, against difficult odds, in building Brea Mall in the midst of a recession—creating employment opportunities and revenue benefits that would assure the city's economic future.

Reaping the rewards of this retail success, Brea found funds to build the Civic & Cultural Center, offer enhanced levels of support for public and social services, recreation and the arts, and create a legacy of developmental opportunity manifest in the later building of Brea Country Hills Elementary School, (the new) Brea Olinda High School, the Marketplace, the Embassy Suites Hotel and today's evolving downtown commercial district.

Many credit Wedin's guiding vision as the force behind the design of Brea's Civic & Cultural Center, which brings together physically the varied governmental entities of local life. Many speak of his foresight in including the center's closed-circuit television system and video production facilities, while others point to his commitment to the arts as the driving force behind Brea's community theater, civic art gallery and Art in Public Places Program.

Wedin left his job with the city in the early 1980's to manage his own economic development firm, but returned to local government in 1988 in the new roles of councilman and mayor.

Though he shuns credit for the city's successes and points with pride to the efforts of others, those who were there when it happened attest to his many accomplishments. Former Mayor William Hamilton (1968-70) has called Wedin the one person, "who, without question, was responsible for providing the outstanding format that has guided Brea to the fine, balanced community that it is," noting that his, "personal and professional skills have made Brea a first-class community that is unchallenged."

the mall its first shoppers, while official ribbon-cutting ceremonies saw executives from Sears, May Co., Broadway and Homart on hand to toast the center's success.

The massive structure's Sept. 28 dedication capped nearly 10 years of behind-the-scenes work by city staff and elected officials. The mall had not come easily or cheaply. Some city leaders had flown so often to Chicago that flight crews knew their names. Charges for travel were well exceeded by costs for site improvements, but the investments quickly paid off. First-year sales figures for Sears alone were 300 percent above projections, and the store manager explained his success as, "just being in a red-hot mall."

The community where residents had rarely been able to buy what they needed in town now rapidly emerged as a retailing magnet, drawing shoppers and tax dollars on a far-reaching regional scale. Restaurants and smaller service and retail centers built near the mall soon attracted their fair share of spending, and Brea's preeminence in the North County economy was established.

The freeway that had made the Brea Mall possible never was joined by other freeways long planned to pass through town. A frequent target of environmentalists, the east-west "Imperial" (sometimes called the "Nixon") stalled in tight financial times, never bisecting Brea along its proposed path at Imperial. This freeway's failure to arrive severely impacted commerce and industry in several nearby cities that had concentrated development in its path, but Brea's businesses faired better due to their proximity to the 57 and its interconnecting routes.

Brea celebrated its 60th birthday in 1977, kicking up its heels at a street dance in St. Angela's parking lot, and rounding out its schedule of events with a picnic, fireworks show and all-church chorale. Groundbreaking ceremonies were held in 1977 at the Brea Financial Commons, and the city dedicated both its new service center and 30-million-gallon water reservoir on Berry Street.

The first former BOUSD Board of Education president to be selected as Brea's mayor, Rex Gaede took office in March of 1977, beginning a term memorable for its local openings and out-of-town excitement. Traveling east to meet with bond raters for discussions on mall financing, Gaede and City Manager Wedin arrived in New York just in time to be caught in the city's historic blackout. A later trip brought Mayor Gaede to the nation's capital, where his cab came under gunfire in the midst of a civil disturbance.

Brea entered the video age in 1978, purchasing equipment for its first city-originated productions with accumulated franchise fees from CableCom/Century Cable. Early studio employees included Cal State Fullerton students working through the school communication department's internship program.

Sometimes-controversial councilman Sam Cooper was chosen mayor in 1978, the same year Dr. C. Gordon Bishop replaced Dr. Bolie as superintendent of schools. Though Dr. Bishop's three-year term would see the BOUSD unify its educational goals and establish its first five-year plan, it also would be marked by a board recall (brought to a head by the selling of buses) and a five-day teachers' strike.

BELOW: Brea, 1967
Well on its way to today, Brea had developed most of its central areas by the late 1960's, and begun stretching out toward the north and east. The remains of the old Union Oil tank farm linger on the west, the just-rising subdivisions near Mariposa School are visible on the north, and the MWD reservoir rests atop the foothills. Within three years, the Orange Freeway would cut a swath through the right-hand side of this setting.
Brea Historical Society

Community Effort
BREAL came to life through the work of many. Alan West coordinated the project, John Rose served as architect, the Rev. Loren Wood was general contractor, Ray Madsen acted as legal counsel and Doug Sharp and Don Forkus helped with plumbing. Doug Tripp coordinated volunteers, Bill and Burt Mashon "kept the books," and Mike Cohen and the Rev. R.C. McFadden screened tenants. Students and retirees pitched in, and even a few youth offenders worked in lieu of jail terms.
Brea Historical Society

Dial-a-Ride came to town in 1978, a new post office was dedicated on Birch, the city park fire station was transferred to a relocatable building at Laurel and Birch, and the structure of government finance was substantially altered when California voters passed Proposition 13, the "Taxpayers' Revolt" Initiative. Led by Brea Rotary, civic groups pooled their resources and ingenuity that year to build BREAL (Brea's Retirement Effort for Abundant Living). Acting on an idea from Alan West, the Rotary Club, the Brea Ministerial Association and the City of Brea joined to build a 30-unit, low-cost senior-housing complex on leased city land at northwest Orange and Ash.

An antique plow was pulled over the site by community leaders in the project's symbolic groundbreaking, and local residents quickly answered the call for help—volunteering labor, soliciting donations and preparing

meals for workers. In the final tally, more than 700 residents contributed 30,000 hours of service to the project. Built entirely without county, state or federal funds, BREAL was financed by a low-interest loan, and came in at half its actual estimated cost.

Breans began receiving paramedic service for the first time in 1979, the cultural arts commission was created by council mandate, and high-visibility efforts to revitalize downtown were observed as the nostalgic "Good Old Brea" project brought Victorian false fronts, landscaping and other beautification efforts to main street's 60 and 70-year-old shops. Though appearances were enhanced, increases in business proved marginal, and the campaign's long-term effectiveness was disappointing. Before another decade had passed, the aging area was slated for redevelopment.

Poised at the brink of the 1980's, Brea had traveled a path of great

ABOVE: Downtown Facelift
"Gingerbread" moldings, old-fashioned signs and facades from San Francisco all become part of a brand-new look for "Good Old Brea."
Brea Historical Society

LEFT: On Needles and Pins
Workmen and patrons observe "Good Old Brea" alterations at Jeanne's Yardage. Owned by Jeanne Gladden, the popular, pink-painted store kept local seamstresses in stitches.
Brea Historical Society

change in its journey from 1960. Dramatic differences could be seen almost everywhere as the decade ended: in the winding streets and greenbelts of a dozen new housing tracts, the manicured acres of expanding industrial parks, the bustling shops of the regional mall, the quiet acres of Carbon Canyon Park and the refurbished blocks of the old downtown.

Opportunity followed close on the taillights of access in the Brea of the 1960's and 1970's. The coming of the freeway was the opportunity the community had hoped for, and the chance to profit from its promise had not passed Brea by. New opportunities now would rise from the fortunes of local commerce, and a fresh set of challenges would become the work of another day.

New Look for a New Age
The expansive angles of Brea's modern, multi-purpose Civic & Cultural Center
soar above Birch Street, cast concrete symbols of a revitalized new regional identity.
Photo by Brian Saul

CHAPTER 9

Into the Future

Cut off from cities to the north by the foothills, and isolated by distance from the centers of south county life, Brea had, from the beginning, followed its own, independent road toward development. In the context of post-war growth, the city lagged nearly a decade behind its neighbors, and few non-residents took note of the sleepy town still surrounded by oil wells and orange groves. But by the late 1970's, Brea had hit its "catch-up" stride, and—before another decade passed, the surprising small north county town would emerge as a regional leader.

By 1980, Brea was a center for business. More than 400 corporations counted offices in the city's eastern and western industrial sectors, and as many as 30 had relocated their regional or national headquarters to Brea.

In the coming decade, major names like American Suzuki, Beckman Instruments, NCR, Norris Industries, Southland Corporation (7-Eleven Stores), Sundstrand Aviation and Fender Musical Instruments would join the city's pioneer company—Union Oil—

and Union would enhance its own local image by building a vast new research center. Banking, insurance, and savings-and-loan giants like Allstate, Mercury, Travelers, the Capital Group and Union Federal would bring their business to Brea, and Security Pacific Bank would build a mammoth new data center employing nearly 2,000 people.

Following the trend of an earlier decade, many of the town's new industrial avenues took their names from the nation's space program. West-side streets like Nasa, Vanguard, Apollo and Columbia were joined by east-side drives such as Saturn, Enterprise, Voyager, Orbiter and Surveyor. All told, 16 such extraterrestrial titles were in use by the mid-1980's.

East-side Industry
World headquarters of the Diagnostic Systems Group of Beckman Instruments, located on Kraemer at Birch.

The community's rising regional profile made way for diversified development in the new decade. As retail centers multiplied and business and industry expanded, further residential building followed, and new homes rose in the foothhills and on east-side lands recently released by the oil companies. New schools, parks, entertainment facilities, civic structures and public art altered the local image, and Brea—the oil and industry town—came of age as a retail, financial, cultural and recreational center.

Orange County's population approached the two-million mark in the census of 1980, and Brea's tally of 27,100 marked nearly 9,000 new residents in only 10 years. Though population had grown tenfold since the building of old city hall, civic business in the late 1970's still was transacted in its cramped quarters on South Brea Boulevard. By 1978, however, work had begun on a startling new addition to the local scene—a modernistic, all-in-one Civic & Cultural Center destined to become the city's new heart.

As early as 1960, local leaders had discussed the need for a new city hall, but high building costs and pressing needs elsewhere called a halt to further planning. The proposed civic structure changed in size, shape and site several times in ensuing years, finally taking its familiar form in the late 1970's on four acres at the mall's northwest corner.

A decision to locate the new civic center adjacent to the mall quickly followed finalization of plans for the retail complex. The emergence of a "Central Area Development Concept" in the early 1970's focused effort on the creation of a new nucleus for local life: a 500-acre, quarter-mile-wide corridor just west of the freeway and south of the railroad tracks.

Here, in an area that would evolve as a hub of regional transit, the city's rising center of commerce (the mall) would be blended—in the "classic European tradition"—with its seat of local government, a regional recreational area (Craig Park), a center of finance (Brea Financial Commons), office structures (Brea Corporate Place), specialty restaurants and entertainment facilities, and a hotel (the Embassy Suites), bringing all major aspects of city life together in a single locale.

In exchange for public works improvements to the mall site, Homart deeded the city a parcel of land on Birch Street across from BOHS, and construction financing for the civic center was arranged through a redevelopment loan. Early planning brought city staff members together with citizen committees and consultants, brainstorming the needs this new structure might serve.

From these sessions came an unprecedented form of government facility—not just a city hall, but an integrated, multi-use Civic & Cultural Center—four buildings (city hall, fire and police headquarters and school district office) combined into one, with the addition of a library, community theater and municipal art gallery.

Warnecke/Dworsky, Architects, garnered the civic structure's design contract, Assistant City Manager Terry Belanger signed on as project manager, and ground was broken in 1978. Sloping upward from the mall and the freeway, the five-level, 270,000-square-foot structure rose around an open atrium, and featured two floors of office space, council chambers, community meeting rooms, a catering kitchen, executive conference center, television production studio, darkrooms and a print shop, two levels of parking and space reserved for rental offices and a soon-to-come 199-seat theater, 6,500-square-foot art gallery and county branch library.

Though a glass canopy-style roof originally was included in the structure's plans, rising costs and

The Center Rendered
The Civic & Cultural Center, as seen in a 1980 design sketch. This drawing shows the structure's unbuilt canopy and mall pedestrian passageway (left), and offers a glimpse of the center's eastern approach before the addition of Embassy Suites. The building design team's credits included Washington, D.C.'s Kennedy Center for the Performing Arts.

concerns over wind stability fore-stalled this feature's construction. Designs also showed a pedestrian "flyover" bridge joining the civic center to the mall (and earliest drawings even linked the library and the high school by a bridge over Birch), but changing fiscal priorities in the coming years derailed such later additions.

As the structural steel took shape and the concrete set, the local press blasted the center—decrying it as a waste of money and tagging it a "concrete monstrosity" and the "Taj Mahal." Construction strikes and inclement weather frustrated progress, but the building's corner-stone was laid in a delayed ceremony March 1, 1980, and the sun shone for official opening festivities three weeks later.

A colorful yet bittersweet "March in March" parade saw residents and civic employees join for a symbolic trek from the old city hall to the new. Sentiment ran high for the familiar, 51-year-old struc-ture—the only real government "home" in Brea's history—and the transition from the "humble, com-fortable" quarters of old city hall to the sweeping expanse of the new was dramatic.

But as the dust settled and the weeks passed, the new center's assets became clear. Its versatile design was spotlighted widely in newspa-per and magazine articles, and its novel form won a prestigious award from the American Institute of Archi-tects. City employees and center patrons noted that ease of access and centralization facilitated service and improved communication between the varied entities of local government, creating a new sense of cooperation among those who before had been physically separate.

The center's price tag rang in at $14.2 million, higher than most cities with a population of 30,000 because it replaced not one, but several structures, but also because it added previously absent art facilities and was built to meet the needs of a projected population of from 60,000

to 80,000. Room for future adminis-trative expansion was designed into the center, with rental income from this as-yet-unneeded space used to defray expenses.

Built at no direct cost to local taxpayers, the civic center became Brea's first tangible asset of an expanding post-mall affluence. Though initially adversely affected by post-Proposition 13 property tax losses, funding for the center later was restored through creation of a mall special assessment district.

Even prior to construction's completion, city employees had moved into their spacious new civic center quarters, and the opening of other areas swiftly followed. Previ-ously transplanted several times, the school district headquarters at northeast Birch and State College took its place on the second floor that fall. Named for veteran administra-tor Vincent Jaster, the 8,000-square-foot school district suite was christened the "Jaster Education Center."

The Brea Gallery opened in September with AT&T's national touring photography exhibit, *American Images*, while the performing arts facility, dedicated as the (Dr. C. Glenn) Curtis Theatre in honor of Brea's famed country doctor, welcomed *I Do, I Do* as its first production the following January. Cal State Fullerton's Cabaret Repertory Theatre became the earliest resident company at the Curtis, and the theater soon also became home to the well-known singing group, the Young Americans, and the newly organized Brea Theatre League.

Though a county branch library always had been part of the center's plans, political intrigue and funding shortfalls tied up county contribu-tions to this project, delaying the start of construction.

Founded in 1921 as the county system's first library, the Brea branch had, in its six decades, been situated in the corner of a garage, two store-fronts, the old city hall and Brea Heights Shopping Center, and opened its new civic-center quarters in September of 1981. Though smaller than anticipated, the 10,000-square-foot library still was the largest in local history.

Final touches to the library capped nearly three years of con-struction at the city work site, and government, the arts and the private

Going Up
A new civic home takes shape as columns are formed and reinforc-ing steel awaits its concrete coating. Afternoon sunlight filters through the unfinished council chambers in this view, which looks northwest from the center's second-floor deck.
Photo Courtesy City of Brea

sector at last rubbed elbows in the completed corridors of a true Civic & Cultural Center.

Though the city's old and new government homes bore little physical resemblance to one another, Brea actually had come full circle with the building of its new civic structure. A pioneer in an earlier era, old city hall originally had housed not only city offices, but (as the site of the library,

police and fire department) had been the county's first real "civic center." Expanding needs and shrinking floor space long since had forced most city departments to other quarters, but the varied aspects of local life again were united in Brea's far larger new civic center.

Vacated but not forgotten, old city hall was named to the National Register of Historic Places in 1984. Occupied for a decade by the American College of Law, the landmark building today serves as home to the Brea Historical Society, which celebrates the city's past through preservation of documents, books, photographs, artifacts and a Heritage Oil Exhibit featuring major contributions from Chiksan, Shaffer Tool Works, Chevron, Shell and Union Oil (since 1983, Unocal).

Though Brea's Civic & Cultural Center was designed to be both flexible and dynamic, several of its unusual assets became apparent only with the passage of time. A shared wall between the art gallery and police department facilitated the booking of high-security exhibits, and glass-walled third-floor offices became handy lookouts for spotting fires. Far more striking was the structure's impact on the community's evolving "sense of place"—lending Brea's small-town look a dramatic dose of big-city style.

The completion of the Civic & Cultural Center marked a turning point in Brea's passage. Its financial footing solidly established in commerce, business and industry, and its major structural needs filled by the city service and civic centers, Brea now turned its attention toward human services, focusing on quality-of-life issues including park development, expansion of cultural and recreational services, and programs for youth and senior citizens. Advancing toward a new century, the coming years brought Brea changes that are still under way today.

The Brea City Council
Cordially Invites You to
the Dedication of
Brea Civic/Cultural Center
800 East Birch Street
on
Saturday, the twenty-second day of March,
nineteen hundred eighty, at 12 Noon

(tours following the ceremonies)

ABOVE: Celebration Invitation
A welcome goes out to residents as the center's dedication ceremonies are set. Note the new building's earliest address—800 Birch—soon changed to today's more familiar form.

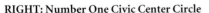

RIGHT: Number One Civic Center Circle
Area Masons and Knights of Columbus join local leaders for the Civic & Cultural Center's 1980 cornerstone laying. Nearly 400 people attended the building's opening ceremonies, which featured music by the BOHS band and speeches by Mayor Sal Gambina and Congressman William Dannemeyer. All-day festivities continued with a barbecue in Carbon Canyon and an "Evening of Fine Art" at Brea Mall.
Brea Historical Society

Time Line to the 90's: Highlights of Brea Life, 1980-1992

1980:

❖ Brea's first Country Fair draws a crowd of 5,000 during its July 4-6 run at City Hall Park. Service clubs, community organizations and city staff come together for planning, and the popular attraction is carried over as an annual event.

❖ Expanded summer parks-and-recreation offerings provide lifestyle enrichment for all ages. By fall of 1992, Community Services will coordinate a broad range of programs (including youth sports, Tiny Tots, day camp and summer-fun club, Volunteens and senior services), a varied list of annual events, and a total of 70 classes, workshops and

City of Brea Community Services

RECREATION

Take Time For Fun!

seminars for children and adults on subjects from bumper bowling and tap dancing to sign language and computer operation, nutrition, parenting and puppetry.

❖ The Brea Theatre League organizes and begins fund-raising for its August, 1981 premiere performance, *You're A Good Man, Charlie Brown.*

❖ Lake Park Brea, the city's fifth and largest mobile-home community, opens on Puente near Central.

❖ Former Mayor Don Fox (1972-74) returns for his second term.

1981:

❖ The city mourns the death of longtime planning commissioner and councilman Richard (Dick) Basse, an avocado rancher known for his wry sense of humor and common-sense

approach to government. Basse Lane commemorates his contributions.

❖ Responding to a proposal from Brean Dean Millen, Cal State Fullerton begins the Brea Community History Project, with assistance from the Brea Historical Coordinating Committee, local businesses and service clubs, and the California Council for the Humanities. Contributions fund the cataloging of local artifacts, files and photos, and the publication of 36 oral biographies.

❖ Brea-born Cruz Reynoso becomes the first Hispanic justice appointed to the California Supreme Court.

❖ July dedication ceremonies open Tamarack Park.

❖ The rusting tin walls of the once-bustling Shaffer Tool Works (Birch at Redwood) are razed to make way for a condominium development.

❖ Orange County watercolorist Don Hendricks is named Brea's first Artist in Residence. Through a grant from the California Council for the Arts, Hendricks visits local schools, teaches adult classes, hosts a video show, curates a gallery exhibit and commits several Brea scenes to canvas.

❖ Assistant Superintendent James Stafford is chosen BOUSD Interim Superintendent of Schools.

❖ Brea Country Hills School opens on 10 acres at 150 N. Associated Road. Sale of 13

district-owned acres east of old BOHS provides partial construction funding for this school, and also covers costs of moving the district office to the new civic center and the district maintenance yard to Berry Street. Additional funds for construction are secured through redevelopment assistance, allowing the school to be built at no cost to local taxpayers and setting a precedent for the later building of the new BOHS.

The Kasuga Lantern
A gift from Brea's sister city of Hanno, Japan, this lantern overlooks a quiet garden at Fire Station 3 on North Kraemer. Hanno became Brea's second international ally in 1980.
Brea Historical Society

Time Line to the 90's

Cooperative Project
Creatively funded through joint school district-city cooperation, Brea Country Hills School was designed as a modular campus to help curb costs. Principal Eileen Moore has guided the school since its opening.
Brea Historical Society

1982:

❖ The long-running *Council Communique*  city newsletter is restyled as the new *Brea Line*.
❖ Olinda Hall (the remodeled old Olinda School at Elm and Sievers) is rededicated as the Brea Senior Citizens Center. One of the first senior centers in the county, the facility undergoes extensive alteration in the late 1980's.

❖ Replacing its earlier Brea lab with a new facility twice its size, Union Oil opens the Fred L. Hartley Research Center on East Imperial Highway.
❖ Olympic gold-medalist Dorothy Hamill skates at Brea Mall's Ice Capades Chalet.
❖ Norma Arias-Hicks takes dual honors as the city's first woman mayor and the county's first Hispanic woman mayor.
❖ Dr. Edgar Z. Seal is selected as BOUSD Superintendent of Schools.
❖ Mayor Dr. Melvin LeBaron hosts the city's first Mayor's Prayer Breakfast and community Christmas tree lighting.

Foundation Guest
Nobel Peace Prize winner Dr. Henry Kissinger, (right) former U.S. Secretary of State, greets local residents Russ and Lorraine Danson at a special appearance in the Curtis Theatre. Soprano Gail Mosher and pop-legend Frankie Avalon appeared on the Brea stage in other Foundation fund-raisers.
From the Russ and Lorraine Danson collection

❖ The Brea Foundation, a non-profit organization established by council resolution, is created to support the community's expanding cultural, recreational and human needs. Through fund-raising events, sponsorships and the proceeds of property management, the Foundation today has channeled more than $1 million to city programs, civic groups and organizations.

1983:

❖ Union Oil, Brea's oldest and largest landowner, defeats a hostile takeover and emerges with the new name "Unocal."
❖ Carrey Nelson becomes the first Brea mayor to visit sister city, Hanno, Japan.
❖ Local police foil an armored-car robbery at Brea Financial Commons. Coming under fire, officers pursue suspects over the city's border into Diamond Bar, where arrests are later made. Sergeant Gary Drlik and Officers Keith Chang, Gary Nowak, Steve Hill and Dan Hunter win honors from Armed Transport of California.

1984:

❖ Old City Hall, the Brea Plunge and the former American Legion Hall on the park's southeast side are named to the National Register of Historic Places by the U.S. Department of the Interior.
❖ The Olympic Torch passes through Brea on its celebrated cross-country trip toward Los Angeles. BOHS track-star Carla Thompson helps

BOHS track-star Carla Thompson

Highlights of Brea Life, 1980-1992

carry the torch through town, while resident (and high jumper) Doug Nordquist competes in the L.A. games.

❖ Chino Hills State Park, an 11,000-acre Carbon Canyon wilderness preserve south and east of the city's borders, receives its official designation. Breans led the battle against an airport in the Chino Hills area, opening the way for this land's recreational use. A limited motor-vehicle access area, Chino Hills today offers quiet space for hiking, camping and equestrian activities.

❖ Two armed robbers enter a major Brea Mall store before opening hours on Christmas Eve and hold several employees hostage. No injuries are reported, but the felons escape undetected.

1985:

❖ Mayor Clarice Blamer declares a "Year of the Arts." Events include the first Mayor's Ball, a major art exhibition and the creation of 300 plaster masks modeled from the faces of Breans by local artist Delaina Hofacre.

❖ Citing cost factors and accessibility problems, the city gives up its plans to develop the old Nike Base as a park.

❖ Fire Station No. 3 opens on North Kraemer and wins the American Institute of Architects' Award of Excellence for functional efficiency, energy conservation and aesthetic quality.

❖ The *Orange County Progress Report* reveals eight major modern industrial parks in Brea, more than a tenth of all those in the county. By 1992, Brea's weekday working population will swell to 110,000.

❖ The Brea Chamber of Commerce opens new quarters at the Civic &

Cultural Center, with Norman Wasserman as executive director. Sherry Norman succeeds him in 1989.

1986:

❖ Redevelopment planning begins for the old downtown.

❖ The six-story, rose-tinted Travelers (Insurance) and neighboring Capital Group buildings open on former high-school farm acreage transformed into the new Brea Corporate Place.

❖ Calvary Chapel relocates from the old Brea Theater to a new site at southwest Lambert and Puente.

❖ On a small plot of level ground atop an eastern hillside, Nov. 1 groundbreaking ceremonies are held for the new BOHS.

1987:

❖ The Red Lantern, a 1920's downtown landmark later known as the Brea Theater, falls to the wrecking ball.

❖ FMC (earlier merged with Chiksan) closes its Puente Street plant, marking the end of Chiksan's nearly 60-year Brea manufacturing career.

❖ Despite efforts to save it, the landmark Sievers House (also called the Neuls or Durkee House) at northwest Berry and Imperial is torn down to make way for a parking lot.

❖ Southern California artist Judy Smith Trasport is commissioned to design a community poster, and turns in the lively work *Our Town*.

1988:

❖ Brea Mall begins an $80-million renovation and expansion program increasing its size by 60 percent. The ice rink falls as a casualty, but makes way for a larger new

Nordstrom, a Robinson's, 75 specialty shops, an expanded food court and three parking structures.

❖ The Brea Memorial Rose Garden is dedicated at City Hall Park.

❖ The aging Brea Plunge is condemned by the health department, but saved from destruction through local efforts to secure a county reconstruction grant. Redesigned to enhance safety, function and aesthetics, the pool re-opens to record crowds the following summer.

❖ The Girls Gym at old BOHS is destroyed in a spectacular nighttime fire.

❖ Igor Olenicoff's award-winning Olen Pointe office and restaurant complex opens its first phase east of the freeway at Lambert and Pointe Drive. Four additional office buildings, two restaurants, a hotel and a theater complex are planned, but remain unbuilt.

Time Line to the 90's

1989:

❖ The two-year Brea Project issues its final report, with recommendations for improved communication and citizen involvement, downtown redevelopment, historic preservation, cultural and recreational expansion, affordable housing, land use and development standards, traffic control and maintenance. A broad-based community effort, the Project involves more than 100 residents in survey teams and citizen task forces.

❖ The uninsured La Vida Hot Springs Hotel burns in a quick-spreading basement blaze. More than 50 firemen from Brea, La Habra and Fullerton battle the flames, but losses reach $200,000. The cafe remains open, and a new hotel is planned.

❖ Los Angeles bar owner Horace McKenna is murdered in a gangland-style shooting at the entrance to his secluded East Carbon Canyon estate.

❖ The Brea Boys and Girls Club organizes under the sponsorship of the La Habra club and former Brea Mayor Carol Weddle.

❖ Hungarian artist Martin Varo becomes the city's second Artist in Residence. Working in an open-air gallery on the lawn of the Civic & Cultural Center, the Fulbright Scholar creates sculptures including the symbolic female figure *Breaking Free*, as well as private works for Embassy Suites.

❖ BOHS' Ladycats win the state basketball championship 70-46 over San Francisco's Mercy High at the Oakland Coliseum. Repeat Ladycat state championships follow in 1991, 1992 and 1993.

❖ Mayor Gene Leyton leads a year-long recognition of local residents and organizations under the theme "Our People Make the Difference." More than 1,000 attend the People's Ball at the Brea Mall.

❖ A state-of-the-art campus for BOHS opens on 50 hillside acres east of the freeway. The first high school in California built without state aid and at no cost to the local taxpayer, the $36-million project is funded primarily through combined sale and lease of the 40-acre old BOHS site, greatly appreciated in value following the building of Brea Mall. Thirteen sites are considered, but Unocal's hilltop lot is selected at the well-under-market price of $30,000 an acre.

Looking Toward Tomorrow
Brea Project Chairman Matt Page (middle) joins (from left) Todd Beckley, Pat Tremayne, Martha Jane Wolking and Jose Mendez in inviting community comment on Brea's future. Residents Isabelle Rhymes (co-chairman), Patrick Davis and George Saunders rounded out the Brea Project steering committee.
Courtesy City of Brea

Highlights of Brea Life, 1980-1992

Lowe Development signs on to guide site transition and the building of the Marketplace, and CRS Sirrene (designer of the Orange County Performing Arts Center) is chosen as architect for the new BOHS. The old high school remains in use until the new campus is complete, the first phase of the Marketplace opens on the site of the former football field, and history repeats itself as an ornamental tower appears in the new school's designs, but remains unbuilt.

Seven years after the start of planning and three years after ground is broken, BOHS's new campus opens to students, and earns honors from the American Institute of Architects.

Key figures in the innovative project include BOUSD Superintendent Dr. Edgar Z. Seal, Project Manager Gary Goff, BOUSD Board Members Brian Burt, Sharon Chase, Lynn Daucher, Frank Davies, Sharon Dean, Dena Edmonson, Bernie Kilcoyne, Leonard MacKain, John Rosell, Susie Sokol and Dan Turner; Unocal's Richard Stegemeier and Roy Green; Lowe Development's Bob Lowe and Robert McLeod, and BOHS alumnus Wayne Wedin.

❖ Brea Canyon High School, an alternative education secondary, opens at 689 N. Wildcat Way.

❖ The Brea Center Baptist Church adds a seminary, credit union and bookstore to its Randolph Avenue address.

❖ The award-winning, two-day workshop "Brea by Design" brings together city staff, community representatives and development professionals to forge a vision for revitalizing the aging downtown. City Manager Frank Benest shines up an old architectural term and dubs the event a "charette."

❖ Water Specialist Andy Corona becomes the 72-year-old city's only employee to die in the line of duty when struck by a car while repairing a ruptured pipeline at Lambert and State College.

❖ The city's Finance Department receives the first of five awards in three years for budgeting and fiscal reporting.

LEFT: Destined for a Hilltop Home
BOHS Co-Principal Gary Goff addresses a crowd of past and present students, faculty and friends as the cornerstone of old BOHS is removed. Split, polished and re-engraved, the symbolic stone is later recycled for use at the new BOHS campus.
Brea Historical Society

RIGHT: Hilltop Handshake
The new Brea Olinda High School gets off to a happy start as Masonic leaders join district dignitaries for ceremonies in December of 1989. District officials present for the school's dedication include (from left) Co-principal Gary Goff, School Board Member Frank Davies and (right) Co-principal Jeanne Sullivan. Three gymnasiums, a stadium, swimming pool, Performing Arts Center and classroom space for 2,000 highlight the Wildcat Way campus.
Photo by Susan Gaede

Time Line to the 90's

1989 CONTINUED:

❖ A concert by the Pacific Symphony opens BOHS' new $3-million Performing Arts Center.

The City of Brea and the Brea-Olinda Unified School District present

A Night of Imagination

**P A C I F I C
S Y M P H O N Y
O R C H E S T R A**

Brea-Olinda High School Performing Arts Center
Inaugural Performance

November 4, 1989

❖ The old BOHS hosts its Last Hurrah, and demolition crews move in on the 63-year-old campus. A poster is commissioned to commemorate the school, its bricks are salvaged and sold as souvenirs, and its former site is marked in the Marketplace by the BOHS Walk of Fame.

❖ The Brea Historical Committee is formed by the city to identify and preserve historic structures and resources, and promote public awareness of the community's past.

❖ Fanning Elementary is named a California Distinguished School.

❖ The automated curbside program "Recycle Brea" begins. Before 1993, this conservation effort will divert nearly 10,000 tons of recyclable material from local landfills.

1990:

The new decade's census logs in 32,873 local residents, a 17.8-percent increase since 1980. Data reveals a rise in the population's median age (from 30 to 33 years), and shows slightly more women than men residing in Brea (50.3 to 49.9 percent).

The region's changing ethnic balance is reflected in a combined "non-White" population of 13 percent (up five points from 1980), with Hispanics and Asians as this segment's largest reporting groups. Local diversity is further reflected in school district figures, which show 36 different languages spoken in the homes of local students.

❖ The historic Wall Building at 105-109 East Ash burns in an Easter-morning blaze.

❖ The city's Communications and Marketing Department receives the first of six awards in a three-year period for print media, video production and marketing.

❖ The city and school district join to prohibit smoking and tobacco use at all civic and school district facilities.

❖ Local historian and teacher Brian Saul begins popular walking tours of the old downtown.

❖ Imperial Plaza East is dedicated at Kraemer with a 50,000-square-foot Lucky Food Center, the largest market then built by Lucky stores.

❖ Refurbished with $1.5 million in improvements, Laurel School is rededicated in its 69th year.

Laurel School, Rededicated in 1990

End of an Era, 1989
Mayor Wayne Wedin (left), joins School District Superintendent Dr. Edgar Z. Seal at the portal of old BOHS as the wrecking ball of progress prepares to take its swing.
Courtesy City of Brea

Highlights of Brea Life, 1980-1992

❖ The Brea Day Worker Job Center opens in a relocatable facility in the downtown redevelopment district. Winner of a 1992 award from Rutgers University, the center finds employment for 1,300 workers in 1991, including 300 permanent placements.

Newly relocated to a Cypress Avenue site, the center continues to provide a place for workers and employers to meet, and also offers instruction in commercial skills and English-language acquisition.

❖ Two early-summer wildland fires in Carbon Canyon threaten Olinda Village and destroy homes over the county line in Sleepy Hollow.

❖ The seven-story, Egyptian-themed Embassy Suites Hotel opens Nov. 17

EMBASSY SUITES H O T E L

as the last key feature in Brea's Central Area Development Concept.

❖ The Brea Improv opens at the Marketplace as the city's first comedy club.

❖ First-stage work begins on the $18-million Imperial Highway Project, a program to widen this "super highway" to six lanes and improve storm drains and water systems.

❖ Affordable housing advances with the opening of the Laurel Creek Townhouse Project on Laurel north of Birch. With the median price of a Brea single-family residence running at $264,000, the city vows to create 1,500 affordable homes within the decade.

By 1992, low-cost housing is enhanced by new construction, "in-fill" development in aging neighborhoods, the Senior Rent-Subsidy Program and three projects by the non-profit Christian organization, Habitat for Humanity.

HABITAT FOR HUMANITY
ORANGE COUNTY

❖ Former City Manager Wayne D. Wedin becomes Brea's mayor, adopting the theme, "Together We Make a Difference."

1991:

❖ Mike Cohen's Brea Northpoint opens in the downtown redevelopment district and earns a Mayor's Award from the Brea Beautification Committee.

❖ Community Services announces the kickoff of a large-scale drug and alcohol awareness program in conjunction with the Brea Police Department, local schools and Kaiser Permanente. Zones near schools and parks are declared "Drug Free," and abusers earn maximum sentences for drug use in these areas.

drug and alcohol
awareness
program

❖ The American Explorers' Youth Center opens on South Brea Boulevard.

❖ "Recycle Brea" wins honors from the Solid Waste Association of North America.

❖ Mexican artist Carlos Terres, a resident of Brea's sister city of Lagos de Moreno, becomes the town's third Artist in Residence. A world-class artist with commissions in Mexico, Spain and Japan, Terres adds four sculptures, a series of paintings and the *Jubilee Mural* to Brea's collection.

❖ Ribbon-cutting ceremonies open the new Veteran's Club House on South Brea Boulevard, operated jointly by the Veterans of Foreign Wars and the American Legion.

❖ Brea's maintenance staff ties a yellow ribbon around the Civic & Cultural Center, a symbolic statement of support for U.S. troops engaged in the (Persian) Gulf War.

❖ Watt Commercial Development signs a contract for the building of a 50-acre commercial center and townhome complex on northwest Brea at Imperial, the first phase of downtown redevelopment.

Plans call for a new "old town," where architecture assumes the look of an earlier age, and Birch Street emerges as a "Towne Plaza," winding

Canyon Transformation, 1990
CPC Brea Canyon Hospital opens a 151-bed acute-care facility at the North Brea Boulevard site of the former Brea Hospital Neuropsychiatric Center.
Brea Historical Society

Time Line to the 90's

1991 CONTINUED:

through fountains and public art, boutiques, theaters and sidewalk cafes

toward a new "channel park" on the west. Ralph's Market, Payless Drug and Petsmart sign on as anchor stores in the 22-acre "Gateway Center" commercial development, with Tom Craig as owner-participant in this Watt/ Craig Joint Venture.

❖   The city's Art Shelter Program, a pioneer effort to bring changing displays of two-dimensional art to local bus stops, is inaugurated on Randolph near Birch. Fifteen such shelters are planned in the Brea program, the first of its kind in California.

❖   Citing concerns over a proposed Unocal mixed-use development that would straddle the Fullerton/Brea border, the city de-annexes (to Fullerton) a 59-acre portion of the Imperial Golf Course.

❖   More than 100 community "designers" gather with city staff and outside consultants to create a vision for Brea's northern "Sphere of Influence," 7.4 square miles of unincorporated hills and canyons that potentially will increase the city's size by 70 percent. Goals and principles for land use and preservation emerge from the workshop series, and the vision document becomes a guidebook for long-range development.

❖   Brea's Parks, Recreation and Human Services Department begins providing contract recreation services to the City of Diamond Bar.

❖   The Harlem Globetrotters meet the Boston Shamrocks in a benefit performance at BOHS.

❖   Developer Darwin Manuel opens Gaslight Square, an office and retail center in the east downtown redevelopment district.

❖   The refinancing of $210 million in redevelopment and civic-center

bonds at lowered rates yields interest savings earmarked for use in upgrading the city's water system, building a community center and completing downtown's ongoing redevelopment.

❖   BOHS is named a California Distinguished School. National Blue Ribbon honors follow in 1993.

❖   Local projects garner two prestigious awards, as the National Privatization Council honors Brea for its combined development of the new BOHS and the Marketplace, and the International Downtown Association recognizes the city for its downtown master plan.

Night Moves
The William Casner House, long a landmark on South Madrona, makes its way across town on a winter night in 1991. Relocated to 121 S. Redwood, the large Airplane Craftsman-style structure currently awaits restoration and new residents.
Courtesy Daily Star-Progress

Highlights of Brea Life, 1980-1992

Sacramento Honorees
Orange County Supervisor Gaddi Vasquez (center) presents Governor's Senior Honor Awards to local residents Joe Falco (left), founder of the Brea Theatre League and chairman of the 1992 Brea Cultural Arts Commission, and John Kumbera, president of Brea's American Association of Retired Persons. Breans took two of three statewide seniors' awards in 1991. *From the Joe Falco collection*

1991 CONTINUED:

❖ Former Mayor Ron Isles (1982) is selected mayor for the city's Diamond Jubilee Year.
❖ The Brea Civic Light Opera stages *Oklahoma!* as its premiere performance.

1992:

❖ A new Brea Church of Jesus Christ of Latter-Day Saints opens on Poplar north of Birch.
❖ The East 100 block of North Brea Boulevard is designated as a future historical district. Tentative plans show the completed area will house the relocated Sam's Place (originally the Brea Bakery), That Frame Place (the former La Habra Valley Bank) and the Kinsler home at 129 S. Orange, plus the renovated Brea Hotel and the rebuilt Wall and Delaney buildings.
❖ A revised agreement with the county states that existing boundaries will be expanded vertically, but not into surrounding terrain at the Olinda/Olinda Alpha Landfill, located in the hills at the terminus of Valencia Avenue.
❖ The community kicks off its Diamond Jubilee with a Feb. 22 birthday party at Brea Mall. The weekend continues with unearthing and opening of the 25-year-old Golden Jubilee Time Capsule at City Hall Park, and the first of three Living History Bus Tours, with re-enactments of memorable scenes from the city's past.

The Curtain Rises
The Brea Theatre League, Stagelight Family Productions, Brea Civic Light Opera and Brea City Orchestra (with Conductor Leon Guide) usher in a busy civic season under the guidance of Community Services Director Ret Wixted, Cultural Arts Manager Emily Keller and Theater Specialist Scott Riordan.

Time Line to the 90's

A Statement of Spirit
The Wildcat wears a unique skin of fur and feathers, combining features of the eagle (a symbol of excellence, intelligence and possibility) and the wildcat (a symbol of power and strength). Dedicated to the students of BOHS, the towering mascot strikes a snarling stance atop its 16-foot-high rock pedestal.

1992 CONTINUED:

Jubilee keepsakes including calendars, visors, T-shirts and sweatshirts, watches, books and the videotape, *A Walk in Time*, go on sale, and a traveling photo collage tours the town.
❖ Carlos Terres' *The Wildcat* is unveiled before an enthusiastic BOHS crowd as the 100th sculpture in Brea's Art in Public Places Pro-

gram. Sculpted in an outdoor, on-campus studio, the cat initially provoked controversy with its unexpected feathers, but in the end, little fur flew. By December, Brea's Art in Public Places program would include 106 pieces, ranking among the nation's largest outdoor art collections.

BREA'S
ART IN PUBLIC PLACES

❖ The City of Brea Gallery under the directorship of Marie Sofi presents *Creative Energy*, the largest exhibit of neon art ever assembled in the United States.
❖ The Living Faith Church opens in Carbon Canyon.
❖ Unocal begins the break down and reconstruction of its natural-gas absorption compressor plant in the hills above Wildcat Way to a site a quarter-mile to the east, the former locale of the Landa Family ranch house.
❖ More than 100 entries line up for May 16's Diamond Jubilee Parade, with Frank Schweitzer as grand marshal and Darwin Manuel as organizer. A picnic follows in City Hall Park.

❖ *Brea...Then and Now*, a 75-year photo retrospective, opens amid old-fashioned festivities at the city gallery June 12. From a field of more than 1,100 entries, 91 photos of today's Brea join vintage prints on loan from the Brea Historical Society. A popular historical home tour rounds out the spring's special events.

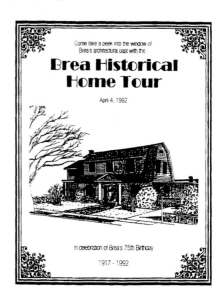

❖ BOHS becomes one of only two statewide sites chosen for installation of Pacific Bell's Knowledge Network information system, and BOHS teacher Glenys Bell receives the Presidential Award for Excellence in Science and Mathematics Teaching.
❖ A boulevard landmark for 58 years, the two-color neon "Brea Welcomes You" sign is damaged by a passing vehicle, and cut from its base and stored for future use in the renovated downtown district.

Dumping Ground
One of only a few landfills remaining in the county, Brea's nearby Olinda/Olinda Alpha site was originally expected to be filled by 1980. Expansion pushed its closing to the year 1997, and then to 2000, and its life later was extended to 2013. Long-range plans show the site will be transformed into a county recreation area.
Photo by Susan Gaede

Highlights of Brea Life, 1980-1992

LEFT: Reaching New Heights
The fire department takes delivery of its first ladder truck, allowing the city full response capability for both single and multi-story structures. Chief Bud Moody welcomes five new firefighters hired to help staff the emergency vehicle.
Courtesy Brea Fire Department

BELOW: So Long, Landmark
Amid a shower of sparks, the Brea Sign is cut from its long-standing site on Brea Boulevard north of Imperial.
Photo by Jack Hancock

❖ Brea Fest, the city's annual "Taste of the Arts," attracts over 5,000 visitors, earning record receipts of $16,400 for the funding of local cultural arts programs.

❖ Unocal announces plans to close its east-side chemical plant and develop this Imperial at Kraemer site as residential. Disassembly work begins, and—for the first time in many years, the tower's Christmas tree fails to light the December sky.

❖ Community workshops unveil Santa Fe Energy's 227-acre Olinda Heights project, the first proposed development in Brea's Sphere of Influence area. Soil remediation starts at the former upper-Olinda townsite, and discussion begins on the fate of the area's oldest remaining oil structures.

❖ Downtown redevelopment moves forward with the resolution of a dispute between the Brea Redevelopment Agency and the Brea Small Businessmen's Coalition, and the razing of Brea Boulevard buildings is followed by the grading of construction sites. By December, west-side structures are nearly gone, and passing motorists watch as the final bricks fall.

❖ The Brea Police Bike Patrol swings into action, cruising shopping

Time Line to the 90's:
Highlights of Brea Life, 1980-1992

1992 CONTINUED:

centers and special events for enhanced mobility and increased citizen contact. Funds for the trial program are channeled from seized drug assets.

❖ Burnie Dunlap succeeds Ron Isles as mayor.

❖ Brea Junior High's 1992 8th-grade California Assessment Program (CAP) tests top the county with an average score of 328—69 points above the state norm.

❖ Built less than three years before, the Brea Mall Robinson's announces it will close its doors as the result of a corporate restructuring. By early 1993, the mall's May Co. re-opens as Robinson's-May, and J.C. Penney

announces plans to take over the Robinson's store.

❖ Preliminary engineering and design work begins for a 32,000-square-foot Community Center planned at the northwest corner of Randolph Avenue and Madison Way. Meeting rooms, a gym, service areas for Tiny Tots, youth and families, outdoor picnic sites and a sculpture garden are included in early proposals for the center.

❖ Refurbished and upgraded with an amphitheater, basketball and volleyball courts, disabled-access playground structures and a 75-tree Jubilee Grove, Arovista Park is rededicated Dec. 5. A year-end recreation update shows one state (Chino Hills), two county (Carbon Canyon and Craig),

Arovista Park
PHASE II OPENING
Celebration!
Saturday, December 5, 1992, 10:00 a.m.

one regional (Tri-City) and eight city (or joint city/school-district shared) recreation areas make modern Brea a leader in leisure.

Radically changed in the space of just two decades, today's Brea bears little resemblance to the town of 20 years past. Nearly a million people pass through the community on a typical weekday, most speeding by on the freeway, but increasing numbers drawn in by the city's bright lights and growing attractions.

The town that for years had only a handful of industries, no movie theater and just a few stores and small cafes now boasts high-rise office structures and sprawling industrial parks, a state-of-the-art civic center and high school, a quality hotel, two art galleries and two performing arts centers, dozens of theaters and restaurants, and hundreds of retail emporiums.

Older than many of its Orange County counterparts, and different in the way it moved toward today, modern Brea is a study in contrasts, a unique blend of hometown USA and progressive urban center. The city that helped build one of Southern California's premiere shopping malls and houses such corporate giants as Unocal and American Suzuki also cheers on the local high-school sports teams, celebrates the 4th of July with fireworks and a country fair, and taps its toes to the Marine Corps Band at summer concerts in City Hall Park.

Two-Wheeled Crime Fighters
The Brea bicycle corps: (left to right, front) Reuben Hernandez, Jerry Brakebill, Debbie Drlik, Rick Edwards, Jon Anderson, Walter McIntyre and Gary Drlik; (back), Bill Vukelich, Dave Jones, Brian Parker, Santo Porto, Clyde Wason, Dave Coovert, Danny Valenzuela and Stewart McCarroll. The Brea Police force also engages a four-legged form of transport in park and wilderness patrols by the Brea Mounted Posse.
Courtesy City of Brea

Though each era in Brea's past has offered its own unique play of events, recurring themes thread through the years, and old problems appear in fresh forms to test the changing times. The twin constraints of inadequate water and transportation bogged down the town's beginnings, and—though each repeatedly was solved—both regularly reappeared as population growth continued. Today, drought conditions still bring the threat of water shortage, and traffic engineers ponder the possibility of gridlock.

Though the city's greatest transformation arrived in the last two decades, gradually accelerating change long has been a pattern of local life. Each passing wave of landowners exploited the region's wealth in different ways, but all found ample resources to meet their needs—grass for grazing and fertile soil for farming, plentiful oil for pumping and a frost-free climate for citrus, and, in the modern era, prime geographic placement for the building of a regional mall.

One way of life faded and another replaced it, and the land took on a new look. The earliest cattle and sheep ranches were plowed into barley fields, which in turn gave way to walnut and citrus groves that later were felled for homes. Soon, as the vast pools of petroleum at last are drained from the soil, the century-old local oil industry will bow out of Brea life, and hills and canyons long dotted with derricks instead will be marked by new development. Downtown will emerge reborn from reconstruction as the cycle of change continues, and other aging areas will step forward for renewal.

Through 75 years, Brea's strength has flowed from sound leadership and farsighted planning mixed with small-town caring and commitment. From the beginning, local volunteers found frequent opportunities to serve, whether fighting fires or building churches, sheltering disaster victims, welcoming combat-bound soldiers, writing the city's first planning study or formulating visions for future growth. Maybe it was the town's early isolation, or the no-nonsense influence of the oil men who built it, but Breans formed an early habit of facing a job head on and doing what they could to get it done.

As the Diamond Jubilee year draws to a close, the community again reaches out toward the promise of decades to come, and prepares to pass this Brea Spirit on to the city's second century.

An anonymous quote from a long-ago pamphlet lends a fitting end to Brea's 75th-anniversary story:

"The young people will have to write their own history and the history of the city of tomorrow. I hope they ask me what I think. I'll tell them that those early days of high wages and hard living made all the difference in this town. All of the industry and the homes, all of the planning and all of the promise, all that is Brea today and all that Brea will be is the harvest of seeds that were planted deep in the oily soil of a quieter time, long ago.

"We used to have a saying here in town, "Oil, Oranges and Opportunity!" It's mostly the opportunity that's left now. But that was the most important thing, after all."

Though this 75th-anniversary volume ends with the events of the Jubilee year, Brea's colorful history continues. In its ongoing effort to celebrate times gone by, the Brea Historical Society seeks photographs, newspapers, written remembrances and other artifacts of the city's past, as well as new members to carry forward its work.

"The past belongs to the future, but only the present can preserve it."

The Face of Brea

"Charlie's Clock," reportedly a Riverside train depot timepiece, came to Brea in the early 1970's to advertise a budding clock shop. The business moved and the clock came down, but residents missed it, so the city bought it and brought it back to town.

Brea...Then and Now:
An Anniversary Album

Brea Style:
Leading the Way in Facilities, Arts and Services

1. *City Central:* Honored with several design awards, the Brea Civic & Cultural Center provides a home for local government, school district and chamber of commerce offices, and also houses a county branch library, civic art gallery and community theater.

2. *Civic Symphony:* The popular Brea Orchestra (under the direction of Leon Guide) performs Klassy Koncerts for Kids and an annual pops series, as well as programs for holidays and seasonal events including the annual Brea Fest.

3. *City of Brea Gallery:* The largest municipal art showcase in Orange County, Brea's gallery spotlights changing exhibits including the prestigious National Watercolor Society and Watercolor West shows. The popular jubilee exhibit *Creative Energy: An Exhibit of Neon Art* (pictured) attracted more than 5,500 visitors.

4. *To Protect and Serve:* Brea firefighters from modern Station No. 3 join local police and emergency communication operators in keeping the city safe.

5. *Civic Center Sunset:* A pillar of the civic center frames the old Horan house on Birch Street, which held out against progress for almost a decade after the building of its impressive next-door neighbor. Randolph Avenue now runs through this property.

6. *Center Stage:* The Brea Civic Light Opera, one of four resident theater companies, presents *Oklahoma!* at the Curtis Theatre. Named for Brea's popular "country doctor," Dr. C. Glenn Curtis, this 199-seat civic theater hosts a busy calendar of musical and dramatic performances.

4

5

6

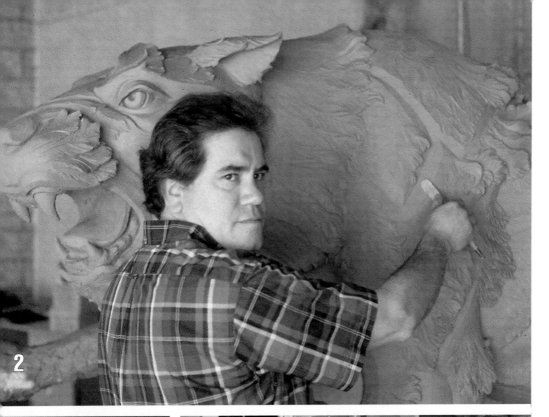

2

4

3

5

6

Art in Public Places: The Gallery That Never Closes

1. *Doublecheck* by J. Seward Johnson, the bronze likeness of a businessman so realistic the letter he holds is readable. This sculpture adorns an office complex on East Birch Street.

2. *The Wildcat:* Artist-in-residence Carlos Terres of Lagos de Moreno, Mexico, sculpts a new mascot in an open-air studio at Brea Olinda High School. The imposing sculpture was bronzed and dedicated during the Diamond Jubilee year.

3. *The Rise of Icarus* by Gidon Graetz reflects the beauty of its surroundings as it sweeps skyward near the intersection of Birch Street and State College Boulevard.

4. *Jupe L'eau* by Pol Bury, Brea's own kinetic "water skirt," captures the attention of shoppers in the mall's Center Court.

5. *The Mustangs* by Ray Persinger, a monument to movement burnished in bronze, graces an East Saturn Street industrial park.

6. *Saturn Sail* by Harold Pastorius, a corten steel structure in vibrant tones, energizes West Saturn Street's industrial sector.

PHOTOS COURTESY CITY OF BREA

Business Brea:
A Center for Commerce and Industry

1. Corporate Headquarters: American Suzuki makes its home in Brea's East Imperial Highway industrial sector.

2. Research Division: Breakthroughs in petro-chemical technology are the buisness of Unocal's Fred Hartley Research Center, also located on East Imperial Highway.

3. Embassy Suites: Brea's seven-story, 229-room Egyptian-themed Embassy Suites opened adjacent to the Civic & Cultural Center in 1989.

4. Brea Mall: The dominant retail center of North Orange County, Brea's elegantly remodeled mall boasts over one million square feet of floor space. Pictured is Nordstrom Court, featuring *La Lune*, by sculptor Niki de St. Phalle.

5. Administrative Offices: Brea Corporate Place, headquarters for the Capital Group—one of many financial interests located in Brea.

Downtown: A Time of Transition

1. *The Clock Ticks:* For old downtown, now in the midst of extensive renewal. This old timepiece will survive the transformation as part of a planned historic block. Photo by Susan Gaede, *Brea...Then and Now.*

2. *Moon Over My Sammy's:* A full moon casts its glow on the bakery-turned-bar called Sam's Place, one of several buildings in the downtown redevelopment area earmarked for relocation in a planned historic block. Photo by Elray Hanna, *Brea...Then and Now.*

3. *The Shape of Things to Come:* Brea's downtown of tomorrow, as seen in an early redevelopment rendering. Watt-Craig Development, Courtesy City of Brea.

The Diamond Jubilee: Brea Celebrates 75 Years

1. Don Fretwell (left) and Robert Halstead unseal Brea's Golden Jubilee time capsule, buried in 1967 at City Hall Park.

2. The Brea Gallery features the community's rich heritage in the photography exhibit *Brea...Then and Now*.

3. Grand Marshal Mickey Mouse greets local fans at the Jubilee Parade.

4. The community's post-parade picnic takes on an international flair with help from Brea's Sister City of Hanno, Japan.

5. Brea Mall provides a festive setting for the city's official birthday party.

6. Girl Scouts Marci Coulson and Courtney Salas of Brea Junior Troop 811 serve old-fashioned lemonade to local sightseers. Photo by Brandon Spencer.

7. Jubilee Home Tours spotlight historic residences and churches. Photo by Brandon Spencer.

Brea's Youth: Faces of the Future

1. *Sound the Alarm: It's Tiny Tots to the Rescue!* Pictured on Lagos de Moreno Park's retired fire truck are (left to right) Devon Allred, Randy Bamsch, Phillip Rangel, Lyle Jackson, C.J. Sandoval, Daniel Brown, Christopher Peluso (at the wheel), Elliott Miller, Shane Burris, Ben Foster, Casey Davis and Travis Gramberg.   Photo by Grace Rouse, *Brea...Then and Now*

2. *Something to Bounce About:* Country Fair kids get a new slant on life as "The Castle" makes its annual appearance. Courtesy City of Brea.

3. *The Better to See You With:* Jeremy Ladebauche enjoys altered visual opportunities, courtesy a Brea Fest face painter. Photo by Lynda Kerney, *Brea...Then and Now*

4. *New Games:* Tiny Tots get a lift from parachute play at Arovista Park. Courtesy City of Brea

5. *A Festive Fourth:* There's fun for everyone at the annual Country Fair, as shown in the smiles of cousins Britlyn Garrett and Loryn Weddle. Photo by Thayer Weddle Garrett, *Brea...Then and Now*

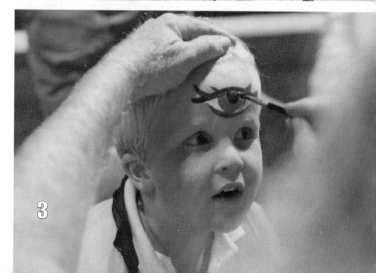

4

5

Going (and Gone), But Not Forgotten...

1. *Moooving On:* Though cattle were once common on the local landscape, only an occasional wayward cow now ventures over Brea's northern border. Photo by Barb Andreas, *Brea...Then and Now.*

2. *The Wall Building Burns:* One of the city's first two-story structures, the Wall was destroyed by fire in 1990, but may rise again as part of Brea's historic block. Photo by Brian Saul.

3. *Sign of the Times:* Long a fixture on Birch at Orange, the S & G Market posts its obituary. Photo by Ron Funk, *Brea...Then and Now.*

4. *A Sentinel Sleeps:* J.D. Sievers' landmark house, the finest residence of Brea's early decades, sat on a knoll near today's Imperial and Berry, but was razed in the late 1980's. Photo by J. Ghandehari, *Brea...Then and Now.*

5. *So Long, Alma Mater:* The front wall of Brea-Olinda High School's main building falls to the wrecking ball of progress, Feb. 18, 1989. Photo by Brian Saul, *Brea...Then and Now.*

6. *Boulevard Days:* Renovated in the 1970's and slated for redevelopment during the Diamond Jubilee year, a stretch of old Brea Boulevard enjoys finer times. Photo by Gary Leper, *Brea...Then and Now.*

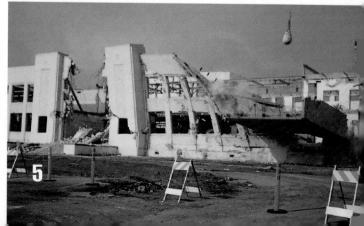

1

3

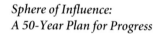

4

Sphere of Influence:
A 50-Year Plan for Progress

1. *An Ambitious Proposal:* A towering oil museum tops a hillside in this sketch, one of many ideas suggested for portions of the sphere's expansive acreage.

2. *The Study:* A proactive plan for development of 7.4 currently unincorporated acres north of Brea's boundaries. More than 100 community members and planning professionals gathered in the fall of 1991 to create a vision for this probable "future Brea."

3. *A Community Team:* Touring the study area in a caravan of small buses.

4. *City of Tomorrow:* Tonner Canyon, now in the last stages of oil production, draws closer to development. Preservation of the land's natural resources ranked high with workshop participants.

5. *Twilight Over the Oilfields:* Resident Ron Funk's photo, *Picture Brea*, grand prize winner in the Jubilee exhibit *Brea... Then and Now.*

6. *The Land As It Stands:* More than 4,700 acres covered with chaparral and clumps of cactus, and crisscrossed by aging oil pipes. Should the entire area be annexed, Brea's size would increase by 70 percent.

5

6

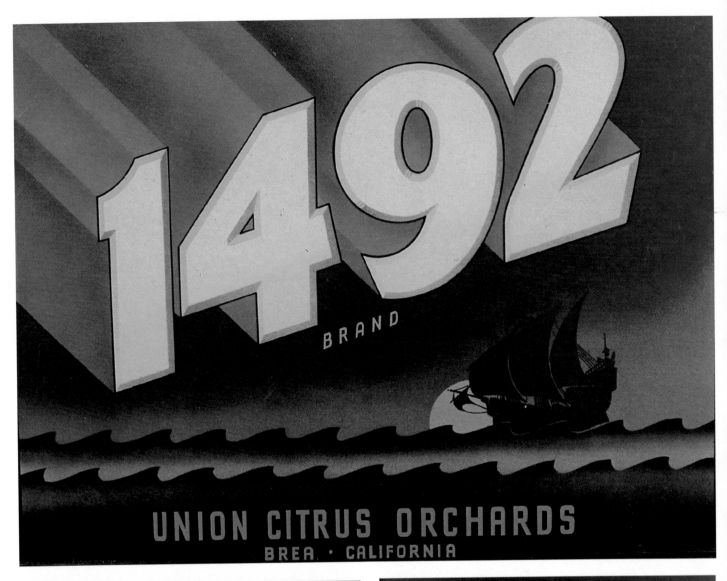

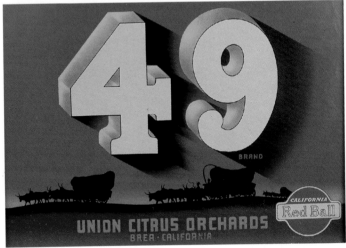

A History of Citrus: Brea's Golden Groves

The Fruit of Union Oil's Orchards: Four grades ranked the quality of local lemons, with the "76" mark reserved for Brea's best.

Brightly designed 10 by 11-inch lithographed labels (such as these rare local examples) identified the contents of wooden shipping crates. Begun as an advertising gimmick, the colorful labels sparked sales, and later gained fame as art forms and collector's items.

Union Citrus Orchards labels from the Dean Millen collection.

LABEL
PHOTOGRAPHY
BY
BILL STRICKLAND

A Celebration Scrapbook

A sampling of Brea's best, both now and in the past. A glimpse at the city's achievements, its humor and its heart.

All in a Name

In its early days, Brea was known as the place with the funny name, and battles raged over just how to pronounce it. Insight on the town's correct sound, as adapted from the 1950 *Brea Progress*.

How do YOU pronounce Brea? Several recent inquiries as to the proper pronunciation of our fair city's name have instigated a round-up of expert opinions.

The consensus of these experts is that Brea should be said "Bray-uh," like a donkey with a British accent, sort of.

The most frequent mispronunciation, however, is "Bree-uh." That mistake is made even by Breans of long residence. A couple of other mispronunciations chop the name down to one syllable—either "Bree" or "Bray." These flagrant errors are usually committed by flatland "furriners" and are therefore excusable. A fourth mistake, usually committed by outlanders—particularly those from the village of Los Angeles—is to tack the Spanish article "La" on the front of the word, as in the street and tar pits of the same name.

Such authorities as Mayor Charles McCart and School officials Vince Jaster and Frank Hopkins agree "Bray-uh" is the right way to say it, and point out the importance of consistency at all costs.

Since Brea's name is the Spanish word for asphalt or tar, the clinching argument comes from Mr. Webster, of the dictionary. Webster's points out that "Bray-uh" is the correct pronunciation, and defines the term as "viscous asphalt formed by the evaporation of petroleum from oil seeps."

The defense rests.

Northern Exposure:
The "Brea" Few People Know

Drive east on Lambert Road to Kraemer, where modern Fire Station 3 stands sentry over the nearby suburbs. Turn north toward the hills, and pass the verdant flora of Village Nurseries. Approach the boundaries of Unocal's vast Stearns Lease, and imagine what unseen sights lie on the less-traveled road ahead.

For those fortunate few who have been beyond the gate, a whole new "Brea" becomes known. Owned since 1894 by Union Oil, Stearns is a place of beauty and contrast, where machinery rubs elbows with willows and wildflowers, and deer and coyotes roam. Though active wells and miles of pipes crisscross its rugged acres, it remains a peaceful place, far removed from the city below. On a clear day, from its heights, you can almost see forever— to the south, the sea and Catalina, and to the north, snow-capped Mount Baldy.

Rich as well as beautiful, Stearns' acres have spawned an aggressive

search for oil. More than 300 wells have been sunk here, and nearly 200 still produce oil. One of the L.A. basin's earliest drilling sites, Stearns remains Unocal's "ace in the hole" —the most prolific of all Southland petroleum fields, with a lifetime predicted yield of 95 million barrels.

A sheep ranch in the pre-oil era, Stearns sold for just 80 cents an acre, but came with some woolly strings: grazing rights for 1,500 sheep for a span of 50 years. Basque rancher Francisco "Frank" Landa and his family lived in a three-room house on the hills' south side, and long after the rest of the family was gone, the Landa's hired hands stayed on to tend the "Sheep Ranch." A few lingering lambs grazed the slopes until the late 1970's, often surprising passing motorists speeding by on the streets below.

The Landa Family, Circa 1920
Francisco (Frank), his wife Dominica (Dominga) and their children Sofia and Simeon (Sam) lived on the "Sheep Ranch" in Brea's hills. Sam later became owner of the popular watering spot still known today as Sam's Place.
From the Fran Newhouse collection

In the old days, there was more going on at Stearns—more people, more bustle and noise. Stearns Camp sat near the mouth of today's Wildcat Way, and smaller clusters of buildings dotted the surrounding slopes. Workers' homes, water wells, storage tanks, offices, absorption and compressor plants, booster stations, even a rifle range and (Arthur) Cy Rubel (company) Park all were built on Union lands in the passing years.

The Stearns field has seen a century of progress, and watched an industry evolve. On foot and on horseback, in "Tin Lizzies" and pick-up trucks, oil workers patrolled these canyons and hills. With cable tools they drilled for a solid year to do what rotary drills now can do in a day. They spudded wells in twisted rock and plumbed progressively lower, laboring at some sites on holes plunging nearly two miles deep in the earth. They heard the rattling chug of steam engines and the throaty buzz of diesels stilled by the modern whir of electric motors, and saw this new power linked to nodding "grasshoppers" rhythmically at work pumping oil from the earth.

From the Brea production office high atop these hills, Unocal Field Manager Eldon East and a staff of nearly 30 supervise today's Stearns site, where secondary recovery with steam and water injection extends the life of an aging field. Some older wells recently have been exhausted, and capped off with yards of concrete. An occasional new well is spudded, but—for the most part— Stearns' "old reliables" pump slowly on, timed to run only part of the day to keep from drying out. After nearly a hundred years, the field's production continues at 2,000 (42-gallon) barrels each day, a daily output in excess of 80,000 gallons.

A Brea Nursery Story

Though citrus is the namesake crop of the county, Brea also earned acclaim through the years as a large-scale producer of nursery stock. Access to quality water and reasonably priced lease land spurred this growing trend, and today's Brea still

boasts a near forest of boxed-to-go ornamental plants.

The history of local growers dates to before Brea's birth, when Roeding and Wood Nursery, a major supplier of citrus seedlings, opened on a large plot of land northwest of today's Berry and Central.

A number of nursery operations later occupied Roeding and Wood's old site, among them the Tomlinson Family's Select Nursery (once one of Southern California's largest producers and shippers of landscape plants). This property later passed to AmFac, and in recent years has taken the name Specialty Plants.

Once Tomlinsons' neighbor to the west, Bob Widner's Buena Park Nursery was located at the northeast corner of Central and Puente in the 1940's and 50's, and is still remembered by Brea old-timers for its extensive use of glass greenhouses.

Property just to the north, where Whittier Avenue ends at Puente, for many years was part of the large Calavo avocado operation, but in recent years instead has become the site of California Living Nursery, a specialist in indoor plants.

A fourth west-side operation, Forest Nursery, also operated in past years on North Puente, but later was bought by Village Nurseries, which greatly expanded its acreage. Village leased land from Union Oil in today's upper North Hills and Fieldstone Terrace areas, in the Edison power-line right-of-way west to Harbor, and at an east-city site stretching from Kraemer to east Eagle Hills. The company maintained offices in Brea for several years, and also operated a retail outlet until the mid-1980's on the northeast side of today's Lambert and Wildcat Way.

Though much of Village's former acreage has been developed, the company today continues to lease two local sites.

Immediately adjacent to Village Nurseries' east-side locale (from east Eagle Hills to Valencia) lies Bergen Nurseries, for many years a wholesaler and specialist in larger landscape plants and trees. Nearby Olinda Nursery, a grower and retailer, sits on 20 Unocal acres on Valencia just south of Birch, while Benny Lou's Nursery occupies 10 Santa Fe Energy acres near the mouth of Carbon Canyon.

A retailer but not a grower, Tokay Gardens (located on Central west of Brea Boulevard) opened as Sandan Nursery in the early 1960's, but gained new owners and its now-familiar name in 1982.

Nothing but Trees, Please
A Story of Brea's Street Names

While Brea's first maps show a garden variety of local street names, a trend toward trees took root quite quickly—and branched out through the years.

Trustees tagged the city's first streets alphabetically by tree, starting with Ash, spreading north and south, and leaving no street out. From their trunk of names came (to the north) Bracken, Cypress and (later) Deodara, while the south sprouted Birch, Cedar, Date, Elm, and finally, Fir.

Though time tampered with the plan, (turning Deodara to Lambert and Cedar to Imperial) the seeds of thought were planted, and new streets blossomed tree names. From Alder to Wisteria, the naming trend grew, until more than 100 local avenues now bloom in shades of nature's nomenclature.

Big-Screen Brea
Cast and crew members of the film *Silver Streak* gather on Brea Boulevard for a shooting sequence in the 1970's.
Photo by Susan Gaede

Brea Breaks Into the "Big Picture"

First "discovered" as a movie set in the 1920's when Mary Pickford filmed *The House with the Golden Windows* on the Graham-Loftus oil lease, Brea has snared its fair share of silver screen roles—in movies both old and new.

In the 1930's, Brea stole scenes in *Black Gold*, starring William Boyd as an oilman who rescues a fellow worker in a rig fire. A backdrop of derricks proved perfect for this

Judy Garland

location scene, shot at the northwest corner of (today's) Brea Boulevard and Lambert Road. Brea Boy Scouts helped with crowd control for the filming, a fact they no doubt remembered when Boyd later became better known as Western-star Hopalong Cassidy.

The next decade saw the town's picturesque "pepper-tree lane" compete with John Garfield and Lana Turner in a scene from *The Postman Always Rings Twice*, shot on Brea Boulevard between (today's) Lambert and Central in August of 1945.

Making a comeback in the 1970's, the town played a cameo role in *Silver Streak,* with Gene Wilder, Richard Pryor and Jill Clayburgh. A street scene in the film offers brief glimpses of the Wall Building on East Ash, since destroyed by fire.

Perhaps in need of a new agent, Brea in 1985 had a final fling in show biz, its new civic center the setting for the one-check *Moving Violations* with Sally Kellerman, Jennifer Tilly, John Murray (Bill's brother), James Keach (Stacy's brother) and burger queen Carla ("Where's the Beef?") Peller.

William Boyd

And...though not a bit like Oz, or even much like Kansas, Brea also played host to at least one appearance by teenage movie-star Judy Garland, whose uncle, Robert Gumm, managed the Brea Theater in the 1930's.

Of Local Note

Guitar Stars...

Few towns of thirty (something) thousand can boast of having been home to a world-famous musical-instrument maker, a bonafide rock star or a top-of-the-charts singing quartet, but Brea is noted for all three.

The famed Fender Musical Instruments company, formerly of Brea, designed guitars for the stars, including Stratocasters used by Beatle George Harrison and heavy-metal rocker Jimi Hendrix. Founded in Fullerton by Clarence "Leo" Fender, the company later was bought by CBS, which operated a Fender manufacturing plant on Saturn Street from 1985-1991.

Grammy Winners...

Singer/songwriter/guitarist James Hetfield, a 1981 graduate of BOHS, hit the big time young as co-founder of today's top-of-the-charts heavy-metal rock group Metallica. Shortly after graduation, Hetfield teamed with drummer Lars Ulrich and two others to form a band that started out playing Los Angeles clubs.

Two relocations and two new members later, the group recorded its debut album (in 1983) for Elektra. A follow-up album, *Ride the Lightning,* went gold the following year, leading to two more LPs, U.S., European and world tours, and the release of...*And Justice for All*, containing the group's 1990 Grammy-award-winning single, "One." A second Grammy followed in 1991 for the band's re-recording of the Queen hit, "Stone Cold Crazy."

The foursome's fifth album, *Metallica*, sold five million copies in

James Hetfield
Courtesy Elektra Records

less than nine months, debuting at *Billboard's* #1 spot and remaining in the top 20 for nearly a year. The band performed its highest-charting single, "Enter Sandman," at the 1992 Grammy Awards, taking a third Grammy before launching a summer stadium tour with Guns N' Roses. A worldwide tour follows in 1992-93.

*A*nd....one last shining example of Brea's contributions to the music world—the star-spangled glove and socks worn by mega-star Michael Jackson in his 1984 world tour were crafted by none other than local resident Bessie Nelson, known as the "Brea Beader."

And Family Acts...

The Singing Osmond Brothers
(From left) Wayne, Morrill, Jay and Alan, made Brea one of their earliest practice sites, rehearsing at the junior high in the early 1960's under the guidance of BJH Choral Director Val Hicks.
From the Leonard MacKain collection

Four Walls and More
A Century of Local Homes

Single sheets of upright board with thin strips of lath in between—no paint, no insulation, no real foundation—these were the "board-and-batten" houses of the early oil leases.

Though they shivered and "shinnied" in the wind, most managed to keep out the rain. Some survived for years, and many wound up in town. Early settlers in Brea townsite felt lucky to have any houses at all. Many lived several months in tents or "tent houses" until finer lodgings were found.

The first Brea homes were compact: a small living room (or parlor), a kitchen, generally two bedrooms and sometimes a dining room. Bathrooms remained outside, but were later "added on," and generally included free-standing, claw-footed enamel bathtubs. With little space, children shared the same bedroom, and often the same bed as well. On cold mornings, everyone

dressed in the kitchen by the large, warm, wood-fired stove. Hot summer evenings were spent outdoors, lounging and talking on friendly, wide front porches.

"Coolers" were used to preserve food. Looking much like built-in closets, these remained open at the floor, allowing cool air to pass in from under the home's foundation. Wire shelves offered space for storage, while a pan of water near the bottom helped to keep things cool. Even so—the butter was always melted. Oak iceboxes with enamelled insides were welcomed in later years, their top shelves stocked with blocks of ice.

Ornate wallpapers and heavy lace curtains adorned the homes of those able to afford them, and—for all, the most prized of possessions was a piano. Most homes were lit by the flickering flame of oil lamps, but natural gas soon helped kindle the glow of gaslights, and some residents kept an open flame burning for outside illumination. By

1920, electricity had sparked change in most local houses.

While Brea built many homes in its first two decades, few followed in the hard years of the Depression and second World War. Post-war houses generally followed a new form, slightly larger, with plaster walls and hardwood floors. Most had a living room, kitchen, dining area, two to three bedrooms, one bath and an ample backyard equipped with a trash-burning incinerator. Many homes were bought by veterans with GI loans.

Trends toward larger homes entered in the late 1950's and early 1960's. Ranch-style houses with more and bigger rooms became popular in these years, and a few tracts were designated "All Electric." The first concentrations of multi-family structures came in the early-1960's, and many town properties first sprouted swimming pools.

"Planned" neighborhoods featuring common pools, clubhouses, tennis courts and playgrounds followed from the mid-1960's, and large condominium developments soon enjoyed similar attractions. Many new houses offered several bedrooms and baths, multiple-car attached garages, and long lists of amenities—most never even imagined by Breans of decades before.

Average Price of a Brea Home	
1920:	**1990: (census)**
$3,000	$240,000

Islands in the Street
Angler Bill Van Arsdale launches his skiff on "Lake Elm" following a 1951 deluge. Van Arsdale, who lived near Elm and Magnolia on the waterfront's west shoreline, found the fishing fine.
Brea Historical Society

They Came From Brea
A Local Hall of Fame

Aviators:

Major Jack "Jake" Armstrong, Air Force test pilot, World War II hero. Holder of the world's closed-course flight speed record, 1954.

Dexter Martin, aviator, flight enthusiast. President of the National Association of State Aviation Officials. Member, OX5 Aviation Pioneers Hall of Fame.

Legislators:

Joe C. Burke (Olindan), Orange County Representative to the California State Assembly, 1915-1919.

Edward (Ted) Craig, (Olindan, later Brean), Assemblyman, 75th District; Speaker of the California State Assembly, 1935.

Jurist:

The Honorable Cruz Reynoso, California State Supreme Court Justice, appointed 1981.

First Hispanic Justice
Brea-born Cruz Reynoso began his legal career fighting for the rights of Imperial Valley farm workers. Appointed by President Jimmy Carter to the U.S. Select Commission on Immigration and Refugees, he later became the first Hispanic member of the California Supreme Court.
From the Dean Millen collection

Cruz Reynoso

Director, Filmmaker:

James Cameron, screenwriter, producer, director.

Entertainers:

James Hetfield: singer/songwriter/guitarist with the heavy-metal rock band Metallica. Winner of three Grammy Awards.

Dicky McNabb, child actor of the 1940's. Dancer and star of the "Our Gang" comedies, including *Good Old Days*.

Oliver (Andy) Ortega, Spanish dancer, World War II "Jeep Show" entertainer.

George Stinson, tenor, 1940's San Francisco Opera star.

George "Foghorn" Winslow (Wenzlaff), Warner Brothers' deep-voiced child star of the 1950's. His movies included *Room For One More* with Cary Grant and Betsy Drake, and *Mister Scoutmaster* with Clifton Webb.

Inventor:

Fred Thaheld, engineer, aeronautical designer. His Guiberson diesel engine today is displayed at the Smithsonian.

James Cameron

Filmmaker
A former local resident and school district employee, James Cameron wrote *The Abyss*, and went on to direct *The Terminator* (with Arnold Schwarzenegger) and the sci-fi classic *Aliens* (winner of two Academy Awards). Cameron took credits as co-writer, producer and director for 1991's box-office blockbuster *Terminator 2: Judgment Day*.

Athletes:

Vic Auer, marksman. National champion, Olympic medalist.

Walter Johnson (Olindan), pitcher, Washington Senators; member, Baseball Hall of Fame.

Randy Jones, pitcher, San Diego Padres. Cy Young Award-winner; member, Orange County Hall of Fame.

Doug Nordquist, high jumper. Two-time national champion; Olympic Festival gold, silver and bronze medalist.

Mothers and Others
The (Often) Unsung Women of Brea

*T*hough history sometimes slighted them, Brea's women played important roles from the city's beginnings. Some success stories:

Then...

❖ **Nellie Alford:**
Owner-operator of the Brea Cafe, a well-patronized dining spot for oil workers in the city's early years. A "popular caterer," she also briefly managed a local hotel.

❖ **Rosalie Williams:**
One of Brea's first businesswomen, Rosalie Williams operated (at separate times) a corset shop, a women's store and boardinghouses in Brea and Olinda. The mother of three, she served briefly as Brea's postmistress, helped organize the Congregational Church and the Woman's Club, served as a member of the Orange County Democratic

Rosalie Rankin Williams
Brea Historical Society

Central Committee and as president of the Olinda PTA.

❖ **Agnes Chansler:**
Carrying the banner of the Heart of Africa Missions, Agnes Chansler spent more than two decades as a

Agnes Chansler

missionary in the Belgian Congo, (now Zaire) starting in 1930.

❖ **Florence Harvey:**
Leader of the movement to form Orange County's public library system, Florence Harvey saw Brea become home to the first county library, and was honored by having its first card issued in her name. She also helped organize the Brea PTA.

❖ **Kathryn Burke:**
Brea's longtime librarian, Kathryn Burke shelved books and answered reference questions from 1925-1948.

❖ **Cuba Hill Hall:**
A representative of Brea's Assembly of God Church, Cuba Hall served with her husband, John, as a missionary on Africa's Gold Coast, arriving in French West Africa in 1931.

❖ **Lulu Launer:**
Wife of Brea City Attorney Albert Launer, Lulu Launer organized the Brea Study Club, which worked to establish a local library and promoted educational programs. She was one of Randolph School's first teachers, and assisted in organizing its PTA and promoting interest in cultural activities.

❖ **Mabel McGee:**
The only woman in Orange County elected to public office in 1918, Mabel McGee was chosen as Brea's city clerk, and also filled appointive positions as tax assessor, recorder and tax collector. Trained as a stenographer, she worked as City Attorney Albert Launer's secretary, and later went into real estate and insurance sales. Miss McGee helped organize Brea's Church of Christ, Scientist—founded in 1918, but later disbanded.

❖ **Grace May:**
Elected as Brea's city clerk in 1924, Grace May served the town for 22 years.

Grace May

❖ **Dorothy Storm:**
Brea's longest-tenured city clerk, Dorothy Storm served in this post a quarter century, from 1959-1984.

And now...

❖ **Norma Arias-Hicks:**
Elected in 1982, Norma Arias-Hicks became Brea's first woman mayor, as well as the first Hispanic woman mayor in Orange County. During her years in office, the city opened a senior center and a fire station, and began the *Brea Line* and Brea Project. She served

Norma Arias-Hicks
Courtesy City of Brea

on the council eight years, and spent six years with the Orange County Hazardous Materials Commission.

❖ **Cleta Harder:**
When Brea's Junior Woman's Club was asked to fill a need, Cleta Harder led the founding of Help for Brain-Injured Children, a rehabilitation and support group. Recently celebrating its 25th year, this organization continues to help disabled children and their families by providing day care and educational services. La Habra's Cleta Harder Developmental School honors her contributions.

❖ **Roberta Carey McDowell Hilliard**
A self-taught artist of modern primitive landscapes, Roberta McDowell graduated from BOHS in 1957 and gained widespread acclaim for her acrylic designs, used in posters, giftware and papergoods.

❖ **Norma Zimmer:**

Norma Zimmer

Singing star of stage and screen, Brean Norma Zimmer was Lawrence Welk's last "champagne Lady."

❖ **Claire Schlotterbeck:**
As president of Hills for Everyone, Brean Claire Schlotterbeck led the successful battle to establish Chino Hills State Park as a wilderness preserve. She most recently served as a Brea Parks, Recreation and Human Services Commissioner.

❖ **Vikki Vargas:**
Now serving as Orange County Bureau Chief for KNBC TV News, Vikki Vargas grew up in Brea, attended Sonora High School, and

Vikki Vargas
Courtesy Orange County Register

got her start at the local CableCom/ Century Cable TV station.

❖ **Bonnie Rosell:**
An exemplary classroom teacher who branched out into staff development, Bonnie Rosell served as director of the Federated Teachers Center in Huntington Beach before beginning her own educational consulting business. The mother of nine and the grandmother of 47, she presents staff development programs throughout Southern California today.

❖ **Clarice Blamer:**
Appointed in the 1980's as Brea's first woman planning commissioner,

Clarice Blamer
Courtesy City of Brea

Clarice Blamer was elected to the city council in 1982 and served for the next eight years. During her tenure as mayor, the city celebrated a "Year of the Arts" and held its first Mayor's Ball. A former member of the Orange County Transportation Commission and a current member of its planning commission, Blamer is the recipient of the YWCA Silver Medallion Award and the North Orange County Business and Professional Women's "Woman of the Year" award.

Signs of the Times

The Remembered Few...

A partial list of those whose names live on in local fame—and why:

❖ **Jack Armstrong:**
Test pilot. (Armstrong Grove, Carbon Canyon Regional Park)

❖ **Richard (Dick) Basse:**
Planning commissioner, councilman. (Basse Lane)

❖ **Truman Berry:**
Walnut/citrus rancher. (Berry Street, Berry Way)

❖ **Edward (Ted) Craig:**
Speaker, California State Assembly, 1935. (Craig Regional Park)

❖ **Dr. C. Glenn Curtis:**
Brea's "country" doctor. (Curtis Theatre)

❖ **William E. Fanning:**
Superintendent, Brea (elementary) School District, 1921-1942 (William E. Fanning Elementary School)

❖ **Vincent Jaster:**
Superintendent, Brea (elementary) School District, 1942-1966. (Jaster Education Center: BOUSD Office)

❖ **Walter Johnson:**
Baseball Hall of Famer. (Walter Johnson Athetic Field, Craig Park)

❖ **Charles McCart:**
Brea Mayor, 1948-1955. (McCart Avenue, McCart Circle)

❖ **John (J.D.) Sievers:**
Citrus rancher, land developer. (Sievers Avenue)

O thers whose names live on, though their claims to fame are less clear:

❖ **Epes Randolph:**
Chief engineer, Pacific Electric Railway (Randolph Avenue). Though Epes Randolph's name remains on this major midtown street and once graced the entire first townsite, Randolph did little to earn the local honor. Once his influence over the Pacific Electric Railway was gone, residents renamed their budding town Brea.

❖ **Patrick Curran (P.C.) Tonner:**
Canyon personality (Tonner Canyon and Tonner Canyon Road). Just over the hills within Brea's Sphere of Influence, Tonner Canyon takes its name from a colorful 19th century character, the "notorious" P.C. Tonner, a hard-drinking young Irish schoolmaster, real-estate agent and sometimes lawyer who served as defense attorney in the Rancho Cañada de la Brea lawsuit. Ironically enough, he lost.

A nd the Forgotten Many....Through the curious quirks of local history, few landmarks celebrate many of those most important in settling this region.

Although **Abel Stearns** once owned everything between Brea and the sea, his name is remembered today only in four Orange County streets, none of them in Brea. While Unocal's local property is still called the Stearns Lease, few signs bearing this name remain.

The Basques who were Brea's first large landowners also are missing, in surnames such as **Hualde, Oxarart, Sarthou, Toussau, Yriarte** and others. Though outside local limits, Fullerton's **Arroues** Drive and **Bastanchury** Road celebrate two of these early area families.

Lyman Stewart, founder of Union Oil, once saw his name used locally for the huge Stewart Station tank farm, refinery and adjacent train stop, but the road that today passes this site instead bears the name "Puente."

Henry Huntington, who built the trolley line, **George Chaffey,** who brought the water, and **Willets J. Hole,** who guided the town's early growth, all are missing from local remembrance. Not one of Brea's first civic leaders has a landmark in his name, although Craig Park's Council Grove collectively honors those who have served in local government.

On a regional scale, two important others are entirely forgotten. The name of rancho owner **Juan Pacifico Ontiveros,** who once called all of Brea, Placentia, Orange and Anaheim his home; and that of **Max von Strobel,** who led Orange County's battle for separation from Los Angeles, both are lost to the county—not a town, a park or even a street to note their passing.

Udder Delight
Dick (left) and Dave DeBoer return to the scene of the crime, boosting Huiberts Dairy's "Bossie" skyward in a reprise of an old BOHS prank. In a mooooving 1982 experience, the BOHS brothers liberated Bossie from the dairy, attached her to cables and dangled her from a light standard at the annual Powder Puff game. The twins and three other "flying farmers" were suspended for the barnyard prank, and the Power Puff game was put out to pasture.
Photo by Susan Gaede

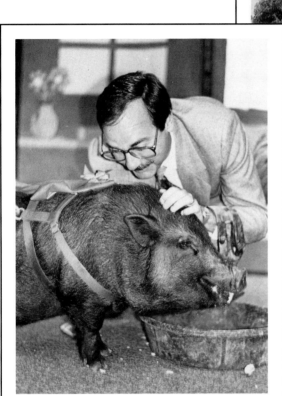

Teachers' Pet
Rocket the potbellied pig hams it up as principal Tim Harvey prepares to pucker—all part of a run-for-fun fund-raiser at Fanning School. Students brought home the bacon in 1992's pledge drive, and—as a consequence, Harvey and several teachers had to "kiss a pig."
Photo by Susan Gaede

Taming the Flame
Celebrating his 102nd birthday, Brean John LaRoche takes aim at his candles with a blow drier. Retired as a tonsorial artist, LaRoche had been barber to Al Capone.
Photo by Susan Gaede

Building Brea
Seven Eventful Decades

From innovative oil tools to missile components and parts for electric cars, products made in Brea have starred in industry for more than seventy years.

In the Forefront, Yesterday...

The 1920's and 30's:

Pioneers in an earlier era, Brea's oil-tool manufacturers of the 1920's and 30's revolutionized the petroleum industry. Early work on the rotary drill and allied inventions was done at Olinda and Brea shops including Baash-Ross and Duro (Enterprise Equipment), and the spectacular (but expensive and often dangerous) gusher became a thing of the past with the introduction of Shaffer Tool Works' patented control gate, famed internationally for well blowout prevention.

The 1940's:

Defense contracts in the 1940's saw Brea's industries fill new needs. Shaffer Tool Works crafted anchor chain, and McGraw & Sons Foundry made lift-gates for troop ships. Chiksan built ball-bearing swivel joints used widely in radar equipment and airplane landing gear, as well as in loading arms of equipment used at the nation's earliest uranium enrichment plant (Oak Ridge, Tenn.), where matter was created for the world's first atomic weapons.

The 1950's:

Diversification in industry marked Brea's post-World War II years. Famed designer Fred Thaheld teamed with Shaffer Tool Works in the building of innovative engines, soon used to power experimental aircraft and agricultural wind machines. Kirkhill brought its customized rubber manufacturing plant to town, crafting an assortment of products from bicycle pedals to

plumbing and aircraft parts. Hart Fruit and Polar Chilled Products blended and shipped millions of gallons of orange juice, Union Research patented dozens of technologies for converting crude oil to high-grade gasoline, diesel and jet fuel, and Collier Carbon and Chemical became a west coast leader in the production of petroleum byproduct fertilizers.

The industrial expansion of the 1950's brought a string of new businesses to town. Early-comers Amercoat (now Ameron), and Tretolite (both producers of industrial chemicals) were joined in the community's new west-side industrial sector by the relocated Chiksan (merged in 1955 with FMC, Food Machinery Corporation). Chiksan in these years became the world's largest manufacturer of oil-field loading systems, its swivel joints used internationally in the transfer of petroleum liquids to field tanks, railroad cars, trucks, barges and tankers.

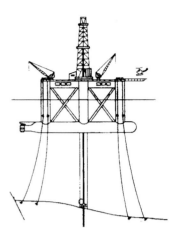

The 1960's:

The scientific advancements of the 1960's saw Brea products put to use both under the sea and in the skies. Beckman Instruments' Mark III atmosphere analyzer tested the air on Triton submarines, Shaffer's advanced oil tools were used for undersea drilling, and Chiksan

patented an improved marine loading arm system. As the nation raced into space, Shaffer manufactured trap doors for the release of aerial projectiles, Chiksan built spaceflight loading arms to handle super-cold liquid fuels, and Kirkhill molded rubber products that went to the moon in the Apollo mission's launching pads and space vehicles.

Today...

The 1970's and 80's:

Industry in Brea continued its strong strides in the years ahead, at the same time the city emerged as a center for retail sales, finance, warehousing and distribution. Beckman and Peritronics designed and built medical instruments, Fender crafted guitars, Consolidated Aero Structure, Del Phi Engineering, Kapco, Macro Dyne and Sundstrand designed and manufactured aircraft and missile components and Unocal's Science Technology Division (Hartley Research Center) transformed crude oil through the use of catalytic "crackers," changing its molecular arrangement to produce petrochemicals and high-value fuels. Many of these companies continue in Brea today.

Behind the closed doors of local businesses, a host of less common objects have been produced in recent years. Kirkhill occasionally crafts Hula Hoops, and J.A.M. Plastics manufactures pocket pen holders (often known as "nerd badges," now the mainstay of a million-dollar industry). A cryogenics lab operated in Brea, and manufacturers turned out beef jerky, potpourri sachets, plaster statuary, robotic dinosaurs and altars for practitioners of the Hari Krishna faith.

And Tomorrow...

The 1990's and beyond:

Still in the front lines for technology, local builders busily craft a safer, cleaner, faster future. The 200 employees of Brea's C.C. Industries currently are at work building large structural wing components used in the new U.S. Air Force/McDonnell Douglas C-17 aircraft, while workers at the smaller local aerospace firm Lucas Western turn out electric motors destined for General Motors' eagerly awaited anti-smog Impact— the first electric car designed to be mass-produced in the United States.

By The Numbers
Brea's Top Employers, 1992

❖ Security Pacific Bank: 1,940
   (data processing)

❖ Beckman Instruments: 1,400
   (clinical instrument
   development and manufacturing)

❖ Unocal Science Technology Division
   (Hartley Research Center): 940
   (petroleum research and
   chemical manufacturing)

❖ Allstate Insurance Regional Offices: 975

❖ Kirkhill Rubber Company: 900
   (rubber components and plastic
   extrusions)

❖ Mercury Casualty: 670 insurance

❖ Albertson's, Inc.: 600
   (retail food distribution)

❖ Brea Olinda Unified School
   District: 600

❖ Brea Community Hospital: 600

❖ American Suzuki Motor Corp.: 517
   (distribution center)

❖ Travelers Insurance: 550

❖ City of Brea: 358

❖ Sundstrand: 302
   (aviation components)

All About the Mall:
Brea's Billion-Dollar "Barley Field"

❖ Built on a turn-of-the-century barley field later owned by Union Oil, Brea Mall opened in 1977 with three anchor stores and 125 specialty shops.

❖ Following an $80-million 1988 renovation, today's mall features 1,250,000 square feet of floor space, including five anchor stores and 175 specialty shops.

❖ Estimates place the total value of the mall's property, buildings and merchandise at a figure closely approaching one billion dollars.

❖ Down a nondescript white hallway through a doorway few pass through lies the heart of it all, the pulse of the mall—the offices of Pembrook Management. Guided by General Manager James Charter, the "mayor" of Brea Mall, a staff of 35 supervises the massive shopping center's cleaning and maintenance, security, and administrative tasks.

❖ An estimated 15 million people visit the mall each year, racking up estimated annual sales of $300 million. Brea Mall is second in the county in shopping center square footage, and also second in sales.

❖ Nordstrom sells more products per square foot than any other mall store. In general, "high-line" stores with expanded selections and more expensive merchandise are the mall's most successful merchandisers.

❖ The mall's anchor stores own their own buildings and pay no rent, but participate financially in the structure's mainte-nance. All other stores are leased, with rental fees based on square footage.

Hats Off to Shoppers
Set in stone, a modern-day gargoyle grins down from his perch at the Brea Mall's Nordstrom parking structure.

❖ Because of maintenance difficul-ties associated with the structure's high ceilings, all light bulbs are routinely changed twice yearly—a task accomplished over several days from the top of a cherry picker.

❖ Fifteen roof-top air-conditioning units cool the mall's cavernous spaces. The structure has no heaters, but round-the-clock lighting builds up warmth.

❖ Mall security personnel are trained in first aid and CPR, and emergency preparedness supplies are maintained at the site.

❖ Often the scene of special events, the mall has played host to the Brea Mayor's Ball and Jubilee Birthday Party, and the BOHS Alumni Association's "Another Hurrah." The scene of fund-raisers for the Fullerton Assistance League and the North Orange County Boys and Girls Club, the building has—for the past four years, also been the site of a popular "camp-in," as several hundred Brea Girls Scouts congre-gate for "Midnight on the Mall."

❖ The exercisers of Club Ped stroll the mall's broad walkways each Tuesday and Friday morning, ambling along its 1 1/2-mile (round-trip) course as maintenance crews prepare for the shopping day's start. Nearly 50 members now take part in the program, begun in 1990 and co-sponsored by the mall and St. Jude's Hospital. A Mothers Fitness and "stroller support" walking group recently began gathering at the mall on Monday mornings.

❖ The mall's Santa (who sports his very own flowing white beard) swoops in each season from Colo-rado, and spends his off-time hours ensconced at the Embassy Suites.

❖ Coins from the mall's fountains are donated to the Brea Lions' Scout Center building fund, with the most recently cleaned and counted batch tallied at $350.

Walk on By
Eulalie and Donald Russell, better known as the "BreaWalkers," kept up the local pace for 50 years, strolling each day along the city's streets. Taking time in later years to stop and collect aluminum cans, the pair recycled to help finance their grandchildren's education. Chosen as "Outstanding Citizens of the Month" by the Brea Woman's Club, the Walking Russells also won honors from the Brea Beautification Committee.
Photo by Susan Gaede

Facts at a Glance, City of Brea

❖ Incorporated: February 23, 1917 as a General Law City.

❖ Council-Manager form of government. Five-member City Council, elected at large for terms of four years; mayor selected annually by vote of the council. Council meetings are conducted on the first and third Tuesdays of each month at 7 p.m. in the Council Chambers, and televised over local cable television.

❖ Members of three commissions (Cultural Arts; Parks, Recreation and Human Services; and Planning), and five committees (Art in Public Places, Affordable Housing, Beautification/ Environmental, Historical, and Traffic) and the Brea Foundation are appointed by Council members to four-year terms.

❖ Operating budget (1992-93): $24,462,969.

❖ City employees: 358, including: **Police Department:** 106 sworn personnel, 26 civilians, 5 reserves; 16 motorcycles, 20 patrol cars and 3 K-9 units. Includes manpower supplied to Yorba Linda on a contractual basis. **Fire Department:** 46 suppression and 10 administrative personnel; four

pumpers, one paramedic/pumper, one attack pumper, one aerial ladder truck and one incident command unit.

❖ Area: 12 square miles; Sphere of Influence: additional 7.4 square miles.

❖ Population: (1993 estimate)
•Daytime 110,000 •Nightime 34,000

❖ Elevation: 375 feet.

❖ Average temperature: 76 degrees.

❖ Average noon humidity: 49 percent.

❖ Average yearly rainfall: 10.04 inches.

❖ Prevailing winds: SW-NW, Mean hourly speed 6 mph.

Caught Up in the Spirit
Seven letters say it all for Brea fan Brian Saul.

S ince Brea's earliest years, sporting competitions and athletic events have earned top scores in the city's leisure life. From the Babe Ruth-Walter Johnson baseball game in the 1920's to the Ladycat state basketball championships of today, athletics have flourished in Brea for more than 70 years.

Ease On Down
Ladycat Nicole Erickson streaks in for a win at
1993's state championship game.
Photo by Charlie Phillips

Great Moments in Sports

*U*p from the obscure years of the early 1980's when team success meant scoring 10 points and celebrating the event over ice cream, Brea Olinda High School's Varsity Ladycats have soared to basketball stardom, dominating Orange County courts for a decade and taking the CIF California State Championship in four of the past five years.

Starting with the team in 1981—a time when only Ladycat referees and scorekeepers sported uniforms and spectators were so sparce no one bothered to pull out the bleachers—Coach Mark Trakh has honed successive squads of Ladycats into hard-working, tough-playing athletes whose motto not surprisingly has become: "Play hard or go home."

Racking up a string of league titles and CIF runner-up honors in the early 1980's, the Ladycats clinched their first Division III championship in 1986, with a score of 54-50 over Foothill. Collecting a series of league and regional titles in the coming years, the team took its first shot at the CIF state championship in 1989, when the Ladycats met San Francisco's Mercy High at the Oakland Coliseum, Trouncing Mercy 70-46, the Ladycats brought home to an eager BOHS the school's first state-level

athletic championship. Taking the title three more times in the next four years, the 'Cats mowed over Hayward's Moreau in 1990 with a score of 54-46 at the Oakland Coliseum, edged out Healdsbury 47-44 in 1992 at Sacramento's Arco Arena, and again brought home top honors in 1993, with a dramatic 42-41 win over Bella Vista at Oakland.

Crediting the Ladycats' continuing success to an outstanding group of athletes willing to practice hard and put the good of the team above their own needs, Coach Trakh calls the Ladycats, "the hardest-working basketball team in California." A place in its award-winning lineup has led to later athletic opportunities for at least a dozen Brea players, all of whom have gone on to colleges and universities on full basketball scholarships.

All-Time Girls CIF State Basketball Champions:
* Brea Olinda High School: 1989, 1990, 1992, 1993

All-Time Girls CIF Basketball Players of the Year:
(Division III)
* 1987: Carrie Egan
* 1989: Aimee McDaniel
* 1990: Aimee McDaniel
* 1991: Jody Anton
* 1992: Jody Anton

When Fame Came Home to Brea:

The Walter Johnson-Babe Ruth Baseball Game

Few local residents today can recall Brea's greatest of all days in sports, for nearly seven decades have passed since the city's battle of baseball giants.

Fame came home to Brea with the return of Walter Perry Johnson. One of the most celebrated pitchers in the history of baseball, Johnson grew up east of old Brea in the oil settlement of Olinda—a town that took its sports seriously. A talented pitcher even as a boy, he was recruited as a teenager to play in Olinda's top-notch, oil-lease league, an honor rarely awarded to youngsters.

From the oil fields of Olinda to Fullerton Union High School, young Johnson polished his fast ball. Playing for Fullerton in 1905, he pitched what some regard as the greatest of all his games, striking out 27 batters in 15 innings for a victory over Santa Ana High.

Soon signed to the major leagues, Johnson starred for the Washington Senators, gaining the nickname "Big Train" for the speeding-locomotive swiftness of his pitch. Baseball great Ty Cobb gave the game one of its most memorable quotes when assessing Johnson's powerful, long-armed throw: "You can't hit," Cobb quipped, "what you can't see."

Johnson played for the Senators 18 years before the team won a league pennant and its first and only World Series against New York's Giants. Baseball lore says his fans stood up to cheer, but remained standing to weep for the man who never quit.

Returning to California following the series, Johnson brought two special things home: his league's Most Valuable Player award and a friendly rival—home-run slugger George H. "Babe" Ruth—baseball's beloved "Sultan of Swat."

Seeing a chance to match the world's greatest hitter and pitcher on a local field, Brea businessmen and Anaheim Elks joined to sponsor a benefit exhibition game. Local stars turned out for Ruth's and Johnson's teams, assisted by a major-league lineup featuring Bob Meusel (Yankee right fielder), Samuel "Wahoo Sam" Crawford (Detroit Tigers center fielder) Ken Williams (St. Louis Browns home-run hitter), and Ernie Johnson (Yankee shortstop and pinch runner).

Businesses and schools for miles around closed in honor of the epic event, held on Halloween afternoon, 1924, at the Brea Bowl, a natural amphitheater near Brea Creek south-west of today's Lambert at Brea. Every ticket was sold and extra bleachers brought in, but the crowd exceeded all hopes. A steady stream of cars stretched for miles, and attendance was estimated at from 5,000 to 15,000.

A left-handed, record-breaking hitter who normally played the outfield, Ruth gave in to promoters, and consented to pitch for his team. Johnson threw for the opposition, but failed to live up to his fame. Pitching few curves, he banked on his fast ball, but his game fell short of the mark. The long season had ended and he had come home, but many fans said he looked tired.

Time-out was called midway in the contest, when a foul tip by Ruth struck a young fan. But the day was saved (and a memory made) when Ruth gifted the boy with a quarter. Though Johnson's team lost 12-1, fans thrilled to two Ruth home runs, and a count of the cash showed a handy profit—all destined for Elks' charities.

Johnson went back to Washington and continued to shine up his stats, pitching two no-hit games, 56 consecutive scoreless innings and 414 career wins for the Senators, and racking up a record 3,497 lifetime strikeouts. Still regarded by many as the greatest fast-ball pitcher of all time, Olinda's most famous citizen was inducted in 1936 into the National Baseball Hall of Fame.

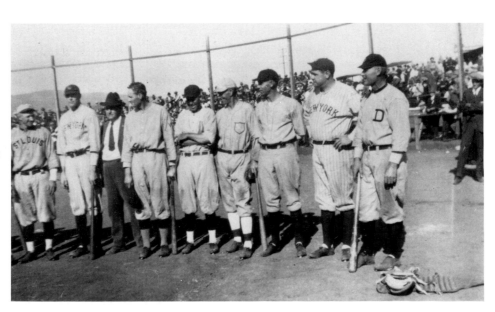

The Johnson-Ruth Big Game Lineup

Touched by Glory:
Brea's Most Famous Baseball

Housed in an unassuming brown building near the entrance to Craig Regional Park is a piece of baseball history few fans have ever seen.

Donated by park namesake Edward (Ted) Craig, a baseball here bears the signatures of game greats Walter Johnson, Babe Ruth, Sam Crawford, Bob Meusel and Ernie Johnson, players in Brea's big exhibition game of 1924.

The signature of San Diego Padre pitcher Randy Jones, BOHS graduate and Cy Young award winner, was added in the 1970's during the ball's presentation ceremony.

Brea Big Game Trivia:

❖ Three players: Johnson, Ruth and Crawford, were later named to the Baseball Hall of Fame.

❖ The Brea Bowl is now the site of Landmark Homes.

❖ The Boy Scout house where the players ate lunch later was relocated, and today is called Pioneer Hall.

❖ The Brea Boulevard at Bracken Street building where the stars changed their clothes for the game is now known as Ron and Wayne's Auto Repair.

**Walter Johnson plaque
located in Craig Regional Park**

The All-American Boy
Brea's Bill Griffith, 1939 Southern California Soap Box Derby champion.
Brea Historical Society

Brea's Soap Box Super-star:
Bill Griffith and his Spider Special

A set of four wheels and two axles, a few scraps of wood and a winning smile: an odd mix, but just the ticket for a teenage soap box star. In 1939, Brean Bill Griffith boasted a coast to victory in just such a car when he and his *Spider Special* streaked in to win at the Southern California Soap Box Derby.

The building of homemade, unpowered coasters caught on strong in the Depression's lean years, and the Griffith brothers of Brea fashioned cars to beat the best. Starting with a small investment in materials, the three Griffith boys designed, built, tested, scrapped, and built again---using the same parts over and over to hone their racers to greater speeds.

Taking to the track in the summer of 1939, 14-year-old Bill Griffith queued up for his premiere public performance, entering the *Spider* at a regional run in Los Angeles. Though many back in Brea knew his car was fast, few gave him much chance to win. With entries numbering more than a thousand, the odds, at best, seemed poor.

But Griffith and the *Spider* won. From a field of 1,128 entries, the Brea boy took top honors in the final round, earning the Southern California championship, a "heap of prizes" and a trip to the Akron, Ohio, national soap-box finals.

Many Breans learned of the exciting news by radio, and thrilled to hear a local boy be interviewed "on the air." Some felt a twinge of envy when they heard how he would travel to the east. In an era when passenger aviation was just beginning, derby-star Griffith would fly.

The local Lions Club had helped finance the *Spider*, and members rallied around their young racer. A caravan of nearly 50 cars escorted him from Brea to Burbank for the overnight flight to Ohio. Less lucky, his family had gone ahead several days earlier to make the long trip by car.

A week of festivities greeted the Griffiths at the All-American and International Soap Box Derby, where events included tours of the city, luncheons, dinners, and speeches by famous people. The boys were housed at the Mayflower Hotel, and given carte blanche for room service.

On a rainy track at the nationals, young Griffith was nosed out in his first heat, but gained satisfaction when the boy who beat him went on to become derby champ. Though he returned without national honors, Southern California welcomed Griffith home as its star, and his victory picture from the L.A. meet was used to promote racing for many years.

They Led Their Teams To Triumph:
BOHS' "Shorty" Smith and Dick Tucker

A small school with big wins in sports, Brea Olinda scored high in hiring twice in its early years, choosing coaches that led their teams to a remarkable record of athletic success.

Stewart "Shorty" Smith first came to BOHS in 1928, just two years after the school's opening. A graduate of Occidental College and a Marine veteran of World War I, he mentored teams at Santa Ana and Fullerton high schools before signing on as athletic director at the new campus to the north. During his 28-year tenure in Brea, Smith's teams amassed a remarkable tally of wins in football, basketball and baseball, bringing home dozens of trophies to shine in BOHS halls.

Highly regarded in Southern California sports circles, Smith gained the title "Mr. Every-thing" for his ability to coach effectively in many sports. In addition to numerous titles and trophies, he may also have left the school another legacy. Some say it was Smith's early claim that his gridiron stars were "fighting like wildcats" that gave BOHS students forever after this now-familiar name.

"Shorty" Smith
Gusher, 1930

In his off-time hours, Smith served as an umpire in the National Softball League, becoming known as one of this group's premiere officials in the 30's and 40's. In 1930, he started the famous Brea-Olinda (Shorty Smith) Relays, one of Southern California's largest track meets—held annually for more than four decades. Smith retired from his 28-year BOHS career in 1956, and was elected four years later to the Southern California High School Hall of Fame.

Hired to coach BOHS basketball and football in 1951, Dick Tucker quickly launched an offensive with his varsity football squad, racking up Orange League championships in eight straight seasons. Tucker was named BOHS director of athletics in 1956, the same year the school took its first CIF football runner-up honors. Varsity gridmen went to the top in 1959, winning the CIF's A-division championship in a 47-21 victory over Beaumont. Tucker's last BOHS team repeated this feat in 1961, with a 20-6 win over St. Bernard.

Dick Tucker
Gusher, 1960

During Tucker's 11 years at BOHS, varsity squads logged an impressive record of 98 wins. Breans delighted in the teams' many successes during these years. Friday became football day for many, and cheering fans filled the stands.

Tucker left BOHS in 1962 to coach football at Orange Coast College, where his impressive record of wins continued. In 23 years as Orange Coast's football mentor, he led his teams to five bowl competitions and two national championships. He continues today as Orange Coast's assistant director of athletics.

BOHS Gridiron Greats:

❖ CIF Southern division runner-ups: 1956, coach Dick Tucker
❖ CIF A-division champions: 1959 and 1961, coach Dick Tucker
❖ CIF A-division champions: 1962 and 1963, coach Glen Hastings
❖ The Oxandabourne Brothers: Ben and Frank (the 1930's)
❖ Gary Holman: (who shared 1960's CIF Southern Section Football Player of the Year award with Mater Dei's John Huarte, later Notre Dame star and Heisman Trophy winner). Arguably BOHS' best all-around athlete, Holman later played baseball for the Washington Senators.
❖ The Ledbetter Family: A local football dynasty that began with Olinda's Otho and Theo (who played under Shorty Smith at Fullerton High before BOHS opened), Talbert (BOHS 1928 team captain), Leo, Charles, Paul, Roy and Rodney; the second generation: Mike, Kit, Rodney, Adrian (CIF 1956 Player of the Year) and Steve (CIF 1961 Player of the Year); and the third generation: Chad, a recent BOHS varsity star.

The Ledbetter Brothers, BOHS Gridiron Greats
Standing (left to right) Tal, Leo, Charles, Paul, Roy and Rodney; and seated Fullerton High stars Otho (left) and Theo (right) flank their mother, Lavonie (Drake) Ledbetter, and father, Guy Ledbetter, who served 23 years as a Brea-Olinda Union High School District Trustee.
From the Ledbetter Family collection

A League of Their Own:
The Many Faces of Brea Baseball

Always baseball towns, Brea (and it precursor, Olinda) have played home to an impressive array of professional pitchers, catchers, fielders and batsmen.

In old Olinda, baseball skill brought built-in benefits. Hired on for oil company jobs because of their game-playing prowess, many oil club members were assigned jobs as "weed whackers" and "poppy pruners." Issued a hoe, rake and shovel and told to abate fire hazards, they were also equipped with bats, balls, mitts and a "tasty lunch box," and instructed to practice when the urge overtook them.

From this fertile field came not only baseball great Walter Johnson, but a handful of other pro players including Jack Burnett of the St. Louis Browns and Willard Hershberger of the Washington Senators. Though later (but still several decades past), Brea added to this roster Jack Salveson, a pitcher for the New York Giants and Hollywood Stars.

And...more recent baseball Breans:

❖ **Charlie Hough:** Drafted by the Dodgers' organization in 1966, Hough was named Pacific Coast League Pitcher of the Year in 1972. He later signed with the Chicago White Sox, and shares a major league record for most strikeouts in one inning (four). He currently resides in Brea.

❖ **Tommy John:** A left-handed pitcher, John played for the Dodgers from 1972-1978, gaining the nickname "Mr. Clutch." He resided in Brea during this period, and later signed on with the Cincinnati White Sox.

❖ **Randy Jones:** Winner of the prestigious Cy Young Award in 1976, San Diego Padre pitcher Randy Jones got his start on the BOHS diamond, where his fast ball brought fans to their feet. Later famed for his frustrating "sinker and slider" pitch, Jones spent 10 years in professional baseball, first with the Padres and later the New York Mets. A popular player known for his good humor, he was inducted in 1985 into the Orange

Local Talent
Cy Young Award-winning Pitcher Randy Jones.
From the Jones Family collection

County Hall of Fame. Jones' family resides in Brea.

❖ **Darrell Miller:** A current Brea resident, Miller played for the California Angels as a catcher and outfielder between 1984 and 1988. The brother of basketball stars Cheryl and Reggie Miller and CSUF volleyball player Tammy Miller, Darrell Miller currently serves as director of community relations for the Angels.

❖ **Claude Osteen:** An 18-year major-league veteran, Osteen played for the Cincinnati Reds, Washington Senators, Houston Astros, Chicago White Sox and L.A. Dodgers during his baseball career. He pitched twice in the World Series with the Dodgers, and helped lead Los Angeles to the title in 1965 over Minnesota's

Twins. Osteen lived in Brea in the late 1960's and early 1970's, and his sons (David, Brian and Erick) attended Mariposa School.

❖ **Bill Russell:** A longtime member of the Dodgers organization, Bill Russell played shortstop for Los Angeles from 1969-1986 and lived in Brea during the 1970's. He currently manages the Albuquerque Dukes.

❖ **Ted Sizemore:** Named Dodger Rookie of the Year in 1969, second-baseman Ted Sizemore played for the St. Louis Cardinals, Philadelphia Phillies, Chicago Cubs and Boston Red Sox during his 12 year-career. He resided in Brea in the 1970's, and his children (Tony and Nicki) attended Mariposa School.

And...Up-and-Coming Stars: (Recent BOHS graduates currently in the Minor Leagues):

❖ **Mike Bradish**—Chicago White Sox

❖ **Todd Eggertsen**—California Angels

❖ **David Leiper**—Oakland Athletics

❖ **Tim Leiper**—Detroit Tigers and Memphis Royals

❖ **Mike Vanderburg**—Baltimore Orioles

Local Star
Former Brea resident and Dodger pitcher Tommy John poses with his wife and son.

He Reached for New Heights:
Olympic High Jumper Doug Nordquist

Two-time holder of the national high jump championship with an all-time record of 7'8 3/4", Brean Doug Nordquist ranked third in the world for this sport in 1986.

Mentored by his third cousin, high-jump champion Dwight Stone, Nordquist entered the 1984 Olympic trials as an unknown, yet emerged as second-place high-jump qualifier. Brea honored its hometown competitor that summer as the Olympic torch passed through town, presenting Nordquist with a plaque and a painting on the steps of city hall.

Though he placed a disappointing fifth in that year's Los Angeles Olympics, Nordquist reached new heights two years later in Moscow, taking a gold medal in the 1986 Olympic Festival Goodwill Games. Olympic Festival silver medals followed in 1987 and 1990, and a bronze came home in 1988.

A graduate of Sonora High School, Fullerton College and Washington State University, Nordquist today resides in La Habra and is employed as a teacher at Santa Fe High.

Flying High
An enthusiastic Doug Nordquist learns he's made a personal best, while Cal State Fullerton Coach Jim Kiefer looks on.
Photo by Jayne Kamin, Los Angeles Times

Kathy Mollica

American Gladiator Grand Champion:
Brea Firefighter Kathy Mollica

The competition had Brea firefighter Kathy Mollica climbing the walls—not to mention hanging from a bungee cord, running an obstacle course and sinking soccer balls in tiny baskets—all while skillfully dodging the knocks of an aggressive opposition.

But, from a field of 10,000 national contenders and 24 final contestants, Mollica sizzled in for the win—emerging as 1991-92 female grand champion on television's *American Gladiators*.

Nicknamed "Flame" during her performance at the program's Los Angeles studio, Mollica first decided to try out for the challenge at the urging of a fellow firefighter. Advancing through a series of competitions, she took top ranking in the *Gladiators'* final round, turning up the heat for Swing Shot, Power Ball and The Eliminator with a mixture of strength, speed, agility and quick thinking.

No stranger to competition, Mollica was picked for her local firefighting post from a field of 300 applicants, and signed on as the city's first woman firefighter in 1990.

Though some assume a woman who battles blazes is only out to prove a point, Mollica insists she's not just playing with fire. Her next career goal is to become a paramedic, followed—she hopes—by a climb up the department ladder, first to engineer, then battalion chief—and, someday, maybe even chief.

As the nation's top woman Gladiator, Mollica walked off with $33,000 in winnings, and took an all-expense paid trip to a Club Med resort. Returning to her Brea post, she came in for some good natured kidding—and a warm welcome by local fans.

On Track:
Record-Breaking Breans

Paul Moore
Gusher, 1935

Breaking the world record by running the 3/4-mile in under three minutes, Brean Paul Moore logged a time of 2.58.7 at Stanford University in 1940, eclipsing by nearly two seconds a record set eight years earlier by Frenchman Jules Ladoumegues.

Coached by BOHS's famed Stewart "Shorty" Smith, Moore apparently stumbled onto his running ability by accident. According to an often-told story, the future track star was playing tennis during his senior year at BOHS, when he took time out to ask if he could get his sweatshirt.

Directed by his teacher to Coach Smith, he was mistaken for another student, and sent off to run in a race. A series of wins followed, capped by more fame for Brea.

Moore's parents, Mr. and Mrs. T. Elwood Moore, were among the city's pioneers, arriving at the townsite in 1911.

And...Stars of Many Sports:
BOHS Southern Section CIF Champions

Track and Field

❖ **Brent Jones:** 1988, 800-meter run, time 1:55:70

❖ **Paul Johnson:** 1976, shot put, mark 60-2 1/4

❖ **Shawn Sinclair:** 1984, 3.0 mile-cross country, time 15:58

Wrestling

❖ **Mike Greenleaf:** 1981 champion, 200-pound division

❖ **Kevin Partelow:** 1983 champion, 105-pound division

Gymnastics

❖ **Karen McDuff:** 1982 champion, side horse vault

Golf

❖ **Kevin Clabord:** 1989 runner-up

Soccer

❖ 1986's Varsity Squad: 2-A division Co-champs, (Coach Manny Toledo)

❖ 1987's Varsity Squad: 2-A division runners-up

❖ **Mike Knaus:** All-Time Boys Soccer Player of the Year: 1986, 2-A division

He Set His Sights on the Gold:
Olympic Marksman Vic Auer

The winner of two Olympic silver medals for marksmanship, Vic Auer broke 30 world records even before graduating from Brea-Olinda High School. Trained by his father, popular BOHS music teacher and Brea Rifle Club founder Leland Auer, the young .22-calibre rifle expert took home hundreds of trophies in the 1950's and 1960's, and three times brought the National Collegiate Title to UCLA.

Auer continued his education at Exeter and Oxford before joining the Air Force, and won both the national and world championships in 1961 and 1962. He took his first Olympic silver medal at Munich in 1972, followed by a silver at Montreal in 1976. Auer won the gold medal at the 1971 Pan American Games in Colombia, and repeated the feat at Switzerland's World Games in 1974.

Turning to coaching, Auer took part in several goodwill tours through the U.S. Department of State, and gained recognition from both the White House and Mayor Tom Bradley for his help with the U.S. Olympic Spirit Team in Los Angeles' 1984 Olympics.

Vic Auer
From the Dean Millen collection

Ice Dancing in France
The skating duo of Kim Krohn and Barry Hagan launch into a routine at their first international competition.
From the Krohn Family collection

Magic Moments on Ice:
The Dance Skating Duo of Krohn/Hagan

One half of one of the United States' best late-1970's ice dancing teams hailed from the sunny city of Brea, as Sonora High graduate Kim Krohn made her mark on the ice.

The ice dancing duo of Krohn and partner Barry Hagan earned honors as Pacific Coast Champions in 1978, a title they held for four consecutive years. Qualifying fourth in this new event at 1980's Olympic trials, Krohn and Hagan went on to win a bronze medal in the 1981 National Championships. The team was hard at work preparing for the 1984 Olympics when Hagan was struck by a car driven by an irate accused shoplifter and thrown through a plate-glass window.

Following Hagan's recoupration, both partners continued to skate. Krohn worked professionally, touring Canada, Japan and Europe, and later "retired" to teach at her old practice rink in Paramount.

BOHS' Championship Swim Teams:
A Winning Way in the Water

Winners of the Orange League Championship for 11 consecutive years (1982-92), the BOHS Girls' Varsity Swim Team stroked to CIF victory five times in the seven years between 1986 and 1992 under the leadership of coach Phyllis Curry, taking Southern Section 2-A division championships in 1986, 1987 and 1988, and 3-A division championships in 1991 and 1992.

Bringing home an impressive share of honors, the BOHS Boys' Varsity Swim Team under coaches Dennis Nelson, Bob Linn, Nancy Windisch and Rod Forsch captured the Orange League Championship eight times in the past decade (1982, 1986-88 and 1990-92). Runners-up in the CIF Southern Section 2-A division in 1987, they returned in 1988 to take the CIF championship over Woodbridge.

The combined BOHS boys' and girls' wins in 1988 marked the first time in CIF Southern Section 2-A swimming history that both division championships had been won by a single school.

BOHS CIF Swimming Champions:
Girls
❖ 200-yd. Freestyle: Denise Weber, 1986,'87,'88
❖ 400-yd. Freestyle Relay: Muriel Bruno, Tammy Flores, Jennifer Niblick, Denise Weber, 1987
❖ 100-yd. Freestyle: Denise Weber, 1988
❖ 200-yd. Individual Medley: Jennifer Kracik ,1988
❖ 400-yd. Freestyle Relay: Erica Dunn, Jennifer Kracik, Robin Palmero, Denise Weber, 1988
❖ 100-yd. Breast Stroke: Debbie Weber, 1991
❖ 100-yd. Butterfly: Erica Dunn 1991, Sachiko White, 1992

❖ 400-yd. Freestyle Relay: Erica Dunn, Amy Clark, Debbie Weber, Sachiko White, 1991
❖ 200-yd. Medley Relay: Tracy Palmero, Debbie Weber, Sachiko White, Erica Dunn, 1991
❖ 400-yd. Freestyle Relay: Amy Clark, Tracy Palmero, Debbie Weber, Sachiko White, 1992

Boys
❖ 100-yd. Breast Stroke: Marc Beck 1986,'87
❖ 200-yd. Individual Medley: Scott DeBoer, 1988
❖ 100-yd. Breast Stroke: Scott DeBoer, 1988
❖ 400-yd. Freestyle Relay: Jeff Anton, Jeremy Hough, Scott DeBoer, Erin Dunn, 1988

The Team to Beat
BOHS's 1987 girls swim squad: (left to right, front) Tammy Flores, Monica Fay, Monika Schoeffler and Robin Palmero
(back) Jennifer Niblick, Mary Byrno, Sue Schwengel, Keri Brown, Denise Weber, Muriel Bruno and coach Phyllis Curry.
From the Phyllis Curry collection

Catch a Wave
Celebrating their CIF success, the 1988 boys' team poses for a snapshot. Left to right, back: Jeremy Hough, Jason Oxley, Ray Schwengel, Coach Jim Armstrong and Jeff Anton; front: Scott DeBoer, Coach Bob Linn and Erin Dunn.
From the Anton Family collection

They Came to Pass:
Harlem's Globetrotters Take on Brea

Though many said Brea would net no results, the mayor still took his best shot—and it was standing room only at the Wildcat court when Harlem's famed hoopsters came out to tip off.

More than two years of local plotting and planning paid off big in September of 1991, as the world-renowned Harlem Globetrotters, "Clown Princes of Basketball," dropped in on Brea for a rare charity exhibition game.

Taking to the court against the Boston Shamrocks, the Globetrotters played out their full repertoire of tried-and-true tricks: the lady's purse and the ball on a rope, the referee soaked by a bucket of water and the audience awash in confetti.

To the strains of "Sweet Georgia Brown," the red, white and blue-bedecked 'Trotters trounced Boston, bringing the crowd of 1,800 to its feet and racking up nearly $13,000 in proceeds for local youth organizations.

The climax to more than two years of negotiations between then-Mayor Wayne Wedin, former City Councilman John Leyton and Globetrotters' owners, the game boosted hopes for both Brea's Boys and Girls Club members and local Boy Scouts and Girl Scouts, with earnings shared equally by both groups and earmarked for ongoing building projects.

The Brea Foundation and the City of Brea present
The Harlem Globetrotters
Charity Exhibition Game
vs. The Boston Shamrocks
**Sept. 6, 1991, 8:00 p.m.
Brea Olinda High School Gym**
All proceeds benefit Brea Lions Scout Center Foundation and the Brea Boys and Girls Club

Connie Jaster James

She Rallied Her Way to Wimbledon:
Tennis Star Connie Jaster James

Brean Connie Jaster James took her first tennis strokes at the age of 12, and went on to reign as queen of the local courts by the late-1950's. The daughter of longtime Brea School District superintendent Vincent Jaster, the young tennis talent was coached by Dick Skeen, who helped guide her early career.

Taking early honors as Orange County Junior Girls Singles Champion (two years running), Jaster went on to broaden her success in the Pacific Northwest Tournament, earning three trophies in the junior women's finals and taking top doubles honors with partner Sukie Mandel.

After completing Fullerton (Junior) College, Jaster transferred to California State College (now University), Los Angeles, playing on a top-notch five-woman team including nationally ranked players Carol Loop and Billie Jean Moffitt (King).

Following a successful 1963 tour on the national circuit, Jaster earner "Player of the Year" honors at Forest Hills, and (with the backing of a hometown booster club) headed for the game's most famous courts at Wimbledon, England. Jaster and doubles partner Nolene Turner reached the quarter finals in this world-class competition.

Competing in Greensboro, North Carolina, Jaster and partner Carol Loop went on to take the National Collegiate Women's Doubles title in 1964. Nationally ranked (19th in singles, 6th in doubles), Jaster continued to tour the U.S. and Canada in coming years, and was named to the 1966 edition of *Who's Who in American Colleges and Universities*.

Later named head coach of the men's tennis team at Iowa's Drake University, Jaster became the first woman to fill this position. She went on to advance the cause of women's tennis in 1975, beating the infamous Bobby Riggs in one of the game's first "battle of the sexes."

Great Moments in Sports Patrons

*T*hese local firms and fans have generously sponsored the inclusion of this "Great Moments" chapter.

Brea Cañon Oil

Brea Civic Light Opera

Brea Trophy and Engraving

Burch Ford

Classic Telecommunications

The Viva Alexander Trust

J. Henri Cleaners

Karen Hawe

Brea's Youth Reach Back to Look Ahead
Winning essayist Mario Calderon (left) receives congratulations from Jane Shellhouse,
sponsor of the $100 cash prize for the top student writing award.

By Mario Calderon

It has been well said that a man without a history is a man without a future. As a teenager raised in the Eighties, I can assure you that a good, pragmatic 80's-man would consider this flippant nonsense. However, as an Hispanic, I've seen too many boys with no sense of their heritage lose themselves in today, in the now, and forget about tomorrow. From personal experience, I can tell you the Eighties attitude is wrong. A man can have no destination if he has no origin.

This basic precept of life holds true for communities of men, as well as for individuals. A city government cannot do the job for which it was created, that of caring for its people, unless it understands those people. And it can never hope to understand its constituents now without knowing what they were before. In the same way, those very same people can never make realistic, long-term plans without knowing the lessons history has recorded. And that, my friends, is why Brea must, under any circumstances, remember, preserve, and examine her past. For without it, Brea's "vision of the future" will hold nothing for her but aimless wandering.

You see, God has, in our history, given the entire world lessons, but Brea is unique in that it has the history of a nation encapsulated within 75 years. From pre-industrial farming, to an industrial oil-boomtown, to a fast-growing metropolitan center for service, Brea has paralleled the entire USA from its conception. We must not waste this advantage! Let us learn from when industry was under-regulated, from when it was over-regulated, from the empty lots on Brea Boulevard, from the huge success of the Brea Mall, from our entire history! We are at a cross-roads, so let's not repeat our mistakes; let's capitalize on our successes! Let's take "the [road] less traveled by, and that [will make] all the difference."

This is the challenge that the human race has faced for all recorded time. And this is the test we have always failed. But maybe, just possibly, if a few of us can find the courage to live up to the ideal, others might follow. So, if you want a bit more experience, a bit more wisdom to make better decisions, then stop a minute, and think back. Think back to our grandparents' time; to the lives of those who died choosing the wrong road. That's where you will always find the answer.

Brea's Youth Look Back

*D*uring the Jubilee celebration, Brea Olinda High School students were invited to submit essays entitled **"Why Brea's Vision for the Future Must Include Preserving Her Past."** The essay contest offered a $100 cash prize to the top entrant, and an opportunity for some illuminating work to be published in this book. Judging was coordinated by local historian and Brea Historical Society past president Inez Fanning, who enlisted Mae Burt and Susan Gaede to read the essays for relevance to the theme. Sponsored by Jane Shellhouse, owner of DNS Weight Loss Center in Brea, the cash prize was awarded to Mario Calderon, a student of BOHS English teacher Rachel Sweet. Mario's essay, and those of the six other finalists, are included here. The effort and value of historical documentation through a book like this was supported from the beginning by school officials. In the words of Dr. Edgar Z. Seal, Superintendent, "this publication will be an outstanding piece of historical literature which will be extremely beneficial to the students, parents and staff of the Brea Olinda Unified School District." Involving high school students in this essay contest was also supported by Dr. Seal. He commended the Brea Historical Society, the high school teachers who encouraged participation, and the students who took time to research Brea's history and offer their insights.

By Michelle Chabot

There once was an acorn that, like all acorns, slowly began its transition into a mighty oak tree. But this acorn was different. Before it became a mighty oak but after it was out of its fragile stage, this young tree showed incredible potential. It was clear that one day this tree would become one of the strongest oaks around, that it would have the most stability, identity, and pride of any tree ever. And what made this

Contest Winners
At the June, 1992, general meeting of the Brea Historical Society, several Brea Olinda High School students were recognized for their outstanding achievement as finalists in the Society's youth essay contest. From the left, top prize winner Mario Calderon, prize sponsor Jane Shellhouse, BOHS English teacher Rachel Sweet, and finalists Michelle Chabot, James Lee, Linda Niwa, Ryann Shyffer and Hannah Tan.

particular tree so special? Its roots. Its history gives it the strength it needs to move into the future; as it grows, its roots grow also. Brea is that tree. We have a fabulous vision for our future, but if we are ever going to achieve all that we hope to achieve, we must never forget our glorious past.

When one thinks of Brea, one phrase comes to mind: community, identity, stability. Brea is a very tightly knit community with a lot of spirit, togetherness, and ambition. However, if Brea moves into her future forgetting her past and never looking back, those qualities which are so characteristic of Brea would be lost forever. History is essential to every form of society. If Brea forgets her history, she is forgetting her identity. The spirit of community, the feeling of togetherness, the sense of identity... without these we would have lost everything. All of our industrial and business success would mean nothing it we forgot our roots.

But we must do more than merely remember; we must cherish our roots. We must teach the future generations Brea's history, We must let our roots grow as we grow, for, like the oak tree, our roots will be what carries us into prosperity. Each day is a new page in Brea's history, a history that, the more it grows, will lead us into our future.

The dirt roads, the old high school, the orange groves...all of it is what has led us to where we are today. Yes, we must move into the twenty-first century, but we must never, ever, lose sight of our roots, For without our roots we will never grow into the mighty oak tree that we desire to become. Our roots give us the stability we need in order to survive the future, the feeling of community we need in order to remain optimistic, and the sense of identity we need in order to never lose sight of reality.

So the tiny acorn of Brea, over seventy-five years old, has grown into a strong tree with the potential to become the mightiest oak around. And the only thing that will lead us into prosperity, the only thing that will make our dreams come true, is our history, our roots.

By James Lee

"History is who we are and why we are the way we are." This timeless statement by David McCullough is the best reason for remembering one's history. Preservation of Brea's history is vital in maintaining communal unity and measuring Brea's progress.

Residents of Brea share a bond not unlike those of other communities. Breans enroll their children in the same schools, shop at the same stores, go to the same movie theaters, encourage their children in the same sports programs, dine at the same restaurants, fill up at the same gas stations, drive on the same roads, etc., yet it would all mean nothing if Brea did not have its own identity. Of what importance is it to say, "I am from Brea," if it is not different from any other city in this nation? Though a city's personality is determined by its present residents, its identity is created by those of yesteryear. Brea's history is what makes Brea unique, for it is the only thing, other than the people, that cannot be duplicated. Failure to preserve Brea's past would mean the loss of its identity, the common heritage and environment that are paramount in maintaining communal unity.

History is the marker by which progress is measured. Without a reference point, how can one claim to have progressed? At Brea's centennial, the question will surely be asked, "How far has Brea come?" If Brea fails to preserve its past, that question cannot be answered. Changes occur with the passing of each generation. But how will the new generation know what these changes are and that it lives in a city much different than the one the older generation lived in if the past is forgotten? It is a natural instinct for a grandparent to tell the grandchildren "what it was like to live way back when." It is this that Brea must seek to preserve, a kind of family history that will satisfy the curiosity of future generations. The founders of Brea deserve to have their legacy preserved if for no other reason than

to assure the present generation that what it does today will in time be remembered.

In the end, Brea's vision for the future must include preserving its past because "history is who we are and why we are the way we are."

By Ryan Shyffer

The past is the key to the future. Without preserving the rich and colorful history of Brea as she moves towards the twenty-first century, we run the risk of forgetting what made the city what it is today.

Brea is quickly becoming a very modern city. Everywhere you look, new and exciting buildings are popping-up. Such structures keep Brea on the leading edge of Orange County and California. Some of the world's leading corporations have been inspired by such structures and have placed branches of their companies here in Brea.

If you look beyond those buildings you will discover many smaller shops and houses that aren't as new: in fact, some of them have survived for nearly three quarters of a century. Just traveling down Brea Boulevard you will find a large number of these buildings retaining their original appearance from decades ago. When I see these small shops and houses, they give me insight as to how the early settlers of Brea lived around the turn of the century.

Many of the residents and businesses in Brea proudly display pictures and relics from throughout Brea's history. One can judge just how far the city has come when he compares the old pictures of acres and acres of farmland to the now present expansion of residential and industrial communities.

Not only the buildings should remain, but also many of the ideas and attitudes should not be forgotten. Brea is a city that was built up from small farms and a few oil wells. The early Breans had to work hard to take a hilly, wild land and transform it into a fertile and prosperous valley. Such attitudes must stay intact to tackle modern day problems that may arise.

I have always thought of Brea as a city with a rich past and a prosperous future. The balance between the memory of the past and the vision of the future must be maintained to keep Brea the city that I have lived in most of my life and of which I have always been most proud.

By Linda Niwa

Brea has evolved into a city of great wealth, pride, and modernization. No longer can you hear the whistle of the trains carting off thousands of fragrant oranges or see the smoke trail billowing out of oil refineries. The bustle of cars zooming down the 57 freeway and the busy shopkeepers of the Brea Mall are now associated with the name Brea. Have we forgotten what our history means? And can we progress into the future without looking or being influenced by the past?

Little Brea emerged in the past few years as a great metropolis of economic growth, spreading her boundaries throughout North Orange County and beyond. Orange groves and oil fields no longer dominate the acreage found here, but that feeling of openness and nostalgia are still ever present. Country fairs and historic landmark tours rekindle that hometown adoration and the feeling that everyone is a neighbor.

We must carry on the preservation of our rustic ardor. Only through keeping this sentiment alive will we allow generations to come feel the warmth and pride we have instilled within our growing community.

Brea's vision into the future is of expansion, but how can we ever forget the past? Those first pioneers planted more than a couple of jobs and a bag of orange seeds; they gave a history to be proud of and a future to behold.

By Hannah Charis Tan

Brea…There is not much glamour or even splendor in such a mundane word as this. Its meaning,

"tar," makes the word seem even less prestigious. Nonetheless, Brea's citizens affectionately call it home.

For many people, Brea is not only a city where their jobs are, but it is also a city where they grew up. This town has helped them become the people they are today because it has provided them with friends, an education, and jobs, the foundations of their lives. Like those long-term citizens, the town itself has a foundation on which it bases its overall structure and personality. This foundation is its past. Brea, like the people who live in it, has characteristics unique in itself.

What would we, as humans, do without our past? If we could destroy or change our past, our personalities, mentalities, and all else that constitutes our very being would change. It would not only alter our future, but it would make our prior lives irrelevant or meaningless. Likewise, Brea's past cannot be altered without directly harming its future. We cannot make her past meaningless.

The remnants of Brea's past, some of which are her old buildings, contain a personality of its own. The many events, like Babe Ruth's exhibition game, and disasters, such as the oil fire in 1926, have beaten, weathered, and tempered her much like seasons, trials and celebrations have fashioned us. Brea's old, and somewhat charred, buildings are relics of what is left of these experiences, much like our wrinkles and scars are what remains from our own lives.

It is experiences such as these which contribute to Brea, and have evoked more sentiment to the word every time it is mentioned. It is also from Brea's past tribulations and revelry that we can learn more about how we can best plan for future endeavors.

Recognition by Sharon Dean, President of the Brea Historical Society during the Jubilee Year, for contest winner Mario Calderon.

By Donald Song

For 75 years our City of Brea has grown and prospered into the sleek, modern commercial center that we see today. Brea continues to grow, in both structure and population. But as we strive to build a better Brea, we cannot help but to look back into the city's rich past and relate it to our goals for the future.

When we envision the first people to settle Brea, we see the hard-working men, women, and children that set the foundation for this city. From these first settlers, Brea's proud heritage began and grew as time progressed. Brea's history still lives, through the old buildings, and, more importantly, through the pride and attitude of its inhabitants. This sense of unity among Breans strengthens our city's special uniqueness, in a county packed with overcrowded, colorless cities.

The only way to uphold this strong sense of unity and pride is to preserve Brea's past, its life and times, and its personality. Progress is inevitable and necessary, but we must find a way to compromise that progress with preservation. Old buildings should be restored and not destroyed. We must check the greedy forces of commercialism that desire to conquer our city. Expansion is good only to a certain point, and after that it becomes the catalyst for overpopulation and slow deterioration; we would become just another city in Orange County.

Only through the knowledge of our city's past will we and the following generations be able to hold that feeling of closeness and family in Brea.

And the past lies in its structure, whether it be the Brea Mall or the old Brea Boulevard.

We must also remember to remind the younger generations to keep the spirit of Brea alive into the future. So here's to our pride, integrity, happiness, and to another prosperous 75 years for good old Brea.

Fifty-nine Years in Brea
The Chicksan Company (later merged with FMC) made its home in Brea from 1928-1987, starting as a small builder of oil tools and growing into an internationally known manufacturer of swivel joints and loading devices.
Brea Historical Society

Partners in Progress

*O*ver the last 80 years, hundreds of families, organizations and businesses have left a legacy of historical significance or made unique contributions to the community of Brea.

*S*ome of these people, their projects, their companies and their heirs are either still with us to relate their stories, or are still making history in this community.

*T*his chapter highlights the pioneer families, civic organizations and businesses who accepted our special invitation to be profiled here.

*T*heir funding enabled us to publish this celebration of the rewards of enduring involvement in both the preservation and the progress of life in Brea.

THE SHAFFER FAMILY

W.D. and Edna (Underwood) Shaffer were committed to Brea's growth in the early years.

"My grandfather managed to run his successful tool works, and be very involved in the community at the same time," recalls Dorothy Sandman Yates of her mother, Esther's, father. "In fact, my grandfather and grandmother (the former Edna Underwood) made something of a family tradition of involvement."

Their three children—Esther Shaffer Sandman, Donald Shaffer, and Betty Shaffer Wilson — all followed in their parents' footsteps, as have their grandchildren and great-grandchildren, many of whom continue to live in the area. The city, the schools, their church, the Lions and Woman's clubs, and the Masonic Lodge all figure as top priorities on the family list.

W.D. served as mayor of Brea from 1936 to 1944. He was on the first school board when Brea-Olinda High School was formed, and his son Donald followed, serving on the city council as well.

Seventeen members of the extended family graduated from Brea-Olinda High School, and later—granddaughter Dorothy's husband, Harold Yates, taught there for 25 years.

W.D. was a staunch member of the Brea Congregational Church. In 1930 he gave the church its pipe organ, and served as organist for the next 15 years. (Much later the organ was moved to the church's new sanctuary, and restored by the Shaffer family.)

For four generations, Shaffer family members have belonged to the Brea Lions Club, and the first meeting of the Brea's Woman's Club was held in Edna Shaffer's house. Later, their daughter, Esther, held high office as Worthy Grand Matron for the statewide Order of Eastern Star.

Dorothy, who has served on the Brea Human Development Commission and chaired the Woman's Club among her many activities, remembers her grandfather with special fondness: "He was a doting grandfather, and a man who was treated with great respect by his friends and neighbors, and by grateful employees whom he kept working — even in slow times."

Shaffer Tool Works manufactured oil equipment until the early 1980's, going through several mergers until it became part of National Lead Co.

The Shaffer heritage of community service continues, however, in other oilfield-related businesses under the Shaffer name and in the family's commitment to Brea's well-being.

Two major inventions for the oilfield had their origin in Brea, thanks to one of the community's best known citizens. W.D. Shaffer—inventor, business success, family man, civic booster, and church leader—created and manufactured the now famous mechanisms. The first, the "flow bean," measured the flow of oil from the well; the second, the "Shaffer Gate," was an important blowout preventer.

W.D. manufactured his inventions in his Brea plant (at Birch and Redwood) and serviced the oil industry worldwide, after starting the Shaffer Tool Works in 1924. The building had housed the Brea Tool Works, which then became Baash-Ross Tool Works before evolving into the Shaffer Tool Works company. Growth of the business—started by the mild-mannered machinist from Springtown, New York—played an important role in Brea development.

At one time, Shaffer Tool was the largest employer in Brea —with seven additional plants in other locations.

The Shaffer children (l-r) Betty, Esther, and Don carried on the family tradition in the community.

THE CRAIG FAMILY

The landmark Craig Regional Park in Brea offers the community 127 acres of greenery for fishing, hiking, biking, playing ball, or just picnicking. Named for Edward (Ted) Craig, the park honors his years of service to Orange County and California.

"My father was well known throughout the state," explains Tom Craig, Ted's son and trustee of the family's Brea interests. "He served in the California legislature, and was Speaker of the House for several years. He was known as a man who did a lot for people, who was a friend no matter what your political party."

In 1899, Tom's grandfather, Isaac, was building wooden oil derricks in Olinda. Moving to Brea in 1912, he went on to build the Brea Hotel, the Congregational Church and the Craig Building. Isaac Craig was instrumental in Brea's incorporation and was one of the first city trustees.

Ted Craig's siblings were successful and adventuresome in their own right, pioneering in different fields. One brother, John, went to Borneo in the 1920's to drill for oil; another, Jim, was a pioneer in offshore drilling in the Gulf of Mexico and England. After retiring, he became a consultant for George Bush. Sister Sarah was superintendent of Los Angeles County libraries; sister Jane's son, Craig Hosmer, became a nine-term U.S. Congressman from Long Beach.

Ted also worked in the oilfields in Texas and Brea, when he came back from WWI service in the U.S. Army Air Corps. But with his qualities of patience and good humor, he soon found his calling as a politician. He served in the modern state's formative years when California was building its highways, aqueducts, bridges, and irrigation systems for agriculture.

Ted's wife Ruth was known as an independent person, long before that present-day quality was valued. Ruth, who could trace her family tree back to 1650 in this country, enjoyed travel and the outdoors. Often she would organize trips to the mountains for her family and other relatives, packing in with a couple of horses and mules.

"Our roads were pretty limited in those days," Tom recalls. "At that time, Imperial Highway was the main link from the ocean to the Imperial Valley. Most everything else was orange groves. And we thought Hollywood was a world away."

Still, Ted and Ruth raised their two sons — Ted, Jr., and Tom — to appreciate the world from their vantage point in Brea. Ted, Jr., didn't have a chance to see much of the world: a pilot, he was killed in World War II.

Tom did become an internationalist. First he earned a business degree from Fresno State, then became a world traveler through a global marketing career in the petroleum industry with Caltex. He lived in India and Africa with his family — wife and four children — in the 1950's and 1960's He continued his international interests through Cessna Jet Marketing, making trips to China, Korea, India and other foreign countries. Now, as a tourist, he travels to challenging and sometimes remote destinations: Russia — including Siberia, into Mongolia, and the Gobi desert.

Currently, Tom Craig keeps the family name involved in local residential and commercial building projects, working with local leaders toward a better Brea for the 21st century.

Ted Craig looking north from Fullerton Dam before the formation of Craig Park. The landmark regional park offers the community 127 acres of greenery for fishing, hiking, biking, playing ball, or just picnicking.

THE FANNING FAMILY

Karl and Inez Fanning have a wealth of family memories. They grew up in the same neighborhood, in pioneer families who helped transform the Brea community from small town to major Southern California city.

Karl is descended from one of Brea's most distinguished founding families. His father, William E. Fanning, was the Brea (Elementary) School District's Superintendent for 28 years, and his mother, the former Stella Lang, was an accomplished artist and civic leader originally from Mt. Pleasant, Iowa.

Karl followed in his father's footsteps as a teacher. A graduate of the University of California at Berkeley in microbiology, he also received a General Secondary Teaching Credential emphasizing biological and physical sciences. Karl taught for 15 years at El Dorado

Karl and Inez Fanning celebrating their 50th wedding anniversary June 28,1991.
Photograph by Turville Photography

Will Fanning, who lived to be 103 years old, was honored with an annual birthday greeting from the children of Fanning school.
Photograph by Susan Gaede.

County High School, Placerville, California. He then returned to Brea to teach at Brea Olinda High School for 21 more years.

His sister, Katherine, taught school briefly before marrying Lyndle Gheen, whose parents Ada and Glenn Gheen, were also Brea pioneers. The couple lives in Eugene, Oregon, and have four grown children and eight grandchildren.

Karl's wife, Inez Jones Fanning, came from a family who pioneered in the area's oil industry. Her father, Richard Ison Jones, left the coal mines of western Colorado with his newlywed bride Margaret to seek his fortune in the oilfields. Through hard work and self education, he built a successful 38-year career with companies that became today's Chevron Corporation.

Inez also studied education, graduating from UCLA. She taught for six

years at Brea's Laurel and Arovista schools, followed by many years of school involvement. She taught piano in private lessons, and served her community well with her music.

Karl and Inez recall that their early lives revolved around the First Christian Church of Brea, with both families serving in a variety of leadership roles .

However, it was Will Fanning who perhaps had the most diverse public career. He was one of seven children, born in Norwalk, California, in 1876 to parents who had crossed the Plains from Arkansas in a covered wagon. Studying in Los Angeles and San Diego, decorated for his service in the Spanish American War, Will introduced many "firsts" to the Brea school system. At the same time he was a leader in the Lions Club, Chamber of Commerce, Veterans' units and civil service programs. Fanning Elementary school is named in his honor.

Community involvement for Karl and Inez also has meant being active in scouting and the Brea Historical Society. Each has served as a Brea Historical Society president, for a total of ten years.

Karl, now retired, serves as docent at Rancho Santa Ana Botanic Gardens, and on the city environmental committee. He is a member of the Orange County Tree Society, and Brea's representative to the Orange County Vector Control Board. Inez has been Brea Woman's Club president several times and was selected Soroptimist Club's Woman of Distinction in 1990.

The Fanning children include: Richard and Joan Fanning of Brea, their children, Christi and Eric; William and Donna Kreps Fanning of Orange; Alan and Diane Fanning of San Jose, and their children, Laura and Jonathan; and Victor and Jean Fanning Nassereddin of Chino Hills, and their children, Amy and Megan.

THE ALEXANDER/DEAN FAMILY

After graduating from high school in 1922, Viva Marie Shoff and her mother came to Brea on a railroad pass. They visited the Pomona Avenue home of their cousins, the W. E. Hurst family, who owned one of Brea's first businesses, the Brea Boiler Works, which was right next door. Although Viva fell in love with California (especially Brea) at first sight, she returned home with her mother to Wymore, Nebraska and worked for a few years. When Forrest Hurst stopped to visit his cousins in the new automobile he had just purchased in Michigan, Viva decided to return to Brea with him. Viva became involved in the social life in Brea very quickly. Employed as a receptionist and bookkeeper for Dr. C. Glenn Curtis, she frequently assisted in emergency medical procedures.

Dayton Burnett Alexander came to Orange County from Durango, Colorado to pursue his musical career. He played the banjo and sang in his band, "Paramount Orchestra — Harmony Plus." Dayton met Viva when he walked into a Santa Ana friend's house while she was playing the piano. Not being a shy person, he immediately brought in his banjo and joined the music fest.

They were married on December 25, 1932, at a house on North Madrona in Brea. Viva's parents and brother, Roy (with wife Mildred), relocated from Nebraska. In 1934, the young couple's son, Franklin, was born at the Cottage Hospital in Fullerton. Soon, local politician Ted Craig was elected Speaker of the State Assembly and needed a secretary. With Dayton's blessing, Viva took Franklin and her parents to Sacramento for one Assembly session.

When she returned to Brea, she and Dayton moved to Santa Ana for a few years, where their daughter, Sharon, was born in 1939. Soon, Dayton was ready to trade in his food sales experience for a grocery store of his own, and in 1944 bought an existing business called The Central Market. A few months later, they bought the old furniture store at 145 S. Pomona Avenue, and moved the market to that location.

Naming it Alexander's Super Market, "Date" and "Vi" developed a successful business. They worked long hours seven days a week to create a warm community feeling where people came to visit as much as to shop. Special services for their regular customers included carrying credit accounts and delivering groceries as far away as the Bartholomae Diamond Bar Ranch. The Lions Club Breakfast was held in the Birch Street parking lot next to the market.

Supplementing dry goods and local produce during WWII, eggs were sold from home-raised chickens and "Grandpa Shoff" became famous for his smoke-cooked German sausage. "Grandma's" freshly-made potato salad was also for sale at the market.

One of Brea's first Christmas tree lots was also on this corner. Dayton went into Los Angeles, ordered a truck load of trees, put 12-year-old Franklin in charge of the lot, and sold every tree. In later years, Dayton added tame reindeer in a fenced yard to delight the children.

The Alexander family was active in community clubs, and also bought a house at 217 N. Pomona Avenue. Their family records comment on the "kind, generous, friendly people of Brea," which was home to Viva until her death in 1990. Dayton passed away in 1965, only a month after the store burned down.

Then Viva, Franklin and Sharon built "Der Wienerschnitzel" on the corner of Birch and Brea. Today, Franklin lives in Anaheim and is a Food Service Specialist with S.E. Rykoff, and his family includes three children and five grandchildren. Sharon married her Brea-Olinda High School classmate, Larry Dean, and they have four sons and one granddaughter. Sharon and Larry still reside in Brea and are involved in many civic and cultural activities.

The family is currently negotiating with the Brea Redevelopment Agency to relocate the Wienerschnitzel to the Southeast corner of Orange and Lambert. After nearly 50 years of watching Brea grow and change with people and businesses coming and going, the Alexander/Dean Family will continue to own a food related business in Brea.

Dayton and Viva Alexander on their honeymoon, 1931.

THE WEST FAMILY

Madelyn West fishing at Mahogony Flats, the Wests' favorite vacation spot.

Leo West was already a third-generation Orange County resident when he moved his young family to Brea in 1938 to work for the Union Oil Citrus Department on land leased from Union Oil. Leo had married the former Madelyn Gardner (whose family also had deep roots in Southern California) in 1929, and they had three sons: Alan, Roger and Gary.

In 1941, Leo became the managing partner of "Valley View Ranch," a 300-acre lemon grove in east Brea — the largest lemon orchard in Southern California. For the next 27 years, from Lambert Road on the north, to Birch Street on the south, from the railroad tracks on the west to Valencia Street on the east, Leo would nurture these citrus groves through every available means. At times this meant being a farmer, a councilman, a family of WWII plane spotters, the mayor, an ambassador, an abatement district official, a Rotarian — and, significantly, a shareholder in the California Domestic Water Company (on behalf of the City of Brea).

Water was always a primary consideration for Leo, for all citrus growers in Southern California, and for all the citizens who had a stake in this young city. Toward the search of

a consistent source of pure water to irrigate the orchard, Leo began his civic leadership journey in 1947 by accepting an appointment to Brea's Planning Commission. After being elected to several terms on the City Council, he became Mayor. To wield more clout for Brea's water interests, he also accepted an appointment to the Orange County Mosquito Abatement District, and was then elected Chairman of the California State Board of Trustees for Vector Control.

For the next decade, Leo West also served on the Orange County Grand Jury, and as a Deputy for the Federal Petite Grand Jury. Back on home turf, Leo and his son Alan were charter members of the Brea Rotary Club in 1957. Leo served them as President in 1962. He was also a guiding force in linking Lagos de Moreno with Brea in a Sister City Program; he helped attract the Kirkhill Rubber Company to Brea; and assisted

Fiftieth wedding anniversary portrait of Madelyn and Leo West, 1979

in the annexation of the Carbon Canyon area to Brea.

In the meantime, Madelyn West kept busy with her own volunteer agenda, fostering education, medical and political interests through a full roster of other Brea organizations. Madelyn served on the Brea Elementary School Board, presided over the Brea Woman's Club, was the charter advisor of the Brea Junior Woman's Club, and was a district representative of Federated Women's Clubs, campaigning in the election of President Dwight Eisenhower.

Madelyn also served many years as a volunteer for the Long Beach Veterans' Hospital. She was a 50-year member of the Brea Congregational Church, having served on many of the church's boards, and on the building committee.

Their Brea community spirit also took hold with their son, Alan, who, by the late 50's, was also active in civic affairs, influencing housing and water interests. Two weeks prior to a dedication ceremony for Brea's 31-million-gallon water reservoir near Berry and Lambert, Alan enlisted the help of Brea engineer Sam Peterson, and they filled 24 one-cup bottles, dipped from the first water to come into the reservoir. Alan's wife Joan typed labels for the bottles, dated October, 1976, which were shared with the dignitaries on hand that Halloween Eve.

In 1978, Alan coordinated the development of an affordable senior housing project called BREAL (Brea's Retirement Effort for Abundant Living). A triumph of volunteerism, BREAL engaged the efforts of Rotary, the Brea Ministerial Association, and the City of Brea to lead more than 700 residents through 30,000 hours to complete the 30-unit complex located at the northwest corner of Orange and Ash. The project won a Disneyland Community Service Award.

BREA HISTORICAL SOCIETY

"The past belongs to the future, but only the present can preserve it." This is the primary purpose of the Brea Historical Society, whose office and museum are at 401 South Brea Boulevard in Old City Hall.

As a non-profit organization established in 1971, the Society promotes a multitude of activities to further that preservation. Its first objective is to collect and preserve historical material relating to the City of Brea. Together, the Society's membership of more than 250 provides a greater understanding of former customs, episodes, and personalities that made the Brea of today.

By showing their support and demonstrating interest in recording Brea's past, these members provide a base that makes this forward-focused group an even more viable part of Brea's future. Through major membership and fund-raising drives, special events, active participation by local industries and businesses, and increased publicity, the Historical Society is growing in scope and influence.

One hands-on task for the Society: It operates a museum to help carry on the city's heritage by illustrating life in Brea at different periods. The Society also publishes materials, including a newsletter for members, and conducts educational programs to further the Society's goals.

One of the group's most popular recent activities was its series of downtown walking tours. The series featured architecturally unique samplings around the city in commercial and residential structures, and garnered great community pride among participants.

To date, the museum holds more than 600 historical photographs, important documents, and artifacts. Indeed, Brea residents are encouraged to make ongoing donations of articles that may have an impact on local history: diaries, manuscripts,

Brea Historical Society Museum
Long a landmark on Brea Boulevard, Old City Hall now serves as the home of the Brea Historical Society. The museum holds more than 600 historical photographs, important documents and artifacts.

scrapbooks, maps, correspondence, mementos, and more. Here, the collection is permanent and housed carefully to preserve the past for scholars and researchers interested in doing major studies on local history.

On the south side of the Old City Hall, there is a permanent exhibit— the Heritage in Oil display, which has been arranged by the Society. It is open by appointment for viewing, and is especially popular with school children.

The Society is run by a board with 11 directors who meet monthly, and is augmented with general society meetings every other month. Activities are supported by memberships for individuals, families, and businesses, as well as donations.

As the city of Brea continues its redevelopment and commercial updating in the 1990's, the Society's photo documentation and collection of area memorabilia have grown increasingly important among residents interested in creating a more promising future by understanding their past.

JUBILEE COMMITTEE

Brea's year-long 75th Birthday was a reflection of the community's pride in its heritage and its promise for the future.

To commemorate this significant anniversary, the City Council appointed a core Jubilee Steering Committee comprised of six residents. The committee set a number of major goals for the Jubliee year: To include all members of the community in various events; to foster goodwill, partnership, and involvement within the community; and to recognize Brea's proud history, exciting present, and challenging future.

With the Jubilee Steering Committee at the helm, the first formal birthday activity launched in September 1991 was a community-wide photo contest that resulted in a Jubilee calendar and a Gallery exhibit, "Brea...Then and Now." Both the calendar and the exhibit featured photographs submitted for the contest and allowed all to view and enjoy Brea's past and Brea's present through the eyes of the community. A Decem-

ber, 1992 Time Capsule and Jubilee Grove Dedication concluded the year of celebration. In between these events, scores of Brea residents and visitors alike enjoyed a variety of activities, met new people and shared common experiences.

Brea's 75th birthday party was held at the Brea Mall on February 22, with festivities lasting till midnight. The next day, the time capsule, sealed in 1967 during Brea's Golden Jubilee, was opened at City Hall Park. It revealed a number of objects, papers, and news articles.

"Living History" bus tours were offered throughout the year, giving people an opportunity to look into Brea's past. Through dramatic reenactment, Breans relived some of the early days of old Olinda and Brea, including the disastrous oil fire of 1926. The Historical Home Tour was popular as well, providing a peek into Brea's architectural past.

In commemoration of the 75th Jubilee, the City released an historic video entitled, "Brea — a Walk in Time." The video features segments of the old downtown and other historic points. Other Jubilee memorabilia included calendars, watches, visors, T-shirts, sweatshirts and Jubilee lapel pins.

Special among the events was the Diamond Jubilee Parade and Community Picnic. The parade featured the Brea Olinda High School marching band, floats, drill teams, equestrian units, local organizations, fire engine companies, and antique automobiles. The Community Picnic which followed the parade at City Hall Park offered pony and train rides, live music, and food booths operated by youth groups. Free swimming at the Brea Plunge was also enjoyed.

Hundreds of volunteers serving on committees and subcommittees throughout the Jubilee year worked diligently to make the events so successful. Mayor Ron Isles served as Chairman, with Mayor Pro-Tem Burnie Dunlap as Co-Chair of the Jubilee Steering Committee. Subcommittee chair and co-chairs included: **Community Involvement:** Pat Fox, Chair; Mary Engwall, Co-Chair; **Business Involvement:** Dave Martin, Chair; Tom Murray, Co-Chair; **Special Events:** Leon Jones, Chair; Carol Wolfert, Co-Chair; **Publicity/Merchandising:** Chris Reimer, Chair; **Parade:** Darwin Manuel, Chair; Bob Wettlin, Co-Chair; **Historical Committee:** Brian Saul, Chair; Kathleen Ralph and Sandy Sarthou, Co-Chairs.

Jubilee Steering Committee:
Front Row—left to right—Mayor Pro Tem Burnie Dunlap, Pat Fox, Mary Engwall, Carol Wolfert
Back Row— left to right—Leon Jones, Dave Martin, Bob Wettlin, Chris Reimer, Brian Saul.
Not pictured: Mayor Ron Isles, Darwin Manuel, Tom Murray, Kathleeen Ralph and Sandy Sarthou.

BREA LIONS' SCOUT CENTER

The former site of Brea's second Boy Scout House soon will again become familiar territory to local Scouts when the Brea Lions' Scout Center — now in its planning stages—opens in Arovista Park.

The Center will serve more than 1,500 Boy Scouts and Girl Scouts, and public and private meetings. Its focus will be on Scouting, as a place for troop and pack meetings, leadership sessions, day camps, Girl Scout bridging ceremonies from one level to another, Boy Scout Courts of Honor, and more.

Recent renovations at Arovista Park called for the demolition of the Boy Scout House. A one-room Olinda school building, dating from around 1910, the clapboard structure had been removed from the canyon during the building of the nearby Carbon Canyon Dam. Trucked into town by Union Oil, it was given to the city for Brea Boy Scouts' use.

By 1990, the 80-year-old structure was beyond repair and too deteriorated for relocation. Its removal left the Boy Scouts of Brea with no place to meet, work, or stow their gear.

Meanwhile, the Girl Scouts had no regular meeting place either. The older scouts usually met in schools, while the Brownies (first through third grades) and the Daisies (kindergarten) gathered in homes.

Leaders for both the Boy Scout and Girl Scout troops got together to discuss the future of Scouting in Brea— a city in which groups were clamoring for the same meeting places. Clearly the Scouts needed their own spot. No city property was available to house them, however, and any new structure would have to be built with private funds.

At this point the Brea Lions Club got involved. The Club has a long-standing tradition of supporting local Scouting: In 1923 the Club built Brea's first Boy Scout House, now known as Pioneer Hall. The structure currently serves the needs of numerous civic groups.

To meet today's needs, the Lions Club was eager to spearhead a massive fund-raising drive for a new Scout Center. The Club committed to raising the funds and presenting the building to the city, just as its predecessor club had done more than 70 years ago.

Leaders from both the Scouts and Lions spent many months conceptualizing the multi-functional building that will serve the Scouts and the Brea community.

Designed by architect Don Schweitzer (grandson of pioneer town trustee Frank Schweitzer (Sr.) and son of former Brea mayor Frank Schweitzer, Jr.), the two-story structure will provide about 10,000 square feet of space. The 5,000 square-foot upper level will consist of a bridge leading to a skylighted atrium with a two-sided fireplace for both the atrium and the main room.

Soundproof, movable walls will partition the large main room into as many as four separate areas. An expanse of windows in the main room will offer a breathtaking view of Arovista Park and the city's adjacent amphitheater. The 5,000 square-foot lower level will provide storage for tents, camping gear, troop supplies and other equipment.

Estimated cost of the building is $1 million — fund-raising efforts continue as the Lions Club works to meet the cost of the Center, which will benefit the community for generations to come.

Bob Martin, a longtime Scout leader and owner of Martinaire, Inc., generously donated the funds to include this tribute to Scouting in Brea.

Scout House for the Future
Funds for a new Scout Center are being raised by the Brea Lions Club. The two-story structure will serve the Scouts and the Brea community for generations to come.

CITY OF BREA VOLUNTEERS

That intangible cornerstone of a thriving community — the one called "spirit" — has nothing to do with buildings, budgets or blueprints. It's all about the activities of countless citizen volunteers. "Brea Spirit" is an invisible cord that connects the city's 75+ year history, adds dimension to today's quality of life, and lends perspective to the future of the community. On behalf of all its citizens, the Brea City Council recognizes the contributions of community volunteers, past, present and future.

The City of Brea recognizes individuals, service organizations, committees and businesses who volunteer and support local programs and activities. Visibly, Brea's dedicated individual volunteers help with many special events, such as ushering at the Theatre, hanging pictures in the Gallery, coaching Youth Sports, teaching at the Job Center, organizing activities at the Senior Center, and serving on the Country Fair Steering Committee. Community service groups and organizations generously

donate time, money or services to city programs. The City's year-end report for volunteer efforts in 1992 alone accounted for an estimated value of $221,259 in contributed services to the city. These numbers reflect 2,511 documented hours of commitment to organized city programs, as well as financial donations and gifts of materials and supplies.

Without volunteers, many programs that add to Brea's quality of life would have to be abolished. They do an outstanding job, and really make a difference! The year-long celebration of its 75th birthday recently earned the city recognition from the California Park and Recreation Society. It received a Self-Esteem Program award because of high community participation. More than 4,400 volunteer hours were logged for all events.

Beyond these highly visible, organized feats from volunteers are countless unrewarded acts by thousands of caring people. In every neighborhood, in every non-profit association, in every religious group,

Early Volunteers
The Brea Fire Department was manned by volunteers, and all dashed to a downtown pick-up point when calls came out for help.
Brea Historical Society

and in individual daily lives, the people of Brea are magnanimously and anonymously helping others. Volunteers support low-cost housing projects for seniors, get involved in business and education partnering, provide transportation for those needing medical attention, bring meals to shut-ins, get involved in literacy programs, support scholarships, and find creative ways to bring renewed meaning to our shared humanity.

Volunteerism has always been a cornerstone of life in Brea, from early bucket brigades to squelch local fires, to hand-rolling bandages for soldiers in foreign ports. From gifts of food baskets for the town's needy, to opening their homes to flood and earthquake victims across the county, citizen volunteers have always shown community spirit in Brea.

SHELL OIL COMPANY

Eighty years ago, when Shell Oil Company's predecessor firm, the American Gasoline Company, first sold its product in the United States, William Howard Taft was president of the United States, and the Ziegfeld Follies reigned on Broadway. As oil discoveries were made around the country, other Shell groups formed to find and produce the valuable crude that was transforming commerce everywhere.

Shell joined other leading oil interests in the Brea community in 1919, when it acquired the oil properties of both the Columbia Oil Company and the Orange Oil Company. The company and its California oilfields became an integral part of the roaring 1920's.

Shell's famous discovery well at Signal Hill, near Long Beach, literally burst out of the ground and shot more than 100 feet into the air. This historic 1921 strike was part of an oil boom, with Signal Hill proving to be one of the most prolific oil fields in U.S. history.

For Shell, this fabulous find gave the company enough local production to allow other West Coast activity. The most valuable of the California properties were those of the Columbia Oil Producing Company, which had leases in fields a few miles east of the Los Angeles city limits. Among them: the Brea-Olinda fields — the officially recognized name for two local areas, one called Brea Canyon and the other Olinda, or sometimes Columbia Olinda.

By the time Shell of California absorbed Columbia in 1922, Columbia's Montebello field properties were producing 580 barrels a day and the Brea-Olinda properties 3,425 barrels daily. At the time, Shell had reservations about the potential value of these properties — though in the long run they proved their worth. The Puente field continued to produce at least small amounts of oil, and the Brea Canyon section of the Brea-Olinda field, drilled deeper as recently as 1950, produced 876,000 barrels of oil that year.

The total Brea-Olinda and Yorba Linda oil fields run by Shell and other operators have been among the most prolific in California, having produced approximately half-a-billion barrels of crude oil for the energy needs of Californians and the nation. Today, Shell Western E&P Inc., the Shell Oil Company affiliate that runs the Shell Brea-Olinda Production Unit portion of these fields, has 28 employees maintaining about 600 producing wells.

Over the years, significant portions of Shell's holdings in the Brea and Yorba Linda area have transitioned from speculative oil field lands to major open space recreational use. Among these are the Carbon Canyon Regional Park and westernmost reaches of the Chino Hills State Park and Firestone Boy Scout Reserve. With consideration for mixed future uses of the remaining property once oil production diminishes, the company is working closely with local cities and other interested parties toward tomorrow's development.

Shell joined other leading oil interests in the Brea community in 1919, when it acquired the oil properties of both the Columbia and the Orange Oil companies.
Brea Historical Society

UNOCAL

In 1890, Unocal was founded less than 100 miles northwest of Brea in Santa Paula, then the center of California's oil country. By 1894, co-founder Lyman Stewart, well known for his "nose" for oil, began buying up land from the Stearns Ranchos Company. He accumulated several thousand acres that became the Stearns Lease. The Brea townsite was established on Stearns land in about 1910. The city was incorporated in 1917 and later annexed some of the Unocal holdings.

Unocal drilled its first well on the Stearns Lease in 1898. Since then, the field has produced 95 million barrels of oil. Of nearly 350 wells drilled, 185 are still producing — including two that were drilled at the turn of the century. The Stearns Lease, now occupying a few thousand acres in the Tonner Canyon area, continues to produce nearly 2,000 barrels of oil per day.

Oil was just the beginning for Unocal and Brea. Since 1951, the company's research activities have

been headquartered at the corner of Imperial and Valencia. The first staff group moved from crowded quarters at Unocal's Los Angeles refinery into their new laboratories on September 1 that year. The research department, which had developed excellent new fuels, lubricants, and other products in the 1930s and 1940s, continued to build on its prestigious reputation. "Hydrocracking" technology developed in the 1950s and 1960s virtually revolutionized refining. Today, Unocal is the world's largest licenser of this technology.

In 1982, Unocal completed an expansion to nearly double the

In 1982, Unocal completed an expansion to nearly double its laboratory space. The facility was renamed the Fred L. Hartley Research Center in honor of the company's longtime chairman.

laboratory space. The facility was renamed the Fred L. Hartley Research Center in honor of the company's longtime chairman.

Research is focused on oil, gas, and geothermal exploration and production; increased efficiency of company operations; and the development of new or improved fuels, agricultural chemicals, and other products. Unocal received 91 U.S. patents in 1991 — a record for the company — and now holds more than 1,100 patents and has granted 200 licenses worldwide.

In 1952, Unocal opened Brea Chemicals to manufacture some of the products developed at the research labs. The plant, also located on Imperial, operated for 40 years. By the time it was shut down in 1992, the original rural character of the neighborhood had undergone a complete transformation into a bustling retail and commercial district.

Unocal continues to play a major role in Brea — helping to preserve and enhance the community's lifestyle while building for the future. The Unocal Land and Development Company is working on a master plan to develop more than 1,300 acres in Brea into golf courses, residential housing, and office and commercial space.

Unocal's prestigious research center has been located at the corner of Imperial and Valencia since 1951.
Photographs courtesy Unocal

DAILY STAR-PROGRESS

In 1917 Brea residents were reading local newspaper ads that touted the latest 35-horsepower automobile—the Overland—for $895, a good buy even then. Twenty-eight cents bought a ticket to Fullerton's Rialto Theater, and just one cent gave them the whole newspaper, the Brea Star.

The Star was a sister to the La Habra Star in the next-door community, and a competitor to the established Brea Progress, already in

Feb. 28, 1918

existence for several years.

The early years were colorful, both for the fledgling newspapers and the new communities they reflected. Some 50 years later, however, the newspapers were joined together as a strengthened enterprise known as the Daily Star-Progress.

The weekly La Habra Star was established by Scotsman A. V. Douglass. Volume I, Number I appeared on July 13, 1916, to serve a village of about 500 persons and 25 businesses.

Also a weekly, the Brea Progress considered its competition mostly

Aug. 13, 1915

friendly, but a force that needed attention. As the older weekly, it had been formerly called the La Habra Valley Progress. The newspaper grew up with its community, around new oil producing and Pacific Electric Railroad efforts, meeting the requirements of the citrus growers in the La Habra Valley, as well as industrial businesses.

The weekly papers survived, however, through depression, recession, wars, various owners, expansions, relocations, and technological advances. They captured and chronicled the flavor of the times, through early settlements, township and cityhood approvals, public works projects in the 1930's, focus on World War II and the subsequent building boom of the 1950's, and so on. Valuable historical accounts were published all along the way, noting new businesses, civic, and social activities that changed the rural area to the suburban/urban tone of the 1990's.

During the years, newspaper owners numbered nine for the La Habra Star and 15 for the Brea Progress before the two enterprises were purchased by Freedom Newspapers, Inc., in 1963. Still the owner today, Freedom Newspapers combined the two several years later, beginning daily publication in 1966, and expanding coverage to include more of the surrounding area.

The daily paper debuted Monday, October 3, 1966, with a strong emphasis on local news. The format in 1966 included a summary column of "World,"

Jan. 25, 1968

"Nation," and "State" news running down the left side of Page one, but still the focus was strictly local news.

Today's newspaper reflects some of the innovations that have taken place. Off-set presses use thin plates to produce clarity in photos, and easier-to-read text. Electronic type production, using computers instead of typewriters, provides tremendous speed in processing, revolutionizing the former hot-lead linotype of the past. Full-color photography is a regular feature now, unlike the early days when photos were a rarity. Still, the spirit of serving the newspaper's local readers remains the same.

Now a weekly newspaper again, the revamped Brea Progress still provides a local format.

A City in Headlines

For more than 75 years, Brea has been front-page news in its own local newspaper, even though the paper has changed names, owners and format many times.

ALFRED GOBAR ASSOCIATES, INC.

"What is the best use of this land?" That is the most common question the consultants at Alfred Gobar Associates, Inc., hears from its clients—whether they are architects, engineers, planners, or developers, or involved with real estate decisions for cities, counties, financial institutions, hotels/motels, industry, public utilities, restaurant chains, or supermarkets.

Alfred Gobar Associates specializes in analyzing economic and business decisions that involve managing and developing real estate assets. By applying management science techniques to land use and real estate decision making, the company helps its clients choose the best possible course. Some of the most practical applications are: What kind of houses to build and where; Estimates of sales volume for shopping centers; Golf course feasibility studies for best placement and use.

Now located at 721 West Kimberly Avenue in Placentia, the staff has worked as a cohesive team since 1966, when the firm was organized as Darley/Gobar Associates, Inc. Several ownership changes ensued, but the

This interior space was originally occupied by Oilfields Bank. Two large vaults are located at the rear of the suite. This portion of the building was extensively rehabilitated in order to accommodate the offices of Alfred Gobar Associates from 1986 to 1991.

research team remained intact, and the company emerged in 1973 as it is known today, under the auspices of principal and president Alfred Gobar, Ph.D.

Dr. Gobar believes the firm's goals can be achieved best by a small group of specialized senior analysts with

support staff. To that end, he maintains an employee population of about 14 persons. As needed, he contracts with other consultants for specialized services in data processing, consumer research, data collection, and so on. This allows the internal staff to concentrate on special strengths: real estate and urban economics, and financial analysis.

Dr. Gobar's own background is highly distinguished. His fields of study include economics, mathematics, physics, and business; his degrees are from Whittier College (B.A. and M.A.), and the University of Southern California (Ph.D.). Prior to his consulting business, he was a professor, worked in industry, and was a venture capital specialist for several small manufacturers.

Over the years, his staff has pioneered the application of econometric models and other quantitative and statistical techniques in its consulting. Resulting benefits mean more intelligent management of land-related assets in terms of risk management, financial rewards, and use of clients' resources.

Dr. Gobar's interest in Brea and the surrounding area has deep roots: His grandfather, Franklin Gobar, was a physician in Fullerton in the early 1900s, and his father was educated in local schools.

As a consultant to the City of Brea for its significant redevelopment, Dr. Gobar notes his pleasure — both professional and personal — in helping the area meet its considerable challenges: "While we use theoretical thought processes in our work, we also have an opportunity to see what we have accomplished when the project takes shape. Our work is very gratifying."

From 1975 until 1991, Alfred Gobar Associates maintained offices in various suites in the Oilfields National Bank building. This historic old building was developed in about 1927 and was occupied at various times by Oilfields National Bank, corporate offices of Shaffer Tool Works, and a variety of other tenants. Dr. Gobar sold the property to the Brea Redevelopment Agency in early 1991 to facilitate revitalization of Brea's old downtown area. The building was torn down in early 1993.

MONTESSORI UNIVERSE OF THE CHILD

Bette Rowell encouraging a love of learning for geography with the Montessori map puzzles and globe.

The education work that Maria Montessori began in 1906 is more timely than ever. Her credo, "Let us give the child a vision of the whole universe," seems custom-made for the 1990's.

The Montessori school at 400 W. Fir Street in Brea, with its well-trained staff and handsome campus, offers a curriculum for pre-schoolers through sixth grade that focuses on the founder's philosophy. First teach independence and responsibility to help the child make choices, and instill the love of learning.

Under the auspices of a family team, the Brea Montessori school enrolls approximately 75 students. Bette Rowell is president, co-director, and teacher in the school; her daughter, Yolanda Rowell Miller, is vice president, director, and teacher; her husband, Edwin Rowell, is school administrator.

The Rowells were introduced to the Montessori Method through their granddaughter, Starshine Rowell, who did exceptionally well in the program. In 1980, Bette and Yolanda — both Montessori trained teachers — opened their school here and, in 1984, added a separate elementary and office build-

ing and enlarged their Day Care facilities.

The method's founder, Dr. Montessori, was a medical doctor in Italy, trained in family practice but denied full access to her profession because of her gender. As a physician, she worked with mentally-ill children. She learned much from them — how they used their hands, how they responded to manipulative tasks, and how they progressed. Why not apply the notion to normal children, she thought, to enhance learning?

And so she devised her self-motivation approach and a program that concentrated on "following the child" at an early age, encouraging sensitivity and discovery. Classroom activity in the Montessori Method, brought to the United States by Alexander Graham Bell, is designed with that in mind.

Working in small groups, each child has his or her own table or a "work rug" on which to work. Each class is comprised of mixed ages (2-6 and 6-12). This allows the children to choose their own interest and skill level, on which the teacher will build.

The curriculum covers primary, for ages two to six, and elementary, for ages six to 12.

Dominant in the early training: **Practical Life** — to enhance early independence; care of person and environment; dexterity; grace; and courtesy. **Sensorial** — using materials in the classroom to help the child develop the five senses. **Mathematics** — using concepts of quantities and symbols for understanding number functions. **Reading and writing** — using highly specialized techniques for early skills. **Science** and **Geography** — with hands-on exposure to the child's immediate environment, and to Dr. Montessori's colorful map puzzles.

The Elementary Curriculum builds from this point, expanded in great detail and generally considered beyond the traditional sixth grade work level. All is interspersed with play time, snacks, naps, lunch breaks, for calming and focusing.

The teacher/child ratio in this state-accredited school is one for every ten students. Special features include an extended day policy — generally a time of recreation for those students who spend the early mornings or later afternoon hours at the school.

A family team, Bette and Edwin Rowell and daughter, Yolanda Rowell Miller, opened Montessori Universe of the Child at 400 W. Fir in 1980.

BANKAMERICA CORPORATION
BANK OF AMERICA, BREA

The year was 1940, when Bank of America's founder A.P. Giannini said, "Serving the needs of others is the only legitimate business in the world today." Over time, his statement has become even more appropriate.

A great many things have changed since then, including the structure and even the name of Giannini's organization—now Bank of America. But his community commitment continues through the bank's Foundation, and its banking practices.

In Brea, the bank—located at 290 South State College Blvd. near Imperial Highway—serves several key types of customers: individuals with checking and savings accounts, small businesses with commercial and personal accounts, redevelopment groups with special lending and deposit requirements.

Also, Bank of America's Southern California Consumer and Residential Production Center operates in the City of Brea. This Center processes, underwrites and services all home and non-home related consumer loans generated by the local retail Branches in Southern California.

Bank of America customers in Brea represent manufacturing, retail, aircraft and insurance, to name a few key industries. Major companies, often with headquarters in other cities, still elect to keep their local accounts in the Brea branch.

As more business and industry came into Brea, Bank of America accommodated new needs, such as a night drop for merchants and special lending programs for companies. The bank's highly sophisticated

computer system, with electronic direct deposit, is important to commercial accounts as well.

Other changes: The branch is open longer hours and has 24-hour Automatic Teller service available with English, Spanish, and Chinese instructions. The bank also operates a 24-hour customer line in English and Spanish.

The Brea branch first opened in 1962, and moved to its current location in 1978. Housed in a handsome structure with an open-beamed ceiling and a light, airy environment, Bank of America's Brea staff emphasizes individual service, in keeping with the tone of the community. Tellers are trained to be solution oriented, and to act as "relationship bankers." A series of "informal days" helps keep

a small-town atmosphere alive as well, such as decorating for the Super Bowl, showing Christmas cartoons and movies during the season, and dressing for Halloween.

Branch banking was a Bank of America first, dating back to the way its founder did business with "the person on the street." That community outreach has translated into special efforts such as the Neighborhood Advantage program to provide special mortgage-financing in targeted areas, and to the bank's Community Reinvestment response to meet challenging economic development needs in California. In Orange County, the programs help cities, chambers of commerce, redevelopment groups, humanitarian causes, and numerous other vital activities.

The Brea branch first opened in 1962, and moved to its current location in 1978. Housed in a handsome structure with an open-beamed ceiling and a light, airy environment, Bank of America's Brea staff emphasizes individual service and relationship banking.

BREA NISSAN

"We call it the third necessity of life in Southern California, right behind food and housing," says John Givans, president of Brea Nissan, speaking about automobiles and the industry that has his career for more than 40 years.

Givans, with his daughter Christy

Brea Nissan's service capabilities include 11 factory trained technicians to serve the latest in technology. In-house sales training is important to keep sales counselors educated on the newest Nissan car and truck models.

Nissan is highly acclaimed by well-known industry publications

"Look at the changes we've seen in our society that directly affect the auto industry," he points out. "With more couples in the workforce, and often long commutes between residence and employment—the average family has three vehicles per household. That's a real evolution since I got into the business in 1950."

Of course, present vehicle engineering and extended factory warranties have changed the industry, too, eliminating substantial repair costs.

As the community has grown, so has Brea Nissan's interaction with schools and youth groups. For example, the dealership provided Fullerton College's campus automotive repair shop with a new Nissan 240SX for lab purposes, and donated nine new Nissan vehicles to other local schools, encouraging automotive repair as a vocation.

John Givans, with his daughter, Christy, believes in investing in the youth of America and supporting a community that has been good to him and his family for two generations.

Givans as executive manager, owns the dealership at 3000 East Imperial Highway that has served the Brea community for more than a dozen years.

Brea Nissan offers a modern showroom on three and a half acres. There are 18 service stalls, about 250 vehicles in its average inventory, and a staff of some 54 employees—many who have been here for five to ten years. Sales, service, and parts all contribute to the dealership's success, yielding more than $15 million in recent annual sales.

such as Road & Track, Car and Driver, and AutoWeek. Honors have been awarded to the top-ranked Maxima, 240SX and NX 2000, the razor-sharp 300ZX Turbo, the Sentra SE-R, and the utilitarian Pathfinder.

Givans started in the automobile business in 1950. Just out of the military after World War II, he went to work for an auto financing firm, then got into sales in downtown Los Angeles. He climbed the management ladder at various dealerships learning all areas of the business before owning his own dealership.

The community has been good to Brea Nissan providing many referral and repeat customers. The dealership generously gives back a portion of its revenues to the youth of the area by sponsoring some 20 Little League teams, ten Pop Warner football teams, a number of swim teams, softball teams and a variety of school events each year. By supporting these organizations, John Givans lives his belief that **"investing in our youth is investing in the future of America."** Mr. Givans also believes in supporting a community that has been good to him and his family for two generations.

PACIFIC MARKETING

Based in reality, but inspired by its philosophy, Pacific Marketing Group (PMG) helps its clients give consumers exactly what they want.

PMG owner/founder Louis L. Knappenberger explains: "Normally a manufacturer develops his product and packaging, then approaches the retailer to sell his goods to the consumer. We turn that entire process around. We find out what the consumer wants and how the retailer can most efficiently sell the product(s). This may mean a change in packaging or a better way of displaying the goods. Then we go to the manufacturer to put all the pieces together. This usually means lower prices to the retailer and the consumer and higher sales for the manufacturer. The advantage is that everyone is looking at the others' needs and all concerned benefit.

PMG attracts business by going after it. They assist with product development, package design, promotional concepts and advertising programs. At that point, PMG can become the product sales representative as well, overseeing new account sales and store service — conducting training and development, and monitoring product placement and display. It operates as a single source for business growth.

As a multi-faceted sales and services network PMG has over 30 years of experience in its specialty — helping suppliers develop products and programs that generate high volume through high-quality products in every price range.

The growth of warehouse retailers in the 1980's has fueled PMG's multi-

Pacific Marketing Group, with a staff of 17 in sales and creative services, is proud to be a part of the Brea Business Community.

million-dollar operations, which reach primarily the 13 western United States, but in some cases across the nation. PMG represents many Fortune 500 companies, as well as regional firms. With associates in every region of the country, PMG can reach markets in any client's target area .

Louis Knappenberger established PMG in 1985 to represent manufacturers and suppliers to the mass marketing retailer. With his partner, Ty Olson, and his wife, Dolores, who manages company operations, Lou employs a staff of 17 in sales and creative services. From their 1,800 square-foot office and showroom nine miles north of Disneyland at 655 North Berry Drive, Suite C, in Brea, staff members use highly computerized systems to produce their superior results.

PMG's long experience in developing brand - and private -

label product lines for volume retailers is a noted specialty.

Knappenberger, who started his career in retailing, worked for two major paint manufacturers before starting PMG. He has lived in Brea since 1977, and is fully committed to several important areas of community service: Lou has served 26 years as a reserve police officer with the cities of Montclair and Brea, California. PMG supports the City of Hope, many activities of Brea Olinda High School, the Brea Police Athletic League; The Senior Center, American Explorers and the Brea Community Emergency Council, which packs holiday meals for the needy.

PMG has also been involved in Paint your Heart, Anaheim for the last two years and the anti-graffiti campaign of Anaheim Beautiful. PMG Marketing Group is proud to be a part of the Brea business community.

CAMPBELL SALES COMPANY

"Take the LFE Road to a Better Education." That slogan is familiar to the students at Brea's Christ Lutheran, Fanning, Mariposa Elementary, and St. Angela Merici schools, because they participate in "Labels For Education," or LFE.

The highly popular program, started 19 years ago by Campbell Soup Company, distributes some $4 million worth of goods to schools across the nation every year through a simple label redemption plan. It was the first promotion of its kind, and is the biggest, with over 80,000 schools registered to participate. This year alone, over 350 million labels will be redeemed.

An important community service, LFE not only allows children from preschool through twelfth, and public libraries, to obtain valuable equipment, it also teaches them firsthand the importance of teamwork and setting goals. As a true grass roots event, LFE helps communities gain free equipment for their schools in tight budgetary times. In fact, enthusiasm for LFE continues to build.

Here's how it works. Campbell's sends out a national mailing annually, asking schools if they would like to register. Once they do, they are listed on Campbell's data base, and the company coordinates the program through local retailers.

Students then collect labels from all sizes of Campbell's Soups and other company food products, and through their school program redeem them for merchandise certificates. There are no presentations to the children or the schools on Campbell's part. Instead, the local stores run the program with

Campbell's merchandising support.

What LFE provides for the students is much more than merchandise. The program is a rallying point, an enthusiasm builder that gets millions of students, teachers, families, and friends in thousands of schools involved, working toward beneficial goals.

The merchandise they are working for encompasses over 1,100 educational and athletic items. Some of the categories in Campbell's 50-page catalog: Art and Music, Audio Visual, Communications, Day Care, Education Accessories, Food Services, Math and Computers, Science, Sports, and Transportation.

Indeed, the program has grown by leaps and bounds since its inception 19 years ago, when it provided mainly audio/visual and playground/athletic equipment.

Typically the programs are timed to coincide with back-to-school (October) and around holidays (November through February).

Locally, Brea's Regional Sales Office handles the LFE program. Located at 120 South State College Blvd., Suite 160, this Sales and Merchandising office oversees Campbell's Southern California market, encompassing 1,200 grocery stores.

Campbell's philosophy in providing the LFE program is to extend the company's pride in its products to help pave the way for better education throughout the nation.

"Labels For Education," (LFE) is a highly popular program, started 19 years ago by Campbell Soup Company. LFE distributes some $4 million worth of goods to schools across the nation every year through a simple label redemption plan.

EMBASSY SUITES

Guests who enter the soaring atrium at the core of the Embassy Suites/Brea realize immediately how extraordinary this hotel really is. Part of an all-suite hotel company known for special amenities, this property claims an identity all its own. Its interior is fashioned after an Egyptian oasis, with an avenue of 30-foot palm trees flanking a reflecting pool and distinctive fountains. Striking original paintings, drawings and sculptures by local artists and school children carry the Egyptian theme throughout the hotel.

Primed to serve both business and leisure guests, the $34 million, 229-suite hotel opened in late 1990 at its 900 East Birch Street address. It is adjacent to the Brea Mall and Civic Center, where the Police Department is housed, and within walking distance of 10 movie theaters and numerous restaurants.

Embassy Suites employs 100 administrative, catering, housekeeping, maintenance, and other personnel,

Fashioned after an Egyptian oasis, with an avenue of 30-foot palm trees flanking a reflecting pool and distinctive fountains, the Brea Embassy Suites Interior is impressive. Striking original paintings, drawings and sculptures by local artists and school children carry the Egyptian theme throughout the hotel.

The hotel's 75-foot outdoor lap pool, whirlpool, sauna, and fitness center get a great deal of attention.

making it one of North Orange County's major employers.

Known as a prestige-oriented organization, Embassy Suites is a wholly-owned subsidiary of The Promus Companies Incorporated, headquartered in Memphis, which also owns Harrah's casinos and hotels, Hampton Inns, and Homewood Suites. Embassy Suites is known as the nation's largest franchisor and operator of upscale, all-suite hotels, located in 31 states, plus Toronto, Canada and Bangkok, Thailand.

Like all Embassy Suites hotels, the Brea facility features two-room suites complete with a living room, separate bath and private bedroom. Each suite comes equipped with a wet bar, refrigerator, microwave oven, dining/conference table, two televisions with remote, two telephones with voice mail, and a sitting area. There are also luxurious penthouse suites.

The suite concept is especially popular with

business travelers, making it easier for them to hold small meetings.

Formal meeting room facilities include a 5,600-square-foot ballroom that holds 430 persons banquet-style; and 15 additional meeting rooms and executive conference suites. Total flexible meeting space is more than 19,000 square feet, and on-site catering gives planners even more convenience.

In Tut's Bar & Grill, which has a 110-seat lounge and 220-seat restaurant, guests are transported back in time to the luxury and classic opulence of Egypt's ancient pharaohs.

Suite rates include a full, cooked-to-order breakfast served daily, and a two-hour manager's cocktail reception each evening. Children under 12 stay free in the same suite as their parents.

Popular with business and leisure travelers alike, the hotel's 75-foot outdoor lap pool, whirlpool, sauna, and fitness center get a great deal of attention.

Embassy Suite management and employees view Brea as a progressive community that invites civic involvement. Many of the staff serve as board members and volunteers for a wide variety of vital organizations.

THE FIELDSTONE COMPANY

The American dream — homeownership — is one of The Fieldstone Company's foremost challenges: *To provide quality houses for first-and second-time move-up buyers in Southern California.*

Since the company was established in 1981, its vision — according to founder and chairman Peter M. Ochs — has been to serve as a model of excellence in homebuilding, with people working together, committed to provide value for customers and service to the community.

Headquartered in Newport Beach, Fieldstone has regional offices in Brea at 145 South State College Blvd., Suite 660, and in San Diego. Based on 1991 sales revenue noted in a Los Angeles Times survey, The Fieldstone Group was Number 2 in Southern California building leaders, with $323 million in sales, and more than 1,200 homes.

The company's more than 200 employees build primarily in Orange, San Bernardino, and San Diego Counties. In Brea, Fieldstone Terrace has taken shape as an enclave of 97 single family homes, with community pool, spa and tennis courts.

Growth for Fieldstone has been steady since its first year, with its housing product matching the shifting demographics of the marketplace. The steady climb reflects Ochs' astute market analysis and strategic planning, with great attention to quality control. Yet Ochs has created a company known as a textbook model of carefully controlled growth.

Ochs began to build his reputation first with American Standard (in 1968), then with the William Lyon Company, serving as president in the late 1970s.

As Fieldstone flourished, Ochs and his management became more and more focused on team problem solving, involving groups of employees in training and brainstorming sessions to improve their jobs,

ABOVE: The management team of Fieldstone, committed to provide value for new homeowners and service to the community of Brea — (standing): Julie Hutchinson, Michael Vairin, Gary Frye and Mike Conlon (seated):Jim Happeny and Julie Taverna.

RIGHT: Fieldstone Terrace in Brea, 97 single family residential homes with community pool, spa and tennis courts.

productivity, and overall profitability. The team concept now extends to subcontractors and suppliers, to improve job coordination and communication, and build a better product.

For his leadership and his company's preeminence in its specialty, Ochs was named 1989 Builder of the Year by Professional Builder magazine. His management theory applied to home building is based on a set of traditional values at his company's core: "Excellence in everything we do. An environment of teamwork and trust. The value of each employee. Commitment to our homebuyers. The importance of profitable operations. Integrity in the

conduct of our business."

Charitable giving is a major focus, as Fieldstone shares its prosperity with the communities it serves. The company makes substantial contributions either directly or through its philanthropic arm, The Fieldstone Foundation, to humanitarian programs — especially for youth, community and educational causes, cultural activities, and Christian ministries. By translating its values into positive action, Fieldstone fosters partnerships with others to produce housing environments for enriched family living.

GERARD ROOFING TECHNOLOGIES

Gerard Roofing Technologies is very much at home on Columbia Street in Brea—the company's U.S. headquarters since 1986.

The company was incorporated in California in 1981 as an importer of a roof tile that had proved popular in New Zealand, where it had been developed.

Gerard Roofing Technologies, America's largest roofing manufacturer of stone-coated steel roof products, started full production in Brea on December 10, 1986, to the sounds of the Brea Olinda High School Marching Band. Featured here is the Montecarlo Gerard Stone-coated Steel, a highly weather-and fire-resistant product.

The Gerard tile is an attractive, Mediterranean-style and highly weather- and fire-resistant product manufactured in stone-coated steel. The tile's sister product, a fire-safe version of America's traditional wood shake, was introduced in 1990. Both products are known for their long life, with 40-year limited weatherproof warranties.

As sales grew, administration and warehousing were moved to several Southern California locations before Gerard decided to establish a U.S. manufacturing site as well. In mid-1985, Gerard chose Brea for its new 46,000 square-foot factory, and began a strong relationship between local contractors and company personnel. The team accomplished capital improvements—installing presses and a production line, and fitting out administration and sales offices—to meet Gerard's construction timetable. When Gerard started full production in Brea on December 10, 1986, producing stone-coated roof tiles out of American coated steel, it was to the sounds of the Brea Olinda High School Marching Band.

Gerard's choice of Brea was the result of a long examination of the company's needs and options. The city's accessibility was a major factor in the decision, as well as its residential comfort for employees, quality recreation, and community pride.

The Gerard plant itself is an attractive building set back from a well-tended, grassy streetscape. The plant is environmentally friendly, with no smoke, smells, or machinery noise emitted. Inside the plant, the same care is taken with materials, manufacturing processes, and transportation methods.

Since Gerard moved to Brea, its plant has produced millions of tiles and shakes that cover many California homes. The company's own R & D section here developed the Gerard shake, a unique and fire-safe substitute for wood shakes, already popular with customers.

In 1990, with burgeoning sales across the sunbelt and along the West Coast, Gerard became a fully integrated member of the $8 billion Alcan Aluminum Corporation's family of companies. Now part of a diversified transnational with the resources to grow further,

Gerard still remains close to its roots.

Many of Gerard's production, administrative, and sales personnel live in or close to Brea, supporting the local economy through wages and salaries. While most of its raw materials for manufacturing must come from outside of Brea, Gerard utilizes many of the services and businesses available within the city.

Gerard also enjoys a close relationship with the city, its fire and police forces. As a member of the Brea Chamber of Commerce, Gerard is involved in many of its programs.

Against a national construction industry trend, Gerard has continued to sell strongly into the 1990's. The Brea company now has offices in Orlando and Miami, Florida, and distributors covering most major states in between. And while the company's success has attracted a number of competitors, Gerard is firmly placed as America's largest roofing manufacturer of stone-coated steel roof products.

Spanish Red Gerard stone-coated steel tile is an attractive, Mediterranean-style product known for its long life.

STRICKLAND'S PHOTOGRAPHY STUDIO

Bill Strickland has been photographing for the last 15 years throughout North Orange County. He created Strickland's Photography Studio to provide a very personalized service and offer a wide range of products and services. A speciality is the very popular glamour portraiture, elegantly done in color or black and white.

In 1990, Strickland's Fine Art Photography took First Place at the Orange County Fair in the Professional Division. Fine art photography can be found on postcards, calendars, and in hotels, restaurants, and professional offices, as well as homes.

Bill is also a wedding specialist. He captures those important memories, not only in full color photographs, but also on videotape. He enjoys the challenge of group photos especially the large family and Bar Mitzvah celebrations.

Advertising photography and product illustration for brochures and catalog sheets are other services available for commercial clients. Bill has won numerous honors, from peoples' choice contests to state contests and fair awards as well. He served seven years on the Board of

Directors for the Professional Photographers of Orange County, with two terms as president of the association.

For custom portraitures, Strickland's Photography offers different themes or environments — indoors with studio props or backgrounds, outdoors for a natural environment and on location for special events. Bill is committed to providing the best service with the best photography.

Strickland's Photography Studio has a new location: 610 South Jefferson, Suite B, Placentia.

BREA OLINDA UNIFIED SCHOOL DISTRICT

Parents and teachers come together on the steps of Randolph School in this PTA picture, circa 1915. "Professor" W.E. Fanning stands back, right.

Celebrating its 90th anniversary in 1993, the Brea Olinda Unified School District has evolved from a single small turn-of-the-century schoolhouse to an eight-campus modern educational system serving more than 5,000 students.

Founded as the Randolph School District in 1903, but lacking funds to build a school, the district opened its first classes to oil workers' children in a one-room Brea Canyon school-house erected by Union Oil.

Ellen Dickinson was hired as the district's first teacher, earning an annual salary of $450 for instructing 13 boys and 17 girls. All studied to-gether, regardless of their age, but when recess arrived, boys and girls were separated by a schoolyard fence.

Milestones of the district's past:

❖ 1903 A local vote creates the Randolph School District, and its first school opens to 30 students. Most arrive on foot, but some travel to

school by horse and pony cart. Sec-ondary students continue their studies at Fullerton Union High School.

❖ 1910 A two-story, four-room school is erected at the southwest corner of today's Lambert and Brea Boulevard. The new school—Brea's very first building—opens with 51 students under the guidance of teachers A. Jenkins and Louise Morton.

❖ 1912 Ralph Jepsen is chosen Brea's first superin-tendent of schools.

❖ 1915 Local pride sparks a change in the district's name from Randolph to Brea, and bonds are voted for a larger school.

❖ 1916 An imposing new school—Brea Grammar—opens on Union Oil land at the northeast corner of today's Lambert and Brea Boulevard.

❖ 1921 Growing Brea becomes a two-school town with the addition of Laurel, built at a cost of $60,000. W.E. Fanning ascends to the post of superintendent following this school's opening.

❖ 1922 The Brea PTA ranks as one of the county's largest and most influential.

❖ 1925 Dismayed with cuts in Fullerton Union High School's curriculum, the separate elementary districts of Brea and Olinda pool their resources to form the Brea-Olinda Union High School District, and plans begin for the building of a local high school.

❖ 1926 Brea-Olinda Union High School rises from a barley field on the town's eastern edge. I. W. Barnett serves as the school's first principal.

❖ 1928 Carl Harvey signs on as BOHS' second principal, guiding his students through 18 formative years marked by major earthquake, the Great Depression and World War II.

❖ 1933-36 Enacted in the aftermath of the Long Beach earthquake, the Field Act requires extensive structural modifications at all three Brea schools.

The pillars that once graced Brea-Olinda High School's entrance on Birch Street were removed after the 1933 Long Beach earthquake.

❖ 1942 Vincent Jaster begins his 24-year tenure as Brea's elementary district superintendent.

❖ 1946 Frank O. Hopkins succeeds Carl Harvey as BOHS principal.

❖ 1948 Brea becomes one of the first two school districts in California to institute driver education and training courses.

❖ 1951 BOHS purchases 10 acres east of the high school to begin a student-run farm. Later acquisitions increase the school's acreage to a total of nearly 65 acres.

❖ 1956 Brea's population shows a growth surge, and Arovista Elementary opens at 900 Eadington Drive. With the addition of this new local elementary, Brea Grammar "graduates" to become Brea Junior High.

❖ 1960 In the wake of Carbon Canyon Dam's construction, the old Olinda School is moved into town to become (today's) Brea Senior Citizens Center.

❖ 1964 The new Olinda School is built by the Army Corps of Engineers in Olinda Village.

Transplanted to its expansive new home, Brea Olinda High gained a bronze mascot, but lost its familiar hyphen — removed by board vote in the late 1980's.
Photo courtesy City of Brea

The bell that called Carbon Canyon students to the old Olinda School makes its home today in the courtyard of the new school, built in 1964.

❖ 1966 The two local elementary districts of Brea and Olinda combine with the high school district to become the Brea-Olinda Unified School District, with Dr. Paul Bolie as first superintendent.

❖ 1966 Mariposa School opens at 1111 Mariposa Drive.

❖ 1971 Fanning School opens at 650 N. Apricot.

❖ 1978 Dr. C. Gordon Bishop becomes superintendent of schools.

❖ 1980 Brea Country Hills School opens at 150 N. Associated Road.

❖ 1980 The school district shifts its base of operation to the new Civic & Cultural Center.

❖ 1982 Dr. Edgar Z. Seal succeeds interum superintendent James

Stafford as BOUSD superintendent of schools.

❖ 1989 A new, state-of-the-art BOHS campus opens on 50 former Union Oil acres east of the freeway as the first privately financed public high school built in California. Following a "Last Hurrah," the old high school falls to the wrecking ball, and is replaced by the Marketplace.

❖ 1989 Fanning Elementary is named a California Distinguished School.

❖ 1991 BOHS is named a California Distinguished School.

❖ 1993 BOHS is named a National Blue Ribbon School. Selected by the U.S. Department of Education in this prestigious biennial competition, the local campus joins only 18 middle schools and high school in California and 260 schools nationwide awarded this honor in 1993.

COLORTEC

In both product and services, Colortec uses a customized approach as the key to its burgeoning business.

A high-quality, four-color separation and image assembly specialist, Colortec provides pre-press services for the printing industry and those with printing needs. The young firm has been so successful, it expects to grow by 50 percent by year's end.

Located at 450 Apollo, Suite E, in Brea, the firm produces color materials that include brochures, catalogs, advertisements, posters, annual reports, flyers and more. The company handles jobs with long lead times, as well as those with fast turnaround.

Using sophisticated electronic equipment (manufactured by Hell, Scitex and MacIntosh) that is at the forefront of the imaging industry, Colortec produces film that goes directly to printers for reproduction. The Colortec system functions as a network that does a number of things: It provides color separations, image alterations and special effects, and integrates copy with the graphics on film.

Established in 1986, Colortec provides pre-press services for the printing industry and those with printing needs.

Amir Ali Saifi, is Colortec principal, owner and master strategist for the expanding business.

Colortec was established in 1986 by Mory Saifi, who has more than 15 years experience in the field. A mechanical engineer by training, Mory became interested in imaging techniques when the technology was still young, but waited until the industry had evolved to a more advanced level before starting his business.

Now Mory is an independent consultant to Colortec. His father, Amir Ali Saifi, is company principal, owner and mastaer strategist for the expanding business. The elder Saifi has an extensive background in business and politics, which helps him evaluate growth and major equipment purchases in this fast-paced field. One of Amir Ali Saifi's strengths: His ability to interpret trends in society to anticipate new business needs.

When the company first opened its doors some six years ago, desk-top publishing was in its infancy, producing black and white images only. The work was accomplished by part manual, part computer methods. Now, using the very latest technological advances in desk-top and other electronic media, Colortec can accept a customer's disk into its system and put it on film through a process that is 100 percent electronic. Such expertise speeds up the process, eliminates revision and saves waste.

Constant training is an integral activity at Colortec to stay ahead of the curve in this evolving science. Keeping the customers aware of technological advances and thoroughly discussing project expectations is all part of the excellent customer service provided by the Colortec staff. Each job is checked thoroughly by the production technician, manager and account executive, before clients review their work. Company specialists assist customers with graphics, and work directly with designers as well, for high-quality results. Colortec customers value this state-of-the art service and anticipate a long-term relationship developing a variety of projects.

The entire operation is handled by ten employees, working two shifts, in a 4,000 square-foot shop. Clients who use Colortec's services encompass a number of fields: book publishers, graphic designers, commercial printers, packaging companies, magazines, large firms, and individuals.

PROTOTYPE GRAPHICS , INC.

Early in 1990, Marsha Romanik, graphic designer and owner of Romanik Designs, made the leap from conventional production of art and design to computer aided methods. To speed up the transition period and make the most of the costly investment in equipment, she signed up for a desktop publishing class at Fullerton College. The teacher of that class, Jim More, in true entrepreneurial spirit, taught part-time, designed projects that caught his interest, and free-lanced in database programming.

A few weeks into the semester, responding to Marsha's abundant classroom questions, More offered "...you don't need a class, you need a business partner". Prototype Graphics, Inc., was the result.

Romanik and More tested the theory that a niche market existed for a design firm that offered a high-quality, ad-agency look to usually mundane publications such as directories and catalogs. Their concept: complement off-the-shelf software with custom programs that would automate many of the grueling tasks inherent in designing and producing such text and picture-intensive publications.

During its first year, Prototype Graphics designed several automotive catalogs, chamber of commerce directories, and the teachers' manual and student workbooks for a kindergarten Bible curriculum containing over 100 full-color illustrations.

An extensive design background allowed Romanik and More to supplement their clients' needs by providing product packaging, logos, brochures, advertising and collateral. Their original niche market concept was already expanding.

Marsha Romanik is well known in Brea for her ongoing design work for the Brea Chamber of Commerce and many local businesses. In 1993, she merged that client base from Romanik Designs into Prototype Graphics, Inc., and opened a new facility at 1516 E. Katella, in Anaheim.

"The merger brings everything together under one roof," says Marsha. "The clients of both companies win, since we've expanded the scope of our services, and really increased efficiency."

Continuing education was more than just a starting place for the company. Both Romanik and More are voracious readers of what's new in their field, and daring enough to apply that knowledge in creating highly effective, eye-catching designs for business.

Marsha Romanik

Jim More

Jim More and Marsha Romanik, partners in a design firm that offers an upscale, high-quality, ad-agency look to usually mundane publications such as directories and catalogs.

Commercial Confusion:
A main-street maze of advertising greets downtown travelers in this photo of Brea Boulevard before the adoption of a citywide signage ordinance.
Brea Historical Society

Patrons

*T*he following families and companies have provided financial support or services and supplies enabling the production and manufacturing of this book. Stars ★ denote their participation in the "Partners in Progress" chapter, which includes historically relevant family biographies or profiles of companies with unique contributions to the development of the community and this literary project.

Agee & Strawn

Alexander/Dean Family ★

Alfred Gobar Associates, Inc. ★

American Business Women's Assoc.
    Horizons Unlimited Chapter

BankAmerica Foundation ★

Beverly's Best Bakery

Brea Cañon Oil

Brea Civic Light Opera

Brea Electric Company

Brea Historical Society ★

Brea Lions Scout Center
    (sponsored by Martinaire) ★

Brea Nissan ★

Brea Olinda Unified School District ★

Brea Trophy and Engraving

Burch Ford

Campbell Sales Company ★

Checkmate Photo/Graphics

City of Brea Volunteers ★

Classic Telecommunications

ColorTec ★

Craig Family ★

Daily Star Progress ★

DNS Weight Loss Center

Embassy Suites - Brea ★

Fanning Family ★

Fieldstone Company ★

Gerard Roofing Technologies ★

GTE Telephone Operations

J. Henri Cleaners

Jubilee Steering Committee ★

Karen Hawe

Montessori - Universe of the Child ★

Pacific Marketing Group ★

Prototype Graphics, Inc. ★

Reynolds Tool Products, Inc.

Schweitzer Family

Shaffer Family (Dorothy Yates) ★

Shell Oil Company ★

Strickland's Photography ★

The St. Paul Companies, Inc.

Sumitomo Bank

Swissims Consulting

Tremayne Family

UNOCAL ★

Wedin Family

West Family ★

Service…20's Style
Flanigan's gas station, automotive center of a
simpler time, stakes out its place at (today's)
corner of Brea Boulevard and Central. A
second Flanigan's Service Station was located
at Flanigan Corners in Olinda.
Brea Historical Society

Bibliography

Ballou, Kathleen. *The Brea Police Department (A History).* Brea: 1973.

Bissell, Ronald M. *Cultural Resources Reconnaissance of the Downtown Brea Master Plan Study Area.* Mission Viejo: RMW Paleo Associates, 1990.

Becker, Kenneth M. and Juanita R. Shinn. *Unocal Report on the Investigations at the Landa House.* Mission Viejo: RMW Paleo Associates, 1992.

Brea, California. *Golden Jubilee. 1917-1967.* Brea: 1967.

Brea Chamber of Commerce. *Portraits of Brea.* Brea: 1991.

Brea Community Services Department. *Brea...Our Town.* Brea: 1988.

Brea-Olinda Union High School/Brea Olinda High School. *Gusher.* Brea: 1928-1992.

Carpenter, Virginia L. *Cañada de la Brea: Ghost Rancho.* Santa Ana: Orange County Historical Society, 1978.

Placentia, A Pleasant Place. Santa Ana: Friis Pioneer Press, 1988.

The Ranchos of Don Pacifico Ontiveros. Santa Ana: Friis-Pioneer Press, 1982.

Cleland, Robert Glass. *Cattle on a Thousand Hills: Southern California; 1850-80.* San Marino: The Huntington Library, 1951.

County of Orange. *Carbon Canyon Regional Park.* Santa Ana: Environmental Management Agency, Interpretive Series No. 3, 1975.

Cramer, Esther R. *Brea, The City of Oil, Oranges and Opportunity.* Brea: City of Brea, 1991.

La Habra: The Pass Through the Hills; the Formative Years of a Southern California Community from 1769. Fullerton: Sultana Press, 1969.

Cramer, Esther R., Keith Dixon et. al., eds. *A Hundred Years of Yesterdays: A Centennial History of the People of Orange County and Their Communities.* Santa Ana: Orange County Centennial, Inc., 1989.

Crump, Spencer. *Henry Huntington and the Pacific Electric; A Pictorial Album.* Los Angeles: Trans-Anglo Books, 1970.

Ride the Big Red Cars; How Trolleys Helped Build Southern California. Costa Mesa: Trans-Anglo Books, 1970.

Donaldson, Stephen E. and William A. Myers. *Rails Through the Orange Groves.* Glendale: Trans-Anglo Books, 1989.

Harding, Purl. *The History of Brea, California: From Early Oil Field Days to 1950.* Brea: *Brea Progress* Publishers, 1950.

Holt, Raymond M. "Oil From a Canyon Called Brea," *Westways,* December 1961, 22-23.

Johnson, Bernice Eastman. *California's Gabrieleno Indians.* Los Angeles: Southwest Museum, 1962.

Long, Raphael. *Pacific Electric's Big Red Cars.* Los Angeles: T. C. Phillips, 1966.

McMillan, Nora Brown. *Memories of Early Olinda.* County of Orange, 1975.

McWilliams, Carey. *Southern California Country; An Island on the Land.* New York: Duell, Sloan, and Pearce, 1946.

Newmark, Harris. *Sixty Years in Southern California, 1853-1913.* New York: Knickerbocker Press, 1916.

Pederson, Barbara L. *A Century of Spirit. Unocal 1890-1990.* Los Angeles: Union Oil Company of California, 1990.

Smith, Sarah Bixby. *Adobe Days.* Cedar Rapids, Michigan: Torch Press, 1925.

Taylor, Frank J. and Earl M. Welty. *Black Bonanza.* New York: McGraw Hill, 1958.

Weaver, John D. *L.A.: El Pueblo Grande.* Pasadena: Ward Ritchie Press, 1973.

Welty, Earl M. and Frank J. Taylor. *The 76 Bonanza.* Menlo Park, California: Lane Magazine & Book Company, 1966.

Yates, Harold Wheeler. *A History of the Brea-Olinda Union High School District.* Thesis, Whittier College, 1961.

Yorba, Mildred MacArthur. "Long Arm From Olinda." *Westways,* October, 1978, 52-55.

Young, Robert A. "Planning via Redevelopment: The Orange County Municipal Experience," *Journal of Orange County Studies,* Spring 1991, 19-29.

Interviews (Published):

The Community History Project of Brea, by the Oral History Program at California State University, Fullerton:

Alexander, Vi (Cathie L. Porrelli: 1982)

Barnes, Ralph (Lawrence B. deGraff: 1982)

Bennett, Dyer (Jean Howlett: 1981)

Bergman, Walter (Phillip Brigandi: 1982)

Burke, Pearl (Rhonda Levinson: 1981)

Chanslor, Perry (Gail Norman-Bilby: 1982)

Estrada, Mary (Jackie Malone: 1981)

Fanning, Karl (Jackie Malone: 1981)

Forkus, Don (Lawrence B. deGraff:1982)

Francesconi, Richard and Jerry McDowell (Lawrence B. deGraff: 1982)

Goodwin, Gladys (Rhonda Levinson: 1981)

Griffith, Warren E. (Beverly E. Schmidt: 1968)

Hall, Frank (Cathie L. Porellli: 1981)

Henderson, Thelma (Bruce Rockwell: 1984)

Holly, Frank M. (Cathie Lou Porrelli: 1982)

Jaster, Vincent (Cynthia Churney: 1982)

Kinsler, Leland (Bruce Rockwell: 1985)

Maggio, Richard (Sonja A. Minasian: 1982)

McBride, Don (Sonja A. Minasian: 1982)

McFadden, Roswell C. (Charles L. Beaman: 1982)

Mestre, Henry (Adolph G. Flores: 1982)

Millen, Dean (Jackie Malone and Dennis Swift: 1981/1986)

Piantoni, Leo (Bruce Rockwell: 1981)

Russell, Charles (Pat Reeder: 1983)

Sandman, Esther (Steven Jones: 1982)

Schweitzer, Frank (Jr.) (Mike Korpi:1977)

Seiler, Catherine (Keam Howlett: 1982)

Serna, Charlotte (Adolph Flores: 1982)

Shaffer, Donald (Steven M. Jones: 1982)

Siebenthal, Voloney (Ann Towner and John Weaver: 1981)

Stafford, James (Mori Higa: 1981)

Warner, Myrtle (Annette Frye: 1973)

Wedin, Wayne D. (Sonja Ann Minasian: 1982)

Winchel, Harry N. (Ann Towner: 1981)

Winder, G. Richard (Pat Reeder: 1983)

Yriarte, John and Patricio (Adolph G. Flores: 1982)

Newspapers:

Alta California

Anaheim Gazette

Brea Good News

Brea Highlander

Brea News-Times

Brea Progress

Brea Star

Daily Star-Progress

Fullerton Tribune

Los Angeles Times

Orange County News-Times

Orange County Register

Whittier News

The Wildcat (BOHS)

Miscellaneous Manuscripts, Papers and Maps:

Brea Chamber of Commerce. Brea Economic Profile. Brea: 1992.

Brea Community History Project (Selections from the Dean Millen Collection)

California State Polytechnic University, Pomona, Department of Urban Planning. Economic Survey Report, City of Brea, 1973.

City of Brea:

Incorporation Papers and Board of Trustee Minutes, 1917-1923.

The Brea Project, Final Report and Recommendations, 1989.

Brea by Design, The Downtown Charette, 1989.

Future Brea, Shaping the Vision, 1992.

County of Orange: Orange County Progress Report: 1965, 1975, 1985.

National Archives, Pacific Southwest Region. Official Log-Book, *S.S. La Brea Hills.*

Southern California Edison Company. An Area Inventory of the City of Brea, 1969.

Miscellaneous Maps of Orange County, Orange County Archives, Santa Ana.

Miscellaneous Records of Los Angeles County, Orange County Recorder, Santa Ana.

Sanborn (Fire Insurance) Maps, Brea: 1915-1933.

Index

C- denotes Color photos which appear in the Anniversary Album between pages 174-175.

General Index

A